OF NO COUNTRY:
An Anthology of the Works of Sir Richard Burton

By the same author:

OF NO COUNTRY:

An Anthology of the Works of Sir Richard Burton

FRANK McLYNN

Illustrations by Howard Phipps

Scribners

A Scribners Book

Copyright © 1990 by Frank McLynn
Illustrations copyright © 1990 by Howard Phipps

First published in Great Britain in 1990 by
Scribners, a Division of
Macdonald & Co (Publishers) Ltd
London & Sydney

British Library Cataloguing in Publication Data

Burton, Sir, Richard. 1821–1890
    Of no country: an anthology of the
    works of Sir Richard Burton.
    1. Exploration. Burton, Sir, Richard,
    1821–1890.
    I. Title.   II. McLynn, F. J. (Frank J.)
    910.92

    ISBN 0–356–17986–9

Typeset by Leaper & Gard Limited, Bristol, England
Printed and bound in Great Britain by
Butler & Tanner Ltd

Scribners
A Division of
Macdonald & Co (Publishers) Ltd
Orbit House
1 New Fetter Lane
London EC4A 1AR
A member of Maxwell Macmillan Pergamon Publishing Corporation

Genius is of no country; her pure ray
Spreads all abroad, as general as the day.

Charles Churchill, *The Rosciad*

To Pauline and Lucy

CONTENTS

INTRODUCTION

A story is told of Orson Welles coming to lecture at a small Midwestern town in the depths of winter. At the local PTA hall he found barely a dozen hardy souls huddling to meet him. He addressed them thus: 'In my life I have been actor, impresario, film director, theatre producer, radio writer, federal administrator, author, goodwill ambassador, illusionist and prestidigitator. Isn't it surprising that there are so many of me and so few of you?' With even greater justice could Richard Francis Burton (1821–90) stake such a claim as multi-talented and multitudinous man. Soldier, consul, explorer and traveller, poet and scholar, anthropologist, ethnologist, archaeologist, occultist, swordsman and war correspondent: these roles merely exhaust the categories where he was recognized as a master or authority; they say nothing about his myriad other enthusiasms and interests.

At the most basic level, all eyewitnesses agree on his overwhelming physical presence. Oscar Wilde's quip 'once seen, never remembered' would certainly not have been made about Burton. Almost six feet tall, broad-shouldered, barrel-chested and, until the illnesses of his later years, a devotee of physical fitness, Burton was a master swordsman, trained pugilist and crack shot. The oriental appearance and Asiatic physiognomy,

1

the dark hair, beetling brow, serpentine eyes, Chinaman moustaches, and the disfiguring cicatrice from Berbera combined to
produce an awesome, diabolic persona, which Burton used to
browbeat and cow opponents. All who met him commented on
his sheer physicality. Ouida cited Othello together with Athos,
Porthos and Aramis as fictional likenesses. Blunt opted for
Balzac's Vautrin. Others reversed the process and called the
Brontë creations Heathcliff and Mr Rochester (both of whom
appeared in 1842) as 'Burtonian'. It has also been alleged that
some of the characters in Disraeli and Bulwer-Lytton novels have
a touch of Burton *avant la lettre* in them. Clearly there was a
sense in which Burton as physical being was an archetype for the
spirit of the early Victorian age.

Linguist, writer, scholar, scientist, explorer, poet, swordsman,
Burton has always had his admirers reaching for superlatives and
Promethean epithets. 'An Elizabethan? A poetic revolutionary?
Matthew Arnold's scholar-gypsy?' wonders Alan Moorehead. A
Janus looking to the medieval past of chivalry and honour and to
the future of science and the triumph over ignorance and superstition, mused his wife Isabel. Verney Lovett Cameron felt that
his fame as an explorer obscured his other achievements, almost
as if the British public was unable to do more than pigeon-hole
him as 'Captain Burton, the well-known traveller'. 'His scientific,
apart from his linguistic and scholarly attainments, were most
wonderful, and if he had cared to make them known to the world, he
would have ranked his as geologist, naturalist, anthropologist,
botanist or antiquarian ... Had he lived in the Elizabethan
instead of the Victorian era he would have been an epoch maker.'

The cliché 'Renaissance Man' jostles for consideration but
connotations of the Renaissance are problematical when applied
to Burton. He was above all a Romantic, and Romanticism is on
one level a rejection of the official ideas and values of the Renaissance. But the fact that so many of his admirers thought his true
spiritual home was in Elizabethan England – and his own predi-
lection for the English of that period lent substance to the claim –
stands in contradistinction to the *Zeitgeist* notion advanced above.
Burton, it seems, was a 'dual man' at every level.

Is any resolution of the contradictions in Burton's personality
possible? Can there be a synoptic view of Sir Richard? Here we
are at once faced with a problem of evidence, for from 1860 on,
much of our knowledge comes from his wife Isabel, a deeply

suspect source. The problem is, *mutatis mutandis*, like trying to get at the truth of the Julian emperors of Rome using Tacitus alone. Some of the account provided is true, but much of it is deeply etched with prejudice and distortion. It is not so much a case of 'All Cretans are liars', for then we could read off the truth from the mirror-image. It is more a case of 'the devil is a liar' with the corollary that one does not know when or how much.

Unless Isabel is quoting directly from her husband's diaries, her *Life* has to be used with great care. The many verbatim accounts of conversations are largely Thucydidean, in the sense that Isabel writes them up *à l'escalier*, or as she would like them to have occurred. There is no external validation or corroborating evidence for her most famous stories. Attempts by Isabel Burton hagiographers to rehabilitate her reputation have usually muddied the waters still further. The classic case is the two-volume *The Romance of Isabel Lady Burton* by W.H. Wilkins. Some of the absurdities can be ignored as the harmless gush of an uncritical admirer, as when Wilkins makes the ludicrous claim for his heroine: 'She could write and speak fluently French, Italian, Arabic and Portuguese, German she knew also ... She was well-read in the literature of all these.' But self-contradiction within a paragraph is scarcely permissible. Wilkins tells us Isabel could never refuse beggars, then says virtually in the same breath that she always went out with little money, so that their begging was futile anyhow. At times he even seems to notice that he is contradicting himself. 'She was very fond of children – that is *en bloc* – she did not care to be troubled with them at too close quarters.' This is like the man who loves the abstraction 'mankind' but hates all individuals of the species, or hates the exploiter without even liking the exploited.

Isabel, then, is the key to both the inner Burton and much of the outer man. Her destruction of his private papers means that any attempt to retrieve the truth about Burton will always be partly her 'truth'. Yet we know enough from Burton himself and others to be reasonably clear why he married her and what the basis of their relationship was. Isabel was herself part of Burton's duality. He was not carnally attracted to her, and sex played little part in their marriage. But she represented stability and a kind of normality – for Burton underrated his wife's peculiarity. She was the safe anchorage to which he could return after harrowing experiences at Dahomey, in the wilds of Dalmatia, or even with

Hankey's Parisian prostitutes. Burton oscillated wildly between frenzied bouts of activity and inexplicable periods of passivity and depression. He had little use for Isabel when he was on the upward spiral, looking ahead to the rapids of the São Francisco river or the gold of Midian and West Africa. But when his spirits dipped and he plummeted into the 'black dog', Isabel came into her own. Her difficulty was that she did not want the role of the passive homemaker, waiting patiently for the hunter to return. She wanted to be at his side, sharing the adventure. For this reason, the eighteen months in Syria were undoubtedly the happiest time of the marriage *for her*.

An anthology of Burton's writings is not the place to discuss his troubled private life. Interested readers are referred to my biography *Snow Upon The Desert*. The outer Burton, Burton face to face with the world, is easier to deal with, largely because his prolific output as author provides a wealth of evidence on the multitudinous man. It is hard to imagine that the diaries and papers Isabel burned would afford more than marginal corrections to the published work on his explorations in Africa, Arabia and South America (the 'black hole' in his life, covering the American journey from mid-April to mid-August 1860 is another matter).

As an African explorer Burton stands firmly in the first division, in a premier league containing himself, Livingstone, Stanley, Speke and Baker. In addition, he possessed creative and scholarly abilities far in advance of the other four. None of the others had his intellectual abilities, his erudition, his scientific curiosity or his linguistic gifts. Additionally, he was one of the great pioneer anthropologists and sexologists. In matters sexual he anticipated Havelock Ellis and Freud, while his ethnological work on Dahomey was hailed for its insight, accuracy, detail and imaginative perception by the modern anthropologist Melville Herskovits. All these aspects of Burton are on display in his books on African travel and exploration. But he was neither single-minded enough nor sufficiently interested in Africa and Africans (in fact he hated black men) to be the supreme technician in African exploration Stanley later became. Additionally, Burton despised the 'Dark Continent' and all its works, while revering the Arabs and claiming that the 'horrors' of the slave trade were largely cant and humbug. Partly for this reason, no significant indigenous oral traditions of his 1857–59 journey survive. This is in contrast to the wealth of such evidence for the others of the 'Big Five' in African exploration: Livingstone, Stanley, Speke and Samuel Baker. But Burton did have one significant feat to his credit: in contrast to Stanley, Baker and the notorious German Karl Peters, he penetrated to the centre of Africa and back without bloodshed. As one of his admirers said of him in 1921 in a centenary lecture: 'No tales of blood disfigure the narratives of his explorations: on his death-bed he could have recalled to his recollection (*sic*) no lives of poor Africans or Asiatics taken away by his orders, no villages in any part of the world plundered.'

Burton's two other great feats of the 1850s, which made him a household name, fall into the category of adventure rather than exploration properly so-called. The pilgrimage to Mecca and the penetration of the forbidden city of Harar were more important ultimately for the ethnological information they threw up, though it was the brazen drama of the two do or die adventures which caught popular imagination. Arguably, when the full balance sheet is drawn up, Burton will be seen to be more important as an anthropologist than an explorer in the true sense.

As an anthropologist, Burton was one of the finest scholars in the field in the nineteenth century. Whether writing on the Fan of Dahomey, the Bedouin of Arabia, the Danakil of Ethiopia, the Ha, Gogo and Kimbu tribes of present-day Tanzania, the Sioux of the Great Plains or the Sind peoples of the Indus valley, Burton's twofold skill as empirical observer and structural semiologist never deserted him. Melville Herskovits was the first modern anthropologist to appreciate Burton's rare talents as a field worker: only Burton's *Mission to Gelele* of the nineteenth-century works on Dahomey stood up to the exact scrutiny of twentieth-century social science. Burton was not an *a priori* theorizer, like Sir James Frazer, but a highly talented field worker, whose unique linguistic gifts enabled him to get inside the idiom of a culture very swiftly. Sexual mores were his especial interest and he may be regarded as the founding father of that strand in modern anthropology that specializes in the close study of 'primitive' sexual behaviour, with Malinowski, Geoffrey Gorer and Verrier Elwin as the best-known practitioners.

As a linguist Burton was a true phenomenon. He mastered twenty-five languages (forty, if we count the variant dialects) and could break the back of any foreign tongue after two months' sustained study. He wrote a grammar of the Jataki dialect in India, compiled dictionaries in Harar, Dahomey and Brazil, as well as making transliterations of proverbs in ten different West African argots. His translations are works of art: accurate, vigorous, brilliant. He moved with ease from the Sanskrit of *Vikram and the Vampire* to Portuguese for Camões's *Lusiads*, to Arabic for the *Arabian Nights* and the *Perfumed Garden*; from Neapolitan Italian for *Il Pentamerone* and on to Latin for the *Priapeia* and *Catullus*. The language of his beloved Arabs was always his first love. Yet Arabic was merely the finest string to his bow. Close behind, as his second favourite, came Portuguese, with Persian in third place. Beyond this were Italian, Spanish, German, Icelandic, Swahili, Hindustani, Sanskrit, Mahratha, Urdu, Pushtu, Jataki, Amharic, Fan, Egba, Ashanti, plus a host of West African and Indian dialects, to say nothing of Latin, Greek, Hebrew and Aramaic. In her feverish desire to convert Richard to catholicism, Isabel might have stopped to consider that glossolalia, the gift of tongues, was traditionally a talent given to God's chosen ones, as the events of Pentecost showed. Burton was a true scholar; but in his zeal not to compromise with the intentions of the author he was translating, he sometimes forgot the other prerequisite for the translator: he must communicate readily with a contemporary audience. There is also a sense in which Burton's awesome linguistic gifts worked against excellence of translation; his friend Frank Harris, after all, recalled that after being steeped in German for two years, he (Harris) could no longer write clear English prose.

As a writer he was prolific, producing forty-three volumes on his travels and explorations. *The Pilgrimage to El-Medinah and Meccah* and *The Lake Regions of Central Africa* are classics, but *First Footsteps in East Africa, Zanzibar, The City of the Saints* (on the Mormons of Salt Lake City) and *Letters from the Battlefields of Paraguay* stand high in the second league.

In many ways Burton was almost a caricature of the Romantic sensibility. Wilfred Scawen Blunt, who had the opportunity to examine Burton at close quarters correctly intuited that even the Arabs would have been sacrificed if Burton's highest ambitions could have been achieved thereby. It is this which most clearly differentiates Burton from T.E. Lawrence as men of Arabia. A student of the subject has summed up like this. 'Burton's personality had a strong romantic streak; his restlessness, his love of travel, adventure and disguise, his somewhat gaudy amoralism and flouting of convention, his varying poses, the grudge he bore his compatriots for not sufficiently appreciating his work, are those of the romantic littérateur-adventurer, and his work betrays the Romantic's intellectual and emotional egotism.'

The financial uncertainty of his early years – and especially the feeling that his mother had thrown away his patrimony – left Burton forever at the mercy of uneasy feelings about money. He complained that the British Museum, by taking the free copy to which it was entitled by law, mulcted authors of their royalties. He moaned and grumbled about the difficulty in getting subscribers to the limited edition of the *Arabian Nights* actually to pay up. Not the least of the paradoxes of Burton was that the man who would brave an Arab dagger, a thuggee's cloth, a Sioux arrow or a Somali lance could not face life on the basis of financial insecurity.

The consular service was even more signally the wrong profession for Burton than the Indian Army had been; at least in India there was a chance of active service. Unable as he was to suffer fools gladly, to defer to intellectual inferiors who were his superiors in a hierarchy, or to take direction, Burton's choice of the Foreign Office as an employer seems highly irrational and even self-destructive. Just as Burton accepted as wife a woman who was a good hewer of wood and drawer of water, but failed to think through the more profound consequences of his action, so in the consular service Burton accepted the chance of travel in faraway places, but overlooked the boredom, the paperwork, the petty small change and bogus politenesses of bureaucratic correspondence and, above all, the need to seek authorization from his superiors for his self-assigned exploration projects. Nor was Burton a master of machiavellianism. The chicanery he employed with his superiors was half-hearted and ill-thought-out (again the lack of patience with details). The Arabian explorer Bertram Thomas thought that, received opinion notwithstanding, Burton gave both the East India Company and the Foreign Office too much rope. His mistake was to ask permission instead of presenting a *fait accompli.* For example, in 1852, instead of asking for three years' leave to cross the Empty Quarter, Burton should have asked for one and then parlayed it into three by dint of 'serious illness', 'kidnapping', 'arrest' and all the other plausible excuses that could arise in the heart of Arabia.

There is no question but that Burton suffered agonies in the strait-jacket of consular service. He once told Frank Harris: 'Do you remember the cage at Loches, in which an ordinary man could not stand upright or lie at ease, and so was done to death slowly by constraint? Places under our government today are cages like that to all men above average size.' Burton's friend Ouida concurred. It was abundantly clear to her that the hero could not shape his own destiny if he was married and in government service; it was, of course, Isabel's responsibility that he was both. But beyond this, she accused the British government of dog-in-the-mangerism. It would not use Burton's great talents on the ground that there was a question-mark against his name – clearly a reference to his report on the Karachi brothels for General Napier in the 1840s. In the eyes of the British establishment there was a clear link between homosexuality and unreliability and even treason – a proposition that seemed to receive a triumphant vindication in the case of Roger Casement. But as Ouida argued, surely correctly, it was a case of 'put up or shut up'. If the Foreign Office had a case against Burton, it should have dismissed him. To keep him on and consign him to limbo on the grounds of his 'unsoundness' was humbug. The consular service was thus inimical to Burton's interests twice over. On the one hand, it was, as described by Ouida, 'a career as fitted to him as the shafts of a tradesman's van to a racer entered for Epsom and Chantilly.' On the other: 'the beheading of Walter Raleigh was, I think, a kinder treatment than the imprisonment of Burton in Trieste.'

Burton also makes a fascinating psychological study. There was a certain ambiguity in his sexuality and an ambivalence in his study of homosexuality, prostitution, pederasty, castration and infibulation. He dallied with Indian and Persian mistresses, experimented with black and Arab women in Africa and Asia, and whoremongered his way through the brothels of Paris. After this his marriage comes as something of a shock. Isabel Arundell, the virginal Catholic, was the least conceivable choice for him, and the record of his sexually unsatisfying marriage suggests, as does the content of his erotic writings, that the sexological works contained an element of sublimation.

Burton in his time played many roles. He was soldier, swordsman, explorer, anthropologist, archaeologist, mining speculator, poet, translator, botanist, zoologist, geologist and dignified consul. He also played the parts (in costume) of Persian merchant in India, Indian doctor in Egypt and Arabia, Moslem merchant in Somaliland and (*in propria persona*) London clubman, devoted husband, iconoclastic critic, raconteur, wit and world-weary cynic. He was in love with the exotic and the erotic, a permanent outsider, a man straddled between cultures, neither wholly British in sensibility nor wholly anything else. He was unquestionably a great man, arguably the most prodigiously gifted of all the 'Eminent Victorians'. There was no one else like him in nineteenth-century England, nor has anyone emerged this century who could challenge his position as colossus across such a wide spectrum of activities. Enigmatic, unintegrated, contradictory, ambiguous, and self-destructive: Burton was all these things. But in his Promethean striving he lived out the meaning of Walt Whitman's archetypal human being: 'Do I contradict myself? Very well then I contradict myself, I am large, I contain multitudes.'

ONE
THE MAN

A scion of the Anglo-Irish upper classes, Burton and his younger brother Edward spent a nomadic childhood in the Europe of the 1820s and 1830s. Their milieu was the expatriate community in France and Italy – people either too unconventional or too disreputable to live in England. Burton grew up ambivalent about all nations and without any strong sense of national identity. His parents gave up trying to control him at an early age. He mingled with gypsies and other vagrants, haunted brothels, and generally led a roistering life. At the age of fifteen he had already had extensive sexual experience with the prostitutes of Naples. His education was acquired from tutors and he gave no serious attention to any subject except the study of languages. From an early age he displayed an astonishing linguistic gift. He mastered French, Italian, modern Greek (picked up in Marseilles), plus dialects such as Neapolitan and Bernais (a mixture of French, Spanish and Provençal). He also became expert in the use of firearms and became one of the outstanding swordsmen of Europe: 'Fencing was the great solace of my life,' he recorded.

Burton's lack of discipline appalled his father, a disillusioned regular army officer, who decided to send Burton, aged nineteen, to Oxford in the hope that he would become a clergyman. Arrival in the 'chill and dolorous North' induced a profound culture shock – a loathing for English mores and customs and a contempt for its rigid and stratified society. He found the dull, flat rainy landscape unbearable after Switzerland and Italy. The houses were mean. The place reeked of toadyism and flunkeyism. The dons were 'queer things' who 'walked the streets'. The standard of tutoring was abysmal. The pronunciation of Latin and Greek was wrong. A fellow student guffawed at the splendid moustaches that had been the envy of the youth of the continental resorts, and when he seemed unable to comprehend a challenge to a duel, Burton was convinced he had fallen among 'grocers'. His brilliance and bravado made him a popular undergraduate, though he claimed to have enjoyed nothing but the fencing and boxing.

Typically, Oxford failed to recognize Burton's intellectual and scholarly abilities. The professor of Arabic refused him as a pupil, thereby depriving himself of contact with one of the greatest Orientalists of the century. Eventually Burton became bored with the mediocrity around him. He deliberately courted rustication, then argued so vehemently with his tutors that he was urged not to return. His departure was quintessential Burton. He insulted the college authorities by suggesting that they were trying to defraud him of his caution-money. Then he drove away in a tandem 'artistically performing on a yard of tin trumpet, waving adieu to my friends, and kissing my hand to the pretty shop-girls.'

From Oxford Burton passed into the Indian Army on a commission and spent seven years on the sub-continent. His time there was immensely productive. He studied eleven different languages, passed qualifying languages in most of them, published original grammars in two. His best Indian years were in the Sind under Sir Charles Napier, one of the few in high authority to recognize Burton's exceptional talents. There he first practised on a large scale his gift for Oriental disguises. As a half-Arab, half-Persian, he went into the bazaars and out among the tribes in the hills.

It was in India that Burton's phenomenal literary energy first became apparent. The list of publications that resulted from the seven years is long and its range wide. Besides linguistic works, there were volumes on the Sind Valley and its peoples, a work on falconry, and monographs on swordsmanship and the use of the bayonet.

Astonishingly, Burton later wrote: 'My career in India had been in my eyes a failure, and through no fault of my own; the dwarfish demon called "Interest" had fought against me, and as usual had won the fight.' This was a reference to his self-destructive tendencies. His 'impolitic habit of speaking the truth' raised question marks against his 'soundness', especially when he devoted so much time to the study of sex and Indian sexual customs: homosexuality, adultery, infanticide, prostitution, etc. Even worse in his superiors' eyes was his habit of lashing all aspects of Anglo-Indian society. His caustic, witty tongue made him many enemies. When he moved to overt political criticism, he became an embarrassment. His analysis of India – as contained in a memorandum submitted to the Court of Directors of the East India Company – contained forceful criticisms of British misrule in India and predicted the outbreak of the Mutiny. Even though events later proved him right, Burton fell foul of the oldest English prejudice of all, that of being 'too clever by half'.

By the time he returned to England on sick leave in 1849, Burton's personality was fully formed. Since his parents were both insubstantial figures in terms of his early 'socialisation', we get a clearer impression of his two grandmothers than of his father and mother, who seem to have opted out of the real world into the fantasy kingdom of hypochondria. It is not possible to establish with any certainty exactly why Burton harboured such deep feelings of misogynism, but there can be no doubting his dislike and suspicion of the female sex. In his autobiographical poem *Stone Talk* (1865) the emotions are clearly on display. Yet misogynism was not the only attitude that would place Burton firmly in a demonology of the modern liberal. A man of the extreme right, with a hankering for the modalities of the Middle Ages, where the code of honour and the sword settled all problems, Burton evinced attitudes that would nowadays be classed as elitist and racist, to go with the sexism already mentioned. His dislikes included socialists and egalitarians of whatever stripe, Jews, blacks, missionaries, do-gooders and even the Irish with whom he could claim kin. In the course of a furious denunciation of the Hungarians – always a favourite target for the European upper classes – Burton manages to work in his dislike of the *gens Hibernica*, as he himself would have expressed it.

*

Trips — Grandmamma Baker
(from *The Life of Captain Sir Richard F. Burton*,
Isabel Burton (1893))

Our father and mother had not much idea of managing their children; it was like the old tale of the hen who hatched ducklings. By way of a wholesome and moral lesson of self-command and self-denial, our mother took us past Madame Fisterre's windows, and bade us look at all the good things in the window, during which we fixed our ardent affections upon a tray of apple-puffs; then she said, 'Now, my dears, let us go away; it is so good for little children to restrain themselves.' Upon this we three devilets turned flashing eyes and burning cheeks upon our moralizing mother, broke the windows with our fists, clawed out the tray of apple-puffs, and bolted, leaving poor mother a sadder and a wiser women, to pay the damages of her lawless brood's proceedings.

Talking of the guillotine, the schoolmaster unwisely allowed the boys, by way of a school-treat, to see the execution of a woman who killed her small family by poisoning, on condition that they would look away when the knife descended; but of course that was just the time (with such an injunction) when every small neck was craned and eyes strained to look, and the result was that the whole school played at guillotine for a week, happily without serious accidents.

The residence at Tours was interrupted by occasional trips, summering in other places, especially at St Malo. The seaport then thoroughly deserved the slighting notice, to which it was subjected by Captain Marryat, and the house in the Faubourg was long remembered from its tall avenue of old yew trees, which afforded abundant bird's-nesting. At Dieppe the gallops on the sands were very much enjoyed, for we were put on horseback as soon as we could straddle. Many a fall was of course the result, and not a few broken heads, whilst the rival French boys were painfully impressed by the dignity of spurs and horsewhips.

At times relations came over to visit us, especially Grandmamma Baker (Grandmamma Baker was a very peculiar character). Her arrival was a signal for presents and used to be greeted with tremendous shouts of delight, but the end of a week always brought on a quarrel. Our mother was rather thin and delicate, but our grandmother was a thorough old Macgregor, of the Helen or the Rob Roy type, and was as quick to resent an affront as any of her clan. Her miniature shows that she was an extremely handsome woman, who retained her good looks to the last. When her stepson, Richard Baker, jun., inherited his money, £80,000, he went to Paris and fell into the hands of the celebrated Baron de Thierry. This French friend persuaded him to embark in the pleasant little speculation of building a bazaar. By the time the walls began to grow above ground the Englishman had finished £60,000, and, seeing that a million would hardly finish the work, he sold off his four greys and fled Paris post-haste in a post-chaise. The Baron Thierry followed him to London, and, bold as brass, presented himself as an injured creditor at grand-mamma's pretty little house in Park Lane. The old lady replied by summoning her servants and having him literally kicked downstairs in true Highland fashion. That Baron's end is well know in history. He made himself king of one of the Cannibal Islands in the South Sea, and ended by being eaten by his ungrateful subjects.

Grandmamma Baker was determined to learn French, and, accordingly, secured a professor. The children's great delight was to ambuscade themselves, and to listen with joy to the lessons. 'What is the sun?' 'Le soleil, madame!' 'La solelle.' 'Non, madame. Le so-leil.' 'Oh, pooh! La solelle.' After about six repetitions of the same, roars of laughter issued from the curtains – we of course speaking French like English, upon which the old lady would jump up and catch hold of the nearest delinquent and administer condign punishment. She had a peculiar knack of starting the offender, compelling him to describe a circle of which she was the centre, whilst, holding with the left hand, she administered smacks and cuffs with the right; but, as every mode of attack has its own defence, it was soon found out that the proper corrective was to throw one's self on one's back, and give vigorous kicks with both legs. It need hardly be said that Grandmamma predicted that Jack Ketch would make acquaintance with the younger scions of her race, and that she never arrived at speaking French like a Parisian.

Grandmamma Burton was also peculiar in her way. Her portrait shows the regular Bourbon traits, the pear-shaped face and head which culminates in Louis Philippe's. Although the wife of a country clergyman, she never seemed to have attained the meekness of feeling associated with that peaceful calling. The same thing is told of her as was told of the Edgeworth family. On one occasion during the absence of her husband, the house at Tuam was broken into by thieves, probably some of her petted tenantry. She lit a candle and went upstairs to fetch some gunpowder, loaded her pistols, and ran down to the hall, when the robbers decamped. She asked the raw Irish servant girl who had accompanied her what had become of the light, and the answer was that it was standing on the barrel of 'black salt' upstairs; thereupon Grandmamma Burton had the pluck to walk up to the garret and expose herself to the risk of being blown to smithereens. When my father returned from service in Sicily, at the end of the year, he found the estate in a terrible condition, and obtained his mother's leave to take the matter in hand. He invited all the tenants to dinner, and when speech time came on, after being duly blarneyed by all present, he made a little address, dwelling with some vigour upon the necessity of being for the future more regular with the 'rint.' Faces fell, and the only result was, that when the rent came to be collected, he was fired at so frequently (showing that this state of things had been going on for some sixty or seventy years), that, not wishing to lead the life of the 'Galway woodcock,' he gave up the game, and allowed matters to take their own course.

Stone Talk ... Being Some of the Marvellous Sayings of a Petral Portion Fleet Street, London, to One Doctor Polyglott, Ph.D.
(1865)

When sudden on my raptured sight
Falls deadly and discharming blight—
Such blight as Eurus loves to fling
O'er gladsome crop in genial spring.
Fast by the side of 'Thing Divine,'
By spirit-parson fresh made mine,   when he sees a
In apparition grim – I saw   mother-in-law,
The middle-aged British mother-in-law!!!

   The pink silk hood her head was on
Did make a *triste* comparison
With blossomed brow and green-grey eyes,
And cheeks bespread with vinous dyes,
And mouth and nose – all, all, in fine,

Caricature of 'Thing Divine.'
 Full low the Doppelgänger's dress
Of moire and tulle, in last distress
To decorate the massive charms
Displayed to manhood's shrinking arms;
Large loom'd her waist 'spite pinching stays,
As man-o'-war in by-gone days;
And, ah! her feet were broader far
Than beauty's heel in Mullingar.
Circular all from toe to head,
Pond'rous of framework, as if bred
On streaky loin and juicy steak;
And, when she walked, she seemed to shake
With elephantine tread the ground.
Sternly, grimly, she gazed around,
Terribly calm, in much flesh strong,

and runs.   Upon the junior, lighter throng,
And loudly whispered, 'Who's that feller?'
'Come! none of this, Louise, I tell yer!'
And 'Thing Divine' averted head,
And I, heart-broken, turned and fled.

He then beholds   And, flying, 'scaped my soul once more;
a Vision of   But not this time, as erst, to soar
Judgement,   Into Tranceland: deep down it fell,
Like pebble dropped in Car'sbrooke well,
Till reached a place whose fit compare
Was furnished lodgings 'bout Mayfair –
In dire September's atmosphere,
When Town is desert, dismal, drear –
With box-like hall, a ladder stair,
Small windows cheating rooms of air,
With comforts comfortless that find
Such favour in the island mind
Bestuffed, and nicknack babery o'er,
Of London blacks a copious store,
Whilst legibly on the tight-fit
'Respectability' was writ.
 And last appeared on that dread stage
That mother-in-law of middle age,
Whose stony glare had strength to say,
'Here lord am I! who dare me nay?'

While voices dread rang in mine ear,
'Wretch! thy eternal home is here:
Though dread the doom, 'tis e'en too good
For one that dines and drinks with Wode!'

This was too much. 'Ruffian,' cried I,   to the disgust
'You beg the question you decry.   of Dr. Polyglott,
Our men and women dress and town   Ph.D.
For mere externals. Bow ye down
Before the master-charm of mind –
Our women's training – education –'
   'There, stop,' cried he, 'your declamation!   The Stone denies
And first of begging questions, sir.   the fitness of
When angry passions dullards stir   women's education.
The first tone of Eristike ($\dot{\epsilon}\rho\iota\zeta\iota\tau\iota\kappa\eta$),
Pitched in a very testy key,
Is, sir, "You beg the question." Logic,
Per se, is e'er amphibologic,
But, *petitio principii*,
Hath finger deep in every pie –
A figure ultra-Judëan,
As his goose-quill who penned ye an
Address to Wat and Laureate Ode;
But this by way of episode.
As for your training boast, I am
Sore tempted t', *ad modestiam*,
Argument, but that Aldrich took
No heed of that in all his book
(And wisely, for 'twould, in this age,
Be formula the most unsage:
The very boys and girls would cry
Shame on the man of modesty).
This reading, writing, ciphering, strumming,
Use of the globes and art of humming,
Or shrieking, dignified as music,
That makes me, if it don't make *you*, sick;
Practice in entering a carriage,
Largest ideas of love and marriage,
Some twenty several sorts of dances
(Saltation market-price enhances),
The science of disposing dress

To set forth charms, hide ugliness;
A thousand rules for choosing hats,
A proper taste in men's cravats,
The art to show the *brodequin's* top
And yet before mid-leg to stop;
To deal with tradesmen all unknown
To parents till the bills are blown,
Or when, upon the marriage day,
The "happy man" is called to pay;
A connoisseurship of champagne,
Slang words, and horses, dogs, and men;
A high aspire to take the chair
In club meant only for the fair;
How to distinguish stones from paste,
And eke to pawn them; how to waste
Time on plays, novels, and romances,
Before the glass to practise glances –
Now soft and sweet, now hard, distressing,
Careless, encouraging, repressing –
And similar feminine arts to net
The foolish fish that like the bait:
Is this your boasted way to show
The young idea how to go?
By Jove! you lavish too much care
In training of a Bayadère!
But t'other day I heard Miss A.
Unto Miss B., her "crony," say,
"I hate your pale-faced things, and own
To liking a nice sailor brown."
The little minx, though hardly ten,
Pronounces on the points of men:
At twenty, think ye, will the nice
Brown sailor but her eye entice?'
    'Nonsense, my Lithy, girls are gay
In moral races, sages say;
But they reform when passed the church,
And leave their lovers in the lurch.
Our boast is home, and every stranger,
Except a Signor or Bushranger,
Who knows our life, must e'er confess
Our hearths are rich in happiness.

Dr. Polyglott,
Ph.D., supports
the virtue of
the married
she-Bull.

Must I suppose this all a dream
Unreal as the Seráb's stream –
Existentless as lights that seem
Before ophthalmic eyes to gleam?'
   'In this rich mine of humbug strain
There runs of fact a slender vein.
There's far less happiness than pride
In crying up one's own fireside:
'Tis mostly done when known the hearer
Holds ball and opera much dearer –
Prefers, as Frenchman does, to sit
Out evenings in th' *estaminet.*
Your "happy hearth" is oft a hell
Where Temper, Spite, and Disgust dwell,
And Ennui sheds her baleful gloom,
Making the place a living tomb;
Till your son, dog-sick, flies it, and
To swindling turns a ready hand,
And your poor daughter, tired of life,
Prefers to be a lackey's wife.
"The homes of Merry England" – zounds!
I hate to hear the well-worn sounds,
Your parrot-poets, pie-poetesses–
Humbugs! – emit. Come now, confess, is
Not the fire-side, where reign immense
Felicity and innocence,
More often far a perfect Cape
Of Storms than Hope? But, mark me, ape,
Your kind's belief in things affords
The strangest contrast to their words:
You know the place is stormy, thus
You call it Hopeful. And what fuss
You make when self-compelled to roam
From British boast, the "happy home"!
'Tis then the sturdy Saxon grows
Watery as a sea-cow's nose,
And maunders like a sick girl o'er
That commonplace his native "shore."
Home is the sole abode of bliss;
Tourist, the exile comfortless;
His heart's the loadstone, home the pole –

The Stone
retorts:

calls happy
home a hell;

Thought streams, home sea to which they roll.
O canting nonsense! Why the deuce
Don't they go home? What is the use
Of this lip-stuff when they might prove
By marching back that home they love?

shows how
gladly we flee;

    'But see, this exile, when returned
To all for which his sick heart yearned,
Growls, grumbles, damns, until once more
Escaped from dearest native shore,
Self-banished as he was before:
Ahasuerus-like, he starts
Once more for hateful "foreign parts."

    'Yet, my Lithophonist, our wives,
Without whom Briton never thrives;

and, when
Dr. Polyglott
Ph.D., reiterates
his assertion,

Our dear domestic better parts,
Whose truthful, faithful, loving hearts
Are our prime boast; whose constancy
It "riles" the outer world to see;
Upon whose bosom man may find
Console from fate, howe'er unkind;
Who, like the Suttees, burn to burn,
And mingle dust in husband's urn —'

    He rolled his head and winked his eyes
In most ill-bred irreverent guise,

shows how
girls are
brought up for
the marriage
market;

And thus proceeded: 'Now don't eat
Abominations in the street.
Your girls brought up to show their faces
At chapels, "sights," and bathing-places,
Pic-nics and archery meetings, where
Liquor abounds, sobriety's rare;
Who deem a ball and ball-room dress
The *ne plus ultra* of happiness;
For *bal masqué* would give their ears;
Who learn each actor's name and years,
And every scandalous anecdote
In town or country ken by rote;
Who know whate'er their mothers know
In mind, perhaps in physique too;
Who quizzically send a friend
To Paris till her waist is thinned:
Such pretty, polking, flirting fools,

That graduate in Folly's schools,
The shortest cuts to sin and crime
Beknown to man in modern time;
Taught from the earliest age to try
Their little hands at coquetry,
To break men's hearts ere Nature lend
Specific remedy to mend
The fractured member; trained to trace
Love-letters with *aplomb* and grace;
The sing'd young lady, wide awake,
Resolved Mamma's advice to take,
No shame to know, to feel no fear
In hunting rent-roll or a peer;
Who limit wedlock's full extent
To diamonds and settlement;
Who views the matrimonial mart
With stony eye and callous heart,
Trots out from her paternal stall
As nag for sale by Tattersall,
To highest bidder is knocked down
Like any slave in Stamboul town,
And swears to honour, love, obey,
The while her heart has gone astray
With some old flame, who bides his day;
The girl whom modish parent teaches
To win and wear marital breeches
By studies physiological,
As they their "natural history" call,
Of Balzac, Kahn, Feydeau, and Walker,
To turn half-addled brains, and talk her
Into believing all the scribble
Wherewith their flimsy goose-quills dribble;
Strong-minded spinsters who prefer
The 'Spital's tainted atmosphere
And Fame to path of hiding life;
Your patriot girls whom the strife
Of brigandism and Secesh
Serves their embryo thoughts t' enmesh;
The advocates of "women's rights;"
Abolitionists whom most delights
To ape the mad Lucretia Mott,

And all the politician lot,
Or those that "go for" Education,
Or those that build on "Emigration":
Such make good wives, such make life sweet
As hours in Newgate or the Fleet.
Immortal Gods, my better friend
From such abhorrent fate defend!

contrasting
them with
Pica;

   'Did'st ever hear of Pica's name –
A noted noble Roman dame?
Yes! Then you know of her 'tis told
She ne'er saw man, or young or old,
After her nuptials. Once among
Her friends a gossip said how strong
Smelt Mister Pica's breath of wine.
The poor dame marvelled, and, in fine,
Declared that all *must* smell the same!
I tell the tale as told by fame.

instancing
Sir Cresswell
Cresswell's court,

And now you have to shift your course
By Court of Probate and Divorce,
Cast loose the tie fast tied by Fate,
Let either wretch unyoke its mate –
Condition'lly that th' whole foul tale
Defile the once pure homestead's pale –
Teach every little miss to see
What Mistress A. with Mr. B.
Was apt to do – teach every boy
Sometime the like delight t' enjoy,
And o'er society to throw
Of lust and crime the hellish glow.

   'Of your fair studies the result,
See hare-brained Hall stand up t' insult
The sense, the "spirit of the age"

and various
vile scandals.

By lectures on concubinage.
Another case: see high-born dame
Lend her fair self to the foul shame
Of confarreation with a black,
The lord of many a dirty lac.
'Twas legal, for the blackamoor
Paid fullest price for his amour;
The lady swore to love, obey,
And honour her dark popinjay.

Yet scarce six months had lapsed
  before,
Un-Desdemona-like, she tore
The tie asunder, on the plea
Of the poor Moor's insanity.
This, braver than Tyndaridæ,
Helped by two well-feed, pompous men
That proved the lord *non compos men-*
tis, by one bolder deed of strife
Settled Othello's hash for life.
And now, his occupation gone,
He walks the Continent alone,
Ne'er to recross the British main
Or to his own return again.'

  'But, Petrus, our paternal love –'
'That kicks you out of doors to rove,
Without an extra hour's delay,
Over the sea and far away,
Only praying you never may
Homewards stray for many a day –

  'Man, are you sporting with your ills?
The rugged ruffian on the hills
Of barbarous Belochistan,
Give him his due, doth all he can
To keep his child at home; for him
He risks with pleasure life and limb,
Robs, murders, fights, and all to feed
The young 'uns, his four spouses breed.'

  'They're savages.'

        'Of course! If not,
The door would be the younkers' lot.
Look at the foreign marts and fairs,
Where you export your sons and heirs
As any other trading wares:
Banish the hapless half-grown boy
(The father's hope! the mother's joy!)
From all he loves, from all in life
That makes life sweet, to bitter strife –
On a grand tour in search of Fortune –
With stony-fisted jade, Misfortune;
Drive him, when barely breeched, to reap

*Dr. Polyglott
Ph.D., instances
the warm paternal
affection of
John Bull.*

*The Stone
replies derisively,*

A golden harvest from the deep.'

    With might and main
He groaned aloud, e'en as might do
The Methodist that wants to show
Bottle and purse are very low,
And thus resumed: 'What weighs me down
In this your God-forgotten town –
What nightly makes me wish I were
In muddy Thames or anywhere
Else – is the horrid degradation
Of the Hetæra's incalcation.
O what potato heels and toes!
How dread her stamp as on she goes,
Wolf-like, upon the human tracks,
Hurls horrid oaths and foul jests cracks
In ghastly mirth, as the Death's head
Grinning before Egyptian "spread;"
Wafting of gin th' infernal stench
Till e'en Cotytto's ghost would blench;
For ne'er, I ween, had met its eyes
Such ultra-Thracian mysteries!
By all the virtues Britons claim,
By all your sense of human shame,
Have you, I ask, no means to stop
The growth of such a poison crop –
To curb a scandal makes your name
Now and hereafter most infame?
I hear it said, were you to cull
From every city every trull
Of abominablest infamy,
And loose them here their chance to try,
No two of them could e'er excel
One of these candidates for hell.
Remain ye idle, careless mute,
While such foul scenes and sights pollute
Innocency's sanctuaries –
Your children's opening minds and eyes;
Or fondly deem ye such things are
To them unknown, unheard of? Far
From this, I may with safety say,

Thereupon the
Stone breaks
into a philippic
against streetwalkers,

Rare is the brat in present day
That learns not with his penny trumpet
The name and nature of a strumpet –
That can't, all sage, discriminate
Betwixt the verb to fornicate,
And with a just discrimen see
The difference of adultery.
'Tis said fruits prove the parent tree
Or sound or else unsound to be.
To judge from spec'mens of your fruit,
The tree must be a Upas shoot,
Within whose ring of poison gloom
Rank Sin and Death luxuriant bloom –
Disease that leaves to far off time
The dreadful legacy of crime;
That, on your children's guiltless heads,
Vials of Heavenly vengeance sheds;
That saps your race's vigour, and
Spreads like a plague o'er every land.
O falsest of false modesty!
Pharisaic hypocrisy!
These crying horrors to ignore,
Nor stretch one hand to salve the sore!
O silly shame, to you confined,
Unto all vile unkindly kind,
Britannia, wake, turn on the gas,
And, with thy trident, to the "Cas;"
Then wend thy melancholic way
Adown the Market named of Hay,
Into the thick night-houses stray,
And end them, like a good old soul,
With Cider Cellar and Coal Hole.'

Politics — Central Europe
(from *The Life of Captain Sir Richard F. Burton,*
Isabel Burton (1893))

'I will now sketch the state of Hungary, whose ambition threatens to make her aggressive, entitled, by the press of England, the "backbone of the Austrian monarchy;" and praised for the "superior political organization" with which she has crushed her Slav rivals.

'Since the days, now forgotten, when Prince Esterhazy first flashed, in London society, his diamond jacket upon the dazzled eyes of the "upper ten thousand," the name of Hungarian has been a passport to favour amongst us. We meet him in the shape of a Kinsky, an Erdödy, or a Hunyadi – well born, well clad, and somewhat unlearned, except in the matter of modern languages. But he is a good rider, a keen sportsman, and a cool player for high stakes – qualities in one point (only) much resembling Charity. He looks like a gentleman in a drawing-room and in the hunting-field; he is quite at home at a fancy ball; he wears his frogged jacket, his tights and his tall boots, his silks, satins, and furs, with an air; his manners are courteous, cordial, and pleasant; in money matters he has none of the closeness of the cantankerous Prussian, none of the meanness of the Italian; and, lastly, he makes no secret of his sympathy with England, with the English, and with all their constitution-manias. What can you want more? You pronounce him a nice fellow, and all, woman especially, re-echo your words, "He is *such* a gentleman!" and – he received the Prince of Wales so enthusiastically!

'But there is another side (politically speaking) to this fair point of view. The Hungarian is a Tartar with a coat of veneer and varnish. Hungary is, as regards civilization, simply the most backward country in Europe. Buda-Pest is almost purely German, the work of the Teutons, who, at the capital, do all the work; you hardly ever hear in the streets a word of Magyar, and the Magyars have only managed to raise its prices and its death-rate to somewhat double those of London. The cities, like historic Gran on the Danube, have attempts at public buildings and streets; in the country towns and villages the thoroughfares are left to Nature; the houses and huts, the rookeries and doggeries are planted higgledy-piggledy, wherever the tenants please; and they are filthier than any shanty in Galway or Cork, in Carinthia or Krain. The Ugrian or Ogre prairies have no roads, or rather they are all road; and the driver takes you across country when and where he wills. The peasantry are "men on horseback," – in this matter preserving the customs of their Hun and Tartar ancestors. They speak a tongue of Turkish affinity, all their sympathies are with their blood-kinsmen the Turks, and they have toiled to deserve the savage title of "white Turks," lately conferred upon them by Europe.

'Fiume, the only seaport of Hungary, is a study of Hungarian nationality. The town is neatly built, well paved, and kept tolerably clean by Slav and Italian labour, the former doing the coarse, the latter the fine work. The port is, or rather is to be, bran-new. Because Austria chooses to provide a worse than useless, and frightfully expensive – in fact, ruinous – harbour for Trieste, whose anchoring roads were some of the best in Europe, therefore (admire the consequence) Hungary demands a similar folly for her emporium, Fiume, whose anchoring roads are still better. After throwing a few million of florins into the water, the works are committed to the charge of the usual half-dozen men and boys; moreover, as the port is supposed to improve, so its shipping and its business fall off in far quicker ratio. Commerce cannot thrive amongst these reckless, feckless people. There is no spirit of enterprise, no union to make force, no public spirit; the dead cities of the Zuyder Zee are bustling New England centres in comparison with Fiume; and the latter, which might have become the emporium of the whole Dalmatian coast, and a dangerous rival to Trieste, is allowing her golden opportunity to pass away never to return. For when Dalmatia shall have been vitalized by the addition of Bosnia and the Herzegovina, her glorious natural basins – harbours that can hold all the navies of the world – will leave Fiume mighty little to do except what she does now, look pretty and sit in the sun.

'All Englishmen who have lived long amongst Hungarians remark the similarity of the Magyar and the southern Irish Catholic. Both are imaginative and poetical, rather in talk than in books; neither race ever yet composed poetry of the highest class. Both delight in music; but, as the "Irish Melodies" are mostly Old English, so the favourites of Hungary are gypsy songs. Both have the "gift of the gab" to any extent, while their eloquence is notably more flowery than fruity. Both are sharp and intelligent, affectionate and warm-hearted; easily angered and appeased, delighted with wit, and to be managed by a *bon mot;* superficial, indolent, sensitive, punctilious, jealous, passionate, and full of fight. Both are ardent patriots, with an occasional notable exception of treachery; both are brilliant soldiers; the Hungarians, who formerly were only cavalry men, now form whole regiments of the Austrian Line. They are officered by the Germans, who will not learn the language, justly remarking, "If we speak Magyar, we shall be condemned for ever to Magyar corps, and when the inevitable split takes place, where shall we then be?" Both are bold and skilful riders; and, as the expatriated Irish Catholic was declared by Louis Le Grand – an excellent authority upon such matters – to be "one of the best gentlemen in Europe," so Europe says the same of the Hungarian *haute volée*.

'As regards politics and finance, Buda-Pest is simply a modern and eastern copy of Dublin. The Hungarian magnate still lives like the Squireen and Buckeen of the late Mr. Charles Lever's "earliest style;" he keeps open house, he is plundered by all hands, and no Galway landowner of the last generation was less fitted by nature and nurture to manage his own affairs. Hence he is drowned in debt, and the Jew usurer is virtually the owner of all those broad acres which bear so little. An "Encumbered Estates Bill" would tell strange tales; but the sabre is readily drawn in Hungary, and the "chosen people," sensibly enough, content themselves with the meat of the oyster, leaving the shells to the owner.

'This riotous, rollicking style of private life finds its way into public affairs; and as a model of "passionate politics," the Hungarian is simply perfect. He has made himself hateful to the sober-sided German and to the dull Slav; both are dead sick of his *outrecuidance;* the former would be delighted to get rid of the selfish and short-sighted irrepressibles, who are ever bullying and threatening secession about a custom tax, or a bank, or a question of union. They are scandalized by seeing the academical youth, the *jeunesse dorée* of Magyar universities, sympathizing with Turkish atrocities, declaring Turkey to be the defender of European civilization, *fackelzuging* the Turkish Consul, insulting the Russians, and sending a memorial sabre to a Sirdar Ekrem (Commander-in-Chief), whose line of march was marked by the fire-blackened walls of Giaour villages, and by the corpses of murdered Christians, men and women and babes. Could the Austro-Germans only shake off the bugbear of Panslavism, they would cut the cable, allow the ne'er-do-well Hungarian craft to drift away water-logged into hypostatic union with that big iron-clad the Turk; they would absorb the whole of Bosnia, the Herzegovina, and Albania; they would cultivate the Slav nationality, and they would rely upon racial difference of dialect and religion to protect them against the real or imaginary designs of Russia. Prince Eugène of Savoy, in the last century, a man of wit, was of that opinion, and so are we.

'Hungary, indeed, is a tinder-box like Montenegro, and much more dangerous, because her supply of combustible is on a larger scale. The last bit of puerile folly has been to press for an Austrian military occupation of Servia; and why? Because an Austrian monitor, being in a part of the river where "No thoroughfare" is put up, was fired upon with ball cartridges by a *schildwache* (sentinel) from the fort walls, and exploded, bungler that she was, one of her own shells. The Hungarians had been raving at the idea of "occupation" in Bulgaria, but the moment they saw an opportunity of breaking the Treaty of Paris, they proposed doing so at once. By-the-by, now that Prince Wrede, a *personâ ingrata*, is removed from Belgrade, you will hear no more of Servian outrages against Austria. To the "Magyarists" we may trace most of the calumnies against the brave and unfortunate Servian soldiery – lies of the darkest dye, so eagerly swallowed by the philo-Turk members of the English Press, and danger of Hungary and her politics of passion. Russians and Turks might be safely put into the ring together, like "Down-Easters" in a darkened room, and be allowed to fight it out till one cried, "Enough!"

'If these views of Hungary and the Hungarians be true – and they are our views – you will considerably discount the valuation set upon them by the Turcophile Press. They were once a barrier against Tartar savagery, a Finnish race, invited by the Byzantine Emperors to act as a buffer against Mohammedanism. The three orders of Magyars – Magnates, Moderates, and Miserables – hate Russia for the sensible and far-seeing part which she played in 1848–49; all excitement is apt to spread; even so in a street dog-fight, every cur thinks itself bound to assist, and to bite and wrangle something or other, no matter what. And where, we may ask, is the power that can muzzle these Eastern ban-dogs? who shall take away the shillelaghs of these Oriental Paddies?

'A taste of Hungarian quality has been given by M. Vambéry in the columns of the *Daily Telegraph*. M. Vambéry was born in Hungary, of Israelitish German parents. Like the sons of Israel generally, he hates Russia, and he loves England, and probably he has good and weighty reasons both for his hate and for his love. He was daring enough to tell us, in his first book of travels, that after dinner with the Turkish Minister at Teheran – and a very good dinner it was – he just disguised himself as a dervish, and travelled perfectly *incog.* for months and months under

Russian eyes, partly through Russian territory. The Russians must have known every step taken by M. Vambéry. He saw only what he was allowed to do; and thus Mr. Schuyler, whose name has, we regret to say, been altered by the irreverent Turcophile to "Squealer," roundly declares that he never visited the places which he has so well described. You will therefore regard M. Vambéry's opinions upon the subject of Turkey with suspicion, and reserve all your respect for his invaluable publications upon the Turanian dialects, his *specialité*. Lieutenant Payer's book will disappoint you; its main merit is that of having been written by a Magyar.

'Do not believe these Ugrians to be "the backbone of the Austrian Empire," whatever they may be to its element of weakness, the Monarchy. And if you are driven to own that the Hungarians "play the leading part in the events of Southern Europe," understand that the chief end and aim of Magyarist policy is to ruin the Slavs. I am a strong Austrian, with a great admiration for the Hungarians, who are to me, personally and individually, most attractive; but this does not blind me to the disadvantages they, *en masse*, bring to Austria. *I believe the Slav to be the future race of Europe, even as I hold the Chinese to be the future race of the East.* In writing politics and history which may live after one is long forgotten, one must speak the truth, and bury repulsions and attractions.

'Were I Emperor of Austria, I should have the police organized on English principles. I should punish with death the first two or three cases of brutal crime. The people are excellent. It speaks highly for the independent Triestines that, with weak laws, and authorities that act as though they dreaded them, the worst crimes are only stabbing when drunk, and suicide; and the latter is entirely owing to the excitability of the climate and the utter throwing off of religion, whilst all moral disgrace or dread is removed by the applause conferred on the suicide, and sympathy with the surviving family – which last is good and noble. I have seen thousands accompanying a *felo de se* to the grave, with verses and laurel leaves and a band of music, as if he had done something gallant and brave. Indeed, one was considered very narrowminded for not joining in his eulogy.'

TWO
THE ARABIAN ADVENTURER

The dispassionate Orientalist does not exist. Burton's particular mania was Arabia and the Arabs. While on a three-year sick leave but still on the Indian list, he tried unsuccessfully to get permission to explore central and eastern Arabia. In the autumn of 1852 he secured a year's leave to study Arabic and, frustrated over the initial project, decided to use the time for a spectacular adventure that would at once establish him as the premier Arabist of his time and place his name on every lip. He decided on a journey to the holy shrines of Mecca and Islam, disguised as an Afghan doctor. This was a highly perilous enterprise, as the penalty for an infidel detected in the sacred cities was death. In a decree in the year 629 Mohammed had ruled Mecca out of bounds to all unbelievers. There had been no relaxation of the rules, and it was still the case in the mid-nineteenth century that any 'Frank' (European) caught in the holy places would be executed. In previous centuries many interlopers had been impaled or crucified. According to Islamic canon, death could be avoided by an offer of circumcision and conversion thrice repeated. But the expectation of due process on discovery was unreasonable. Almost certainly the offender would be despatched on the spot.

Burton's aim was to take ship from Suez down the Red Sea,

then disembark and trek inland with the other hadjis to Medina and Mecca. He planned to make his journey when the three separate traditional caravans, from Cairo, Damascus and Baghdad, swept down the Arabian peninsula. There would be safety in numbers in more senses than one by losing himself in the human torrent of fanatically devout pilgrims.

This human tidal wave descended on Medina in time for the first twelve days of the Moslem year, for the hadj was a ritualistic affair and every visitor to Mecca had to perform his obeisance in a given order. Just before entering the sacred confines of Mecca, every pilgrim had to wash, shave and change into the *ihram*, mandatory wear in Mecca, consisting of two pieces of seamless white cloth, one wrapped around the loins, the other round the neck and left shoulder. The first compulsory call in Mecca was the Kaaba – a square, windowless stone building in the middle of the courtyard of the Great Mosque with a single door for entry, seven feet above the ground. The Kaaba was swathed in a mantle of black brocade known as the Kiswah, embossed with gold-lettered inscriptions from the Koran. On the Kaaba's south-east outside corner was the holiest relic of all – the Black Stone. Islam held that the stone had been given to Abraham, father of the Arab peoples, by the angel Gabriel; originally white, it had long since blackened by the sins of the hadjis who kissed it. Ironically, the monolith was almost certainly a pagan icon which Mohammed, implacable foe of idolatry, had syncretized into his new religion.

Having circled the stone cube seven times, the pilgrim had then to walk across the courtyard of the Great Mosque to the well of Zemzem, traditionally said to have been the one from which Hagar drew water for Abraham's son Ishmael. After drinking and washing from the well, the visitor would run six times between Mounts Safa and Marwa just outside the city, in a symbolic re-enactment of Hagar's quest for water and redemption. Eight days of prayer and fasting in Mecca followed. On the ninth day there was a general exodus to the heights of Arafat, to hear the Imam preach a sermon at the spot where Mohammed left his instructions to his disciples. On the tenth day at Muzlalifa the pilgrim had to throw seven stones seven times (forty-nine pebbles in all) at the pillars of Muna, in memory of Abraham, said to have driven off the devil with a fusillade of stones at this spot. On the final day it was the duty of the hadji to sacrifice a sheep and distribute the meat to the poor. The pilgrimage was then at an end.

To achieve his objective Burton had to live, think and breathe like an Arab – a feat of total immersion in his role no method actor could hope to emulate. He even had himself circumcised. He sustained the deception for many months in the company of Muslim pilgrims, all the time writing and sketching beneath his burnous. At the supreme moment, when he was simulating the ecstasy of kissing the Black Stone in the Kaaba, the holy of holies, in Mecca, his curiosity was such that he opened one eye and recorded his opinion that the stone was an aerolite.

The result of the journey was one of Burton's literary master-pieces. The descriptions of events just before entering Mecca show that Burton could write as dramatically as the best adventure writers when the subject was to his taste. He is patently in love with the Arab world in a way he never was with Africa. But significantly, his *Personal Narrative of a Pilgrimage to El-Medinah and Meccah*, written in Cairo and Bombay over a period of twelve months, was a more detached work then T.E. Lawrence's *The Seven Pillars of Wisdom*. Where Lawrence is poetic, Burton is tough-minded. Where Lawrence is introspective, Burton is scientific and taxonomic. Both men were soldiers, scholars and adventurers, but where Lawrence produced a luminous self-portrait, Burton effaced himself and instead exposed the world of Islam.

From Al-Suwayrkiyah to Meccah
(from *Personal Narrative of a Pilgrimage to El-Medinah and Meccah*
(1855–6))

Having pitched the tent and eaten and slept, we prepared to perform the ceremony of *Al-Ihram* (assuming the pilgrim-garb), as Al-Zaribah is the Mikat, or the appointed place. Between the noonday and the afternoon prayers a barber attended to shave our heads, cut our nails, and trim our mustachios. Then, having bathed and perfumed ourselves, – the latter is a questionable point, – we donned the attire, which is nothing but two new cotton cloths, each six feet long by three and a half broad, white, with narrow red stripes and fringes: in fact, the costume called *Al-Eddeh*, in the baths at Cairo. One of these sheets, technically termed the *Rida*, is thrown over the back, and, exposing the arm and shoulder, is knotted at the right side in the style *Wishah*. The

Izar is wrapped round the loins from waist to knee, and, knotted or tucked in at the middle, supports itself. Our heads were bare, and nothing was allowed upon the instep. It is said that some clans of Arabs still preserve this religious but most uncomfortable costume; it is doubtless of ancient date, and to this day, in the regions lying west of the Red Sea, it continues to be the common dress of the people.

After the toilette, we were placed with our faces in the direction of Meccah, and ordered to say aloud, 'I vow this Ihram of Hajj (the pilgrimage) and the Umrah (the Little pilgrimage) to Allah Almighty!' Having thus performed a two-bow prayer, we repeated, without rising from the sitting position, these words, 'Oh Allah! verily I purpose the Hajj and the Umrah, then enable me to accomplish the two, and accept them both of me, and make both blessed to me!' Followed the *Talbiyat*, or exclaiming —

'Here I am! O Allah! here am I –
No partner hast Thou, here am I;
Verily the praise and the grace are Thine, and the empire –
No partner hast Thou, here am I!'

And we were warned to repeat these words as often as possible, until the conclusion of the ceremonies. Then Shaykh Abdullah, who acted as director of our consciences, bade us be good pilgrims, avoiding quarrels, immorality, bad language, and light conversation. We must so reverence life that we should avoid killing game, causing an animal to fly, and even pointing it out for destruction; nor should we scratch ourselves, save with the open palm, lest vermin be destroyed, or a hair uprooted by the nail. We were to respect the sanctuary by sparing the trees, and not to pluck a single blade of grass. As regards personal considerations, we were to abstain from all oils, perfumes, and unguents; from washing the head with mallow or with lote leaves; from dyeing, shaving, cutting, or vellicating a single pile or hair; and though we might take advantage of shade, and even form it with upraised hands, we must by no means cover our sconces. For each infraction of these ordinances we must sacrifice a sheep; and it is commonly said by Moslems that none but the Prophet could be perfect in the intricacies of pilgrimage. Old Ali began with an irregularity: he declared that age prevented his assuming the garb, but that, arrived at Meccah, he would clear himself by an offering.

The wife and daughters of a Turkish pilgrim of our party assumed the Ihram at the same time as ourselves. They appeared dressed in white garments; and they had exchanged the Lisam, that coquettish fold of muslin which veils without concealing the lower part of the face, for a hideous mask, made of split, dried, and plaited palm-leaves, with two 'bulls'-eyes' for light. I could not help laughing when these strange figures met my sight, and, to judge from the shaking of their shoulders, they were not less susceptible to the merriment which they had caused.

At three P.M. we left Al-Zaribah, travelling towards the South-West, and a wondrously picturesque scene met the eye. Crowds hurried along, habited in the pilgrimgarb, whose whiteness contrasted strangely with their black skins; their newly shaven heads glistening in the sun, and their long black hair streaming in the wind. The rocks rang with shouts of *Labbayk! Labbayk!* At a pass we fell in with the Wahhabis, accompanying the Baghdad Caravan, screaming 'Here am I'; and, guided by a large loud kettle-drum, they followed in double file the camel of a standard-bearer, whose green flag bore in huge white letters the formula of the Moslem creed. They were wild-looking mountaineers, dark and fierce, with hair twisted into thin Dalik or plaits: each was armed with a long spear, a matchlock, or a dagger. They were seated upon coarse wooden saddles, without cushions or stirrups, a fine saddle-cloth alone denoting a chief. The women emulated the men; they either guided their own dromedaries, or, sitting in pillion, they clung to their husbands; veils they disdained, and their countenances certainly belonged not to a 'soft sex.' These Wahhabis were by no means pleasant companions. Most of them were followed by spare dromedaries, either unladen or carrying water-skins, fodder, fuel, and other necessaries for the march. The beasts delighted in dashing furiously through our file, which being lashed together, head and tail, was thrown each time into the greatest confusion. And whenever we were observed smoking, we were cursed aloud for Infidels and Idolaters.

Looking back at Al-Zaribah, soon after our departure, I saw a heavy nimbus settle upon the hill-tops, a sheet of rain being stretched between it and the plain. The low grumbling of thunder sounded joyfully in our ears. We hoped for a shower, but were disappointed by a dust-storm, which ended with a few heavy drops. There arose a report that the Badawin had attacked a party of Meccans with stones, and the news caused men to look exceeding grave.

At five P.M. we entered the wide bed of the Fiumara, down which we were to travel all night. Here the country falls rapidly towards the sea, as the increasing heat of the air, the direction of the watercourses, and signs of violence in the torrent-bed show. The Fiumara varies in breadth from a hundred and fifty feet to three-quarters of a mile; its course, I was told, is towards the South-West, and it enters the sea near Jeddah. The channel is a coarse sand, with here and there masses of sheet rock and patches of thin vegetation.

At about half-past five P.M. we entered a suspicious-looking place. On the right was a stony buttress, along whose base the stream, when there is one, swings; and to this depression was our road limited by the rocks and thorn trees which filled the other half of the channel. The left side was a precipice, grim and barren, but not so abrupt as its brother. Opposite us the way seemed barred by piles of hills, crest rising above crest into the far blue distance. Day still smiled upon the upper peaks, but the lower slopes and the Fiumara bed were already curtained with grey sombre shade.

A damp seemed to fall upon our spirits as we approached this Valley Perilous. I remarked that the voices of the women and children sank into silence, and the loud Labbayk of the pilgrims were gradually stilled. Whilst still speculating upon the cause of this phenomenon, it became apparent. A small curl of the smoke, like a lady's ringlet, on the summit of the right-hand precipice, caught my eye; and simultaneous with the echoing crack of the matchlock, a high-trotting dromedary in front of me rolled over upon the sands, – a bullet had split its heart, – throwing the rider a goodly somersault of five or six yards.

Ensued terrible confusion; women screamed, children cried, and men vociferated, each one striving with might and main to urge his animal out of the place of death. But the road being narrow, they only managed to jam the vehicles in a solid immovable mass. At every matchlock shot, a shudder ran through the huge body, as when the surgeon's scalpel touches some more sensitive nerve. The Irregular horsemen, perfectly useless, galloped up and down over the stones, shouting to and ordering one another. The Pasha of the army had his carpet spread at the foot of the left-hand precipice, and debated over his pipe with the officers what ought to be done. No good genius whispered 'Crown the heights.'

Then it was that the conduct of the Wahhabis found favour in my eyes. They came up, galloping their camels, –

'Torrents less rapid, and less rash, –'

with their elf-locks tossing in the wind, and their flaring matches casting a strange lurid light over their features. Taking up a position, one body began to fire upon the Utaybah robbers, whilst two or three hundred, dismounting, swarmed up the hill under the guidance of the Sharif Zayd. I had remarked this nobleman at Al-Madinah as a model specimen of the pure Arab. Like all Sharifs, he is celebrated for bravery, and has killed many with his own hand. When urged at Al-Zaribah to ride into Meccah, he swore that he would not leave the Caravan till in sight of the walls; and, fortunately for the pilgrims, he kept his word. Presently the firing was heard far in our rear, the robbers having fled. The head of the column advanced, and the dense body of pilgrims opened out. Our forced halt was now exchanged for a flight. It required much management to steer our Desert-craft clear of danger; but Shayak Mas'ud was equal to the occasion. That many were not, was evident by the boxes and baggage that strewed the shingles. I had no means of ascertaining the number of men killed and wounded: reports were contradictory, and exaggeration unanimous. The robbers were said to be a hundred and fifty in number; their object was plunder, and they would eat the shot camels. But their principal ambition was the boast, 'We, the Utaybah, on such and such a night, stopped the Sultan's Mahmil one whole hour in the Pass.'

At the beginning of the skirmish I had primed my pistols, and sat with them ready for use. But soon seeing that there was nothing to be done, and wishing to make an impression, – nowhere does Bobadil now 'go down' so well as in the East, – I called aloud for my supper. Shaykh Nur, exanimate with fear, could not move. The boy Mohammed ejaculated only an 'Oh, sir!' and the people around exclaimed in disgust, 'By Allah, he eats!' Shaykh Abdullah, the Meccan, being a man of spirit, was amused by the spectacle. 'Are these Afghan manners, Effendim?' he enquired from the Shugduf behind me. 'Yes,' I replied aloud, 'in my country we always dine before an attack of robbers, because that gentry is in the habit of sending men to bed supperless.' The Shaykh laughed aloud, but those around him looked offended. I thought the bravado this time *mal placé;* but a little event which took place on my way to Jeddah proved that it was not quite a failure.

As we advanced, our escort took care to fire every large dry Asclepias, to disperse the shades which buried us. Again the scene became wondrous wild:–

> 'Full many a waste I've wander'd o'er,
> Clomb many a crag, cross'd many a shore,
>   But, by my halidome,
> A scene so rude, so wild as this,
> Yet so sublime in barrenness,
> Ne'er did my wandering footsteps press,
>   Where'er I chanced to roam.'

On either side were ribbed precipices, dark, angry, and towering above, till their summits mingled with the glooms of night; and between them formidable looked the chasm, down which our host hurried with shouts and discharges of matchlocks. The torch-smoke and the night-fires of flaming Asclepias formed a canopy, sable above and livid red below; it hung over our heads like a sheet, and divided the cliffs into two equal parts. Here the fire flashed fiercely from a tall thorn, that crackled and shot up showers of sparks into the air; there it died away in lurid gleams, which lit up a truly Stygian scene. As usual, however, the picturesque had its inconveniences. There was no path. Rocks, stonebanks, and trees obstructed our passage. The camels, now blind in darkness, then dazzled by a flood of light, stumbled frequently; in some places slipping down a steep descent, in others sliding over a sheet of mud. There were furious quarrels and fierce language between camel-men and their hirers, and threats to fellow-travellers; in fact, we were united in discord. I passed that night crying, 'Hai! Hai!' switching the camel, and fruitlessly endeavouring to fustigate Mas'ud's nephew, who resolutely slept upon the water-bags. During the hours of darkness we made four or five halts, when we boiled coffee and smoked pipes; but man and beasts were beginning to suffer from a deadly fatigue.

Dawn (Saturday, Sept. 10th) found us still travelling down the

Fiumara, which here is about a hundred yards broad. The granite hills on both sides were less precipitous; and the borders of the torrent-bed became natural quays of stiff clay, which showed a water-mark of from twelve to fifteen feet in height. In many parts the bed was muddy; and the moist places, as usual, caused accidents. I happened to be looking back at Shaykh Abdullah, who was then riding in old Ali bin Ya Sin's fine Shugduf; suddenly the camel's four legs disappeared from under him, his right side flattening the ground, and the two riders were pitched severally out of the smashed vehicle. Abdullah started up furious, and with great zest abused the Badawin, who were absent. 'Feed these Arabs,' he exclaimed, quoting a Turkish proverb, 'and they will fire at Heaven!' But I observed that, when Shaykh Mas'ud came up, the citizen was only gruff.

We then turned Northward, and sighted Al-Mazik, more generally known as Wady Laymun, the Valley of Limes. On the right bank of the Fiumara stood the Meccan Sharif's state pavilion, green and gold: it was surrounded by his attendants, and he had prepared to receive the Pasha of the Caravan. We advanced half a mile, and encamped temporarily in a hill-girt bulge of the Fiumara bed. At eight A.M. we had travelled about twenty-four miles from Al-Zaribah, and the direction of our present station was South-west 50°.

Shaykh Mas'ud allowed us only four hours' halt; he wished to precede the main body. After breaking our fast joyously upon limes, pomegranates, and fresh dates, we sallied forth to admire the beauties of the place. We are once more on classic ground – the ground of the ancient Arab poets,–

'Deserted is the village – waste the halting place and home
At Mina, o'er Rijam and Ghul wild beasts unheeded roam,
On Rayyan hill the channel lines have left their naked trace,
Time-worn, as *primal Writ that dints the mountain's flinty face;'*–

and this Wady, celebrated for the purity of its air, has from remote ages been a favourite resort of the Meccans. Nothing can be more soothing to the brain than the dark-green foliage of the limes and pomegranates; and from the base of the Southern hill bursts a bubbling stream, whose

'Chaire, fresche e dolci acque'

flow through the gardens, filling them with the most delicious of melodies, the gladdest sound which Nature in these regions knows.

Exactly at noon Mas'ud seized the halter of the foremost camel, and we started down the Fiumara. Troops of Badawi girls looked over the orchard walls laughingly, and children came out to offer us fresh fruit and sweet water. At two P.M., travelling South-west, we arrived at a point where the torrent-bed turns to the right: and, quitting it, we climbed with difficulty over a steep ridge of granite. Before three o'clock we entered a hill-girt plain, which my companions called 'Sola.' In some places were clumps of trees, and scattered villages warned us that we were approaching a city. Far to the left rose the blue peaks of Taif, and the mountain road, a white thread upon the nearer heights, was pointed out to me. Here I first saw the tree, or rather shrub, which bears the balm of Gilead, erst so celebrated for its tonic and stomachic properties. I told Shaykh Mas'ud to break off a twig, which he did heedlessly. The act was witnessed by our party with a roar of laughter; and the astounded Shaykh was warned that he had become subject to an atoning sacrifice. Of course he denounced me as the instigator, and I could not fairly refuse assistance. The tree has of late years been carefully described by many botanists; I will only say that the bark resembled in colour a cherry-stick pipe, the inside was a light yellow, and the juice made my fingers stick together.

At four P.M. we came to a steep and rocky Pass, up which we toiled with difficulty. The face of the country was rising once more, and again presented the aspect of numerous small basins divided and surrounded by hills. As we jogged on we were passed by the cavalcade of no less a personage than the Sharif of Meccah. Abd al-Muttalib bin Ghalib is a dark, beardless old man with African features derived from his mother. He was plainly dressed in white garments and a white muslin turband, which made him look jet black; he rode an ambling mule, and the only emblem of his dignity was the large green satin umbrella born by an attendant on foot. Scattered around him were about forty match-lock men, mostly slaves. At long intervals, after their father, came his four sons, Riza Bey, Adbullah, Ali, and Ahmad, the latter still a child. The three elder brothers rode splendid dromedaries at speed; they were young men of light complexion, with the true Meccan cast of features, showily dressed in bright coloured silks, and armed, to denote their rank, with sword and gold-hilted dagger.

We halted as evening approached, and strained our eyes, but all in vain, to catch sight of Meccah, which lies in a winding valley. By Shaykh Abdullah's direction I recited after the usual devotions, the following prayer. The reader is forwarned that it is difficult to preserve the flowers of Oriental rhetoric in a European tongue.

'O Allah! verily this is Thy Safeguard (*Amn*) and Thy (*Harim*)! Into it whoso entereth becometh safe *(Amin)*. So deny *(Harrim)* my Flesh and Blood, my Bones and Skin, to Hell-fire. O Allah! save me from Thy Wrath on the Day when Thy Servants shall be raised from the Dead. I conjure Thee by this that Thou art Allah, besides whom is none (Thou only), the Merciful, the Compassionate. And have Mercy upon our Lord Mohammed, and upon the Progeny of our Lord Mohammed, and upon his Followers, One and All!' This was concluded with the 'Talbiyat,' and with an especial prayer for myself.

We again mounted, and night completed our disappointment. About one A.M. I was aroused by general excitement. 'Meccah! Meccah!' cried some voices; 'The Sanctuary! O the Sanctuary!' exclaimed others; and all burst into loud 'Labbayk,' not unfrequently broken by sobs. I looked out from my litter, and saw by the light of the Southern stars the dim outlines of a large city, a shade darker than the surrounding plain. We were passing over the last ridge by a cutting called the Saniyat Kuda'a, the winding-place of the cut. The 'winding path' is flanked on both sides by watch-towers, which command the *Darb al-Ma'ala* or road leading from the North into Meccah. Thence we passed into the Ma'abidah (Northern suburb), where the Sharif's Palace is built. After this, on the left hand, came the deserted abode of the Sharif bin Aun, now said to be a 'haunted house.' Opposite to it lies the Jannat al-Ma'ala, the holy cemetery of Meccah. Thence, turning to the right, we entered the Sulaymaniyah or Afghan quarter. Here the boy Mohammed, being an inhabitant of the Shamiyah or Syrian ward, thought proper to display some apprehension. The two are on bad terms; children never meet without exchanging volleys of stones, and men fight furiously with quarterstaves. Sometimes, despite the terrors of religion, the knife and sabre are drawn. But their hostilities have their code. If a citizen be killed, there is a subscription for blood-money. An inhabitant of one quarter, passing singly through another, becomes a guest; once beyond the walls, he is likely to be beaten to insensibility by his hospitable foes.

At the Sulaymaniyah we turned off the main road into a byway, and ascended by narrow lanes the rough heights of Jabal Hindi, upon which stands a small whitewashed and crenellated building called a fort. Thence descending, we threaded dark streets, in places crowded with rude cots and dusky figures, and finally at two A.M. we found ourselves at the door of the boy Mohammed's house.

The First Visit to the House of Allah
(from *Personal Narrative of a Pilgrimage to El-Medinah and Meccah* (1855–6))

There at last it lay, the bourn of my long and weary Pilgrimage, releasing the plans and hopes of many and many a year. The mirage medium of Fancy invested the huge catafalque and its gloomy pall with peculiar charms. There were no giant fragments of hoar antiquity as in Egypt, no remains of graceful and harmonious beauty as in Greece and Italy, no barbarous gorgeousness as in the buildings of India; yet the view was strange, unique – and how few have looked upon the celebrated shrine! I may truly say that, of all the worshippers who clung weeping to the curtain, or who pressed their beating hearts to the stone, none felt for the moment a deeper emotion than did the Haji from the far-north. It was as if the poetical legends of the Arab spoke truth, and that the waving wings of angels, not the sweet breeze of morning, were agitating and swelling the black covering of the shrine. But, to confess humbling truth, theirs was the high feeling of religious enthusiasm, mine was the ecstasy of gratified pride.

Few Moslems contemplate for the first time the Ka'abah, without fear and awe: there is a popular jest against new comers, that they generally inquire the direction of prayer. This being the Kiblah, or fronting place, Moslems pray all around it; a circumstance which of course cannot take place in any spot of Al-Islam but the Harim. The boy Mohammed, therefore, left me for a few minutes to myself; but presently he warned me that it was time to begin. Advancing, we entered through the Bab Benu Shaybah, the 'Gate of the Sons of the Shaybah' (old woman). There we raised our hands, repeated the Labbayk, the Takbir, and the Tahlil; after which we uttered certain supplications, and drew our hands down our faces. Then we proceeded to the Shafe'is' place of worship – the open pavement between the Makam Ibrahim and the well Zemzem – where we performed the usual two-bow prayer in honour of the Mosque. This was followed by a cup of holy water and a present to the Sakkas, or carriers, who for the consideration distributed, in my name, a large earthen vaseful to poor pilgrims.

The word Zemzem has a doubtful origin. Some derive it from the Zam Zam, or murmuring of its waters, others from Zam! Zam! (fill! fill! *i.e.* the bottle), Hagar's impatient exclamation when she saw the stream. Sale translates it stay! stay! and says that Hagar called out in the Egyptian language, to prevent her son wandering. The Hukama, or Rationalists of Al-Islam, who invariably connect their faith with the worship of Venus, especially, and the heavenly bodies generally, derive Zemzem from the Persian, and make it signify the 'great luminary.' Hence they say the Zemzem, as well as the Ka'abah, denoting the Cuthite or Ammonian worship of sun and fire, deserves man's reverence. So the Persian poet Khakani addresses these two buildings:–

'O Ka'abah, thou traveller of the heavens!'
'O Venus, thou fire of the world!'

Thus Wahid Mohammed, founder of the Wahidiyah sect, identifies the Kiblah and the sun; wherefore he says the door fronts the East. By the names Yaman ('right-hand'), Sham ('left-hand'), Kubul, or the East wind ('fronting'), and Dubur, or the West wind ('from the back'), it is evident that worshippers fronted the rising sun. According to the Hukama, the original Black Stone represents Venus, 'which in the border of the heavens is a star of the planets,' and symbolical of the generative power of nature, 'by whose passive energy the universe was warmed into life and motion.' The Hindus accuse the Moslems of adoring the Bayt Ullah.

'O Moslem, if thou worship the Ka'abah,
Why reproach the worshippers of idols?'

says Rai Manshar. And Musaylimah, who in his attempt to

found a fresh faith, gained but the historic epithet of 'Liar,'
allowed his followers to turn their faces in any direction, mentally
ejaculating, 'I address myself to thee, who hast neither side nor
figure;' a doctrine which might be sensible in the abstract, but
certainly not material enough and pride-flattering to win him
many converts in Arabia.

The produce of Zemzem is held in great esteem. It is used for
drinking and religious ablution, but for no baser purposes; and
the Meccans advise pilgrims always to break their fast with it. It is
apt to cause diarrhœa and boils, and I never saw a stranger drink
it without a wry face. Sale is decidely correct in his assertion: the
flavour is a salt-bitter, much resembling an infusion of a
teaspoonful of Epsom salts in a large tumbler of tepid water.
Moreover, it is exceedingly 'heavy' to the digestion. For this
reason Turks and other strangers prefer rain-water, collected in
cisterns and sold for five farthings a gugglet. It was a favourite
amusement with me to watch them whilst they drank the holy
water, and to taunt their scant and irreverent potations.

The strictures of the *Calcutta Review* (No. 41, art 1), based upon
the taste of Zemzem, are unfounded. In these days a critic cannot
be excused for such hasty judgments; at Calcutta or Bombay he
would easily find a jar of Zemzem water, which he might taste for
himself. Upon this passage Mr. W. Muir (Life of Mahomet,
vol. 1, p. cclviii.) remarks that 'the flavour of stale water bottled
up for months would not be a criterion of the same water freshly
drawn.' But it might easily be analysed.

The water is transmitted to distant regions in glazed earthen
jars covered with basket-work, and sealed by the Zemzemis. Religious men break their lenten fast with it, apply it to their eyes to
brighten vision, and imbibe a few drops at the hour of death,
when Satan stands by holding a bowl of purest water, the price of
the departing soul. Of course modern superstition is not idle
about the waters of Zemzem. The copious supply of the well is
considered at Meccah miraculous; in distant countries it facili-
tates the pronunciation of Arabic to the student; and everywhere
the nauseous draught is highly meritorious in a religious point of
view.

We then advanced towards the eastern angle of the Ka'abah,
in which is inserted the Black Stone; and, standing about ten
yards from it, repeated with upraised hands, 'There is no god but
Allah alone, Whose Covenant is Truth, and Whose Servant is

Victorious. There is no god but Allah, without Sharer; His is the Kingdom, to Him be Praise, and He over all Things is potent.' After which we approached as close as we could to the stone. A crowd of pilgrims preventing our touching it that time, we raised our hands to our ears, in the first position of prayer, and then lowering them, exclaimed, 'O Allah (I do this), in Thy Belief, and in verification of Thy Book, and in Pursuance of Thy Prophet's Example – may Allah bless Him and preserve! O Allah, I extend my Hand to Thee, and great is my Desire to Thee! O accept Thou my Supplication, and diminish my Obstacles, and pity my Humiliation, and graciously grant me Thy Pardon!' After which, as we were still unable to reach the stone, we raised our hands to our ears, the palms facing the stone, as if touching it, recited the various religious formulæ, the Takbir, the Tahlil, and the Hamdilah, blessed the Prophet, and kissed the finger-tips of the right hand. The Prophet used to weep when he touched the Black Stone, and said that it was the place for the pouring forth of tears. According to most authors, the second Caliph also used to kiss it. For this reason most Moslems, except the Shafe'i school, must touch the stone with both hands and apply their lips to it, or touch it with the fingers, which should be kissed, or rub the palms upon it, and afterwards draw them down the face. Under circumstances of difficulty, it is sufficient to stand before the stone, but the Prophet's Sunnat, or practice, was to touch it. Lucian mentions adoration of the sun by kissing the hand.

Then commenced the ceremony of *Tawáf*, or circumambulation, our route being the *Mataf* – the low oval of polished granite immediately surrounding the Ka'abah. I repeated, after my Mutawwif, or cicerone, 'In the Name of Allah, and Allah is omnipotent! I purpose to circuit seven circuits unto Almighty Allah, glorified and exalted!' This is technically called the Niyat (intention) of Tawaf. Then we began the prayer, 'O Allah (I do this), in Thy Belief, and in Verification of Thy Book, and in Faithfulness to Thy Covenant, and in Perseverance of the Example of the Apostle Mohammed – may Allah bless Him and preserve!' till we reached the place Al Multazem, between the corner of the Black Stone and the Ka'abah door. Here we ejaculated, 'O Allah, Thou hast Rights, so pardon my transgressing them.' Opposite the door we repeated, 'O Allah, verily the House is Thy House, and the Sanctuary Thy Sanctuary, and the Safeguard Thy Safeguard, and this is the Place of him who flies to Thee from (hell)

Fire!' At the little building called Makam Ibrahim we said, 'O Allah, verily this is the Place of Abraham, who took Refuge with and fled to Thee from the Fire! – O deny my Flesh and Blood, my Skin and Bones to the (eternal) Flames!' As we paced slowly round the north or Irak corner of the Ka'abah we exclaimed, 'O Allah, verily I take Refuge with Thee from Polytheism, and Disobedience, and Hypocrisy, and evil Conversation, and evil Thoughts concerning Family, and Property, and Progeny!' When fronting the Mizab, or spout, we repeated the words, 'O Allah, verily I beg of Thee Faith which shall not decline, and a Certainty which shall not perish, and the good Aid of Thy Prophet Mohammed – may Allah bless Him and preserve! O Allah, shadow me in Thy Shadow on that Day when there is no Shade but Thy Shadow, and cause me to drink from the Cup of Thine Apostle Mohammed – may Allah bless Him and preserve! – that pleasant Draught after which is no Thirst to all Eternity, O Lord of Honour and Glory!' Turning the west corner, or the Rukn al-Shami, we exclaimed, 'O Allah, make it an acceptable Pilgrimage, and a Forgiveness of Sins, and a laudable Endeavour, and a pleasant Action (in Thy sight), and a store which perisheth not, O Thou Glorious! O Thou Pardoner!' This was repeated thrice, till we arrived at the Yamani, or south corner, where, the crowd being less importunate, we touched the wall with the right hand, after the example of the Prophet, and kissed the finger-tips. Finally, between the south angle and that of the Black Stone, where our circuit would be completed, we said, 'O Allah, verily I take Refuge with Thee from Infidelity, and I take Refuge with Thee from Want, and from the Tortures of the Tomb, and from the Troubles of Life and Death. And I fly to Thee from Ignominy in this World and the next, and I implore Thy Pardon for the Present and for the Future. O Lord, grant to me in this Life Prosperity, and in the next Life Prosperity, and save me from the Punishment of Fire.'

Thus finished a Shaut, or single course round the house. Of these we performed the first three at the pace called Harwalah, very similar to the French *pas gymnastique*, or Tarammul, that is to say, 'moving the shoulders as if walking in sand.' The four latter are performed in Ta'ammul, slowly and leisurely; the reverse of the Sai, or running. These seven Ashwat, or courses, are called collectively one Usbu. The Moslem origin of this custom is too well known to require mention. After each Taufah or circuit, we, being unable to kiss or even to touch the Black Stone, fronted towards it, raised our hands to our ears, exclaimed, 'In the Name of Allah, and Allah is omnipotent!' kissed our fingers, and resumed the ceremony of circumambulation, as before, with 'Allah, in Thy Belief,' &c.

At the conclusion of the Tawaf it was deemed advisable to attempt to kiss the stone. For a time I stood looking in despair at the swarming crowd of Badawi and other pilgrims that besieged it. But the boy Mohammed was equal to the occasion. During our circuit he had displayed a fiery zeal against heresy and schism, by foully abusing every Persian in his path; and the inopportune introduction of hard words into his prayers made the latter a strange patchwork; as 'Ave Maria purissima, – arrah, don't ye be letting the pig at the pot, – sanctissima,' and so forth. He might, for instance, be repeating 'And I take Refuge with Thee from Ignominy in this World,' when 'O thou rejected one, son of the rejected!' would be the interpolation addressed to some long bearded Khorasani, – 'And in that to come' – 'O hog and brother of a hoggess!' And so he continued till I wondered that none dared to turn and rend him. After vainly addressing the pilgrims, of whom nothing could be seen but a mosaic of occiputs and shoulder-blades, the boy Mohammed collected about half a dozen stalwart Meccans, with whose assistance, by sheer strength, we wedged our way into the thin and light-legged crowd. The Badawin turned round upon us like wild-cats, but they had no daggers. The season being autumn, they had not swelled themselves with milk for six months; and they had become such living mummies, that I could have managed single-handed half a dozen of them. After thus reaching the stone, despite popular indignation testified by impatient shouts, we monopolised the use of it for at least ten minutes. Whilst kissing it and rubbing hands and forehead upon it I narrowly observed it, and came away persuaded that it is an aërolite. It is curious that almost all travellers agree upon one point, namely, that the stone is volcanic. Ali Bey calls it 'mineralogically' a 'block of volcanic basalt, whose circumference is sprinkled with little crystals, pointed and straw-like, with rhombs of tile-red feldspath upon a dark background, like velvet or charcoal, except one of its protuberances, which is reddish.' Burckhardt thought it was 'a lava containing several small extraneous particles of a whitish and of a yellowish substance.'

Having kissed the stone we fought our way through the crowd

to the place called Al-Multazem. Here we pressed our stomachs, chests, and right cheeks to the Ka'abah, raising our arms high above our heads and exclaiming, 'O Allah! O Lord of the Ancient House, free my Neck from Hell-fire, and preserve me from every ill Deed, and make me contented with that daily bread which Thou hast given to me, and bless me in all Thou hast granted!' Then came the Istighfar, or begging of pardon; 'I beg Pardon of Allah the most high, who, there is no other God but He, the Living, the Eternal, and unto Him I repent myself!' After which we blessed the Prophet, and then asked for ourselves all that our souls most desired.

THREE
THE AFRICAN EXPLORER

After his adventures in the Hejaz, Burton looked for another Islamic shrine to infiltrate: Harar in Somaliland. He sought the aid of some British officers to take part in the exploration of Somaliland; among them was Lt. John Hanning Speke (1827–64), later his collaborator in Africa. At first Burton planned to enter Harar in disguise, but in the end he entered the city openly as a would-be emissary from Britain. The Amir welcomed him but kept him under a kind of city arrest until fear of British intervention led him to release his unwelcome guest. In the extract printed from *First Footsteps in East Africa* Burton gives an ironic, stoical account of his dangerous exploit.

On the basis of his successes in the Islamic holy places and the sensation caused by his books on the subject, between 1854 and 1855 Burton obtained permission for a second expedition to Somaliland. Again accompanied by Speke (and two other Army officers), Burton reached the horn of Africa and camped near Berbera. In April 1855 his camp was attacked. Speke was badly wounded, and one of the other officers killed. Burton himself took a javelin through the face; it transfixed his jaw and emerged on the opposite cheek. The white men were very lucky to escape with their lives and beat a confused retreat.

After recuperating in England from his wounds, Burton saw service in the Crimean War. Predictably he again fell foul of the high command and of the notorious Lord Raglan who, champion of the commission purchase system, detested Indian Army officers who actually had experience in warfare. Burton commanded a force of cavalry irregulars – a task well suited to his talents – but again his contempt for the imbecility of his superiors shone through, and by the end of the conflict he was as much *persona non grata* to the 'top brass' as W.H. Russell, *The Times* correspondent, who first alerted the British public to the horrors and official incompetence in the war.

In the mid-nineteenth century Africa was truly the 'Dark Continent' – most of its interior was still unexplored. Reports reaching the East African coast suggested that there was an 'inland sea' or 'slug-shaped' lake called Tanganyika. Burton proposed to chart the limits of this lake, study the ethnography of the tribes in the area, and report on trade prospects in the interior. His private ambition was to find the source of the Nile, the 'Mountains of the Moon' just north of the Equator of which Ptolemy the ancient geographer had spoken. The Indian Company agreed to the request for a two-year leave of absence, and the enterprise was sponsored both by the Royal Geographical Society and by the Foreign Office, which contributed £1,000 to the expenses.

While making preparations in London, Burton again met Speke and agreed to take him on the expedition, on the basis of Speke's knowledge of geodesy acquired in Tibet. The clash between these two powerful personalities was of an almost mythical kind, Hector against Achilles, Arjun versus Karna. Speke was born into a moneyed, aristocratic Wiltshire family but, unlike Burton, he had no intellectual interests at all. His greatest love was big-game hunting, and he had spent much of his early life, like Burton, in the army in India, and on hunting leave in the Himalayas. Tall, fair-haired, the very epitome of the English gentleman, Speke with his diffident manner concealed ambition and will power of frightening intensity. Unknowingly, on the Somali expedition Burton had seriously alienated him, by sending him on a subsidiary expedition, by calling his journal notes amateurish and, worst of all, by appearing to attribute cowardice to Speke during the night attack at Berbera.

Speke the glory-hunter bitterly resented serving as second-in-command to Burton. *He* wanted the greatest fame as an explorer

of Africa. Beneath the contingent and ephemeral points of difference between the two men was an unbridgeable psychological
chasm. Burton's personality was fundamentally bisexual.
Because of his parents' inadequacy, his early bonding had been
with his brother Edward. When Edward became a catatonic
depressive after taking a terrible beating from some angry
villagers in Ceylon, and spent the rest of his life in an asylum,
Burton tried to fill the gap with young men who would be substi-
tute brothers. There was a long of line of these: John Steinha-
euser, Walter Scott, Charles Tyrwhitt Drake. In one of those
curious coincidences in which Burton's life abounded, all these
men met early or tragic deaths.

Burton, in a word, wanted a fraternal relationship with Speke.
Since Speke was himself a repressed homosexual, there would
seem to have been no obvious barrier. But Speke had psychological demons of his own to wrestle with. His mother-fixation, the
basic element in his homosexuality, led him to entertain
murderous feelings towards his large family of siblings, and especially towards his elder brother. These homicidal feelings manifested themselves in two main ways. Whenever Speke achieved a
triumph, such as sighting a new river, he would celebrate with
the slaughter of the first animal that came to hand. Speke gives us
many examples of his bloodlust in big-game hunting; he would
fire away with insensate rage at a herd of hippo long after he had
bagged enough and to spare in terms of meat supply. The other
manifestation was even more odd. Speke liked to kill pregnant
female deer and antelope, then rip out the foetus and gorge
himself on the flesh of the embryo, which he professed to find a
great delicacy. This hatred of the unborn mammal can be seen as
a transmogrified hatred of the other offspring actually born to his
beloved mother.

Speke's oddity did not end there. At his very first meeting with
Burton he told him he had come to Africa to be killed. In many
other men, especially in the Victorian era, this could be dismissed
as tired-of-life hyperbole. But the entire tenor of Speke's life, his
many brushes with death, his excessively developed instincts of
aggression and slaughter, and, especially, the manner of his
death, suggest that more profound unconscious forces were at
work.

In 1857 an expedition under Speke and Burton departed from
Zanzibar for the interior, following the established Arab caravan

routes. It took them 134 days to get as far as Tabora. They then pressed on to Lake Tanganyika and took boats to the northern end, hoping to find the true source of the Nile. But the key river Ruzizi proved to be an influent, not effluent, which destroyed the theory that Lake Tanganyika could be the source of the Nile.

The expedition returned to Ujiji and thence to Tabora (Unyanyembe). Here Burton made the greatest mistake of his life. By this time he was tired of Speke, whose jealous, essentially philistine English temperament was so alien to his own. Also, Burton hated and despised Africans, and the Arab settlement of Tabora was a haven for him, with his love of all things Islamic. He therefore consented to allow Speke to strike north in pursuit of another lake, said by rumour and folklore to be even bigger than Tanganyika. In this way, while Burton lolled at Tabora, Speke discovered the true source of the Nile, at Lake Victoria.

The evidence for Speke's claim was impressive, and at some level Burton already knew his companion had scooped the great prize. But Burton refused to accept Speke's theory that Lake Victoria was the fountain of the Nile and subjected Speke to ridicule: 'The fortunate discoverer's conviction was strong; his reasons were weak – were of the category alluded to by the damsel Lucetta, when justifying her penchant in favour of the lovely gentleman Sir Proteus: "I have no other but a woman's reason. I think him so because I think him so."'

Relations between the two plummeted, and the return journey to the East coast (reached in January 1859) was accomplished largely in sullen silence. The journey was the greatest feat of East African exploration to date. Burton's meticulous anthropological notes on the Gogo, the Kimbu, the Ha and other leading tribes of the Lake Regions make his record of the expedition *the* principal source of the history of Tanzania c.1830–55. Burton's great achievement was marred only by his visceral hatred of the black man (illustrated in the first extract), which was to get worse as he grew older. Here was another paradox about Burton. He could get inside the idiom of any culture, even one he hated and despised. The gap between Burton the scholarly anthropologist and Burton the stereotypical Victorian theorist of race was an unbridgeable crevasse.

Burton was always a self-destructive individual. Even when he had achieved great things, a certain boredom or hauteur always prevented him from capitalizing on them. Not so Speke, the ruthless glory-hunter. The two men arrived in Zanzibar with relations between them at rock-bottom. Burton then made the mistake of vacationing in the Red Sea while Speke hurried home to England to address the Royal Geographical Society and establish himself as the true professional African explorer, as against Burton's dilettantism. Sir Roderick Murchison, president of the Royal Geographical Society, who never liked Burton, immediately commissioned Speke to head a second expedition to fix the sources of the Nile. Burton arrived in England to find that Speke had swept the board clean. The result was a feud that lasted until Speke's death.

In the three extracts reproduced here from *The Lake Regions of Central Africa*, there is no mention of Speke. Nor is there elsewhere in the book; Burton simply cut him out and referred to 'my companion'. Burton's East African book lacks the drama of Stanley's journeys, but his careful, meticulous, scientific observation is everywhere in evidence.

First Footsteps in East Africa; or, An Exploration of Harar (1856)

At 10 A.M. on the 2nd January, all the villagers assembled, and recited the Fatihah, consoling us with the information that we were dead men. By the worst of footpaths, we ascended the tough and stony hill behind Sagharrah, through bush and burn and over ridges of rock. At the summit was a village, where Shirwa halted, declaring that he dared not advance: a swordsman, however, was sent on to guard us through the Galla Pass. After an hour's ride, we reached the foot of a tall Table-mountain called Kondura, where our road, a goat-path rough with rocks or fallen trees, and here and there arched over with giant creepers, was reduced to a narrow ledge, with a forest above and a forest below. I could not but admire the beauty of this Valombrosa, which reminded me of scenes whilome enjoyed in fair Touraine. High up on our left rose the perpendicular walls of the misty hill, fringed with tufted pine, and on the right the shrub-clad folds fell into a deep valley. The cool wind whistled and sunbeams like golden shafts darted through tall shady trees – 'bearded with moss, and in garments green' – the ground was clothed with dank grass, and around the trunks grew thistles, daisies, and blue flowers, which, at a distance might well pass for violets.

Presently we were summarily stopped by half a dozen Gallas attending upon one Rabah, the Chief who owns the Pass. This is the African style of toll-raking: the 'pike' appears in the form of a plump spearman, and the gate is a pair of lances thrown across the road. Not without trouble, for they feared to depart from the *mos majorum*, we persuaded them that the ass carried no merchandise. Then rounding Kondura's northern flank, we entered the Amir's territory: about thirty miles distant, and separated by a series of blue valleys, lay a dark speck upon a tawny sheet of stubble – Harar.

Having paused for a moment to savour success, we began the descent. The ground was slippery black soil – mist ever settles upon Kondura – and frequent springs oozing from the rock formed beds of black mire. A few huge Birbisa trees, the remnant of a forest still thick around the mountain's neck, marked out the road: they were branchy from stem to stern, and many had a girth of from twenty to twenty-five feet.

After an hour's ride amongst thistles, whose flowers of a bright red-like worsted were not less than a child's head, we watered our mules at a rill below the slope. Then remounting, we urged over hill and dale, where Galla peasants were threshing and storing their grain and loud songs of joy: they were easily distinguished by their African features, mere caricatures of the Somal, whose type has been Arabized by repeated immigrations from al Yemen and Hadramaut. Late in the afternoon, having gained ten miles in a straight direction, we passed through a hedge of plantains, defending the windward side of Gafra, a village of Midgans who collect the Gerad Adan's grain. They shouted delight on recognizing their old friend, Mad Sa'id, led us to an empty Gambisa, swept and cleaned it, lighted a fire, turned our mules into a field to graze, and went forth to seek food. Their hospitable thoughts, however, were marred by the two citizens of Harar, who privately threatened them with the Amir's wrath, if they dared to feed that Turk.

As evening drew on, came a message from our enemies, the Habr Awal, who offered, if we would wait till sunrise, to enter the city in our train. The Gerad Adan had counselled me not to provoke these men; so, contrary to the advice of my two companions, I returned a polite answer, purporting that we would expect them till eight o'clock the next morning.

At 7 A.M., on the 3rd January, we heard that the treacherous Habr Awal had driven away their cows shortly after midnight. Seeing their hostile intentions, I left my journal, sketches, and other books in charge of an old Midgan, with directions that they should be forwarded to the Gerad Adan, and determined to carry nothing but our arms and a few presents for the Amir. We saddled our mules, mounted, and rode hurriedly along the edge of a picturesque chasm of tender pink granite, here and there obscured by luxuriant vegetation. In the centre, fringed with bright banks, a shallow rill, called Doghlah, now brawls in tiny cascades, then whirls through huge boulders towards the Erar river. Presently, descending by a ladder of rock scarcely safe even for mules, we followed the course of the burn, and emerging into the valley beneath, we pricked forward rapidly, for day was wearing on, and we did not wish the Habr Awal to precede us.

About noon we crossed the Erar river. The bed is about one hundred yards broad, and a thin sheet of clear, cool, and sweet water covered with crystal the great part of the sand. According to my guides, its course, like that of the hills, is southerly towards the Webbe of Ogadayn: none, however, could satisfy my curiosity concerning the course of the only perennial stream which exists between Harar and the coast.

In the lower valley, a mass of waving holcus, we met a multitude of Galla peasants coming from the city market with new potlids and the empty gourds which had contained their butter, ghi, and milk; all wondered aloud at the Turk, concerning whom they had heard many horrors. As we commenced another ascent, appeared a Harar Grandee mounted upon a handsomely caparisoned mule and attended by seven servants who carried gourds and skins of grain. He was a pale-faced senior with a white beard, dressed in a fine Tobe and a snowy turban, with scarlet edges: he carried no shield, but an Abyssinian broadsword was slung over his left shoulder. We exchanged courteous salutations, and as I was thirsty he ordered a footman to fill a cup with water. Half way up the hill appeared the 200 Girhi cows, but those traitors, the Habr Awal, had hurried onwards. Upon the summit was pointed out to me the village of Elaoda: in former times it was a wealthy place belonging to the Gerad Adan.

At 2 P.M. we fell into a narrow fenced land, and halted for a few minutes near a spreading tree, under which sat women selling ghi and unspun cotton. About two miles distant on the crest of a hill, stood the city – the end of my present travel – a long sombre line strikingly contrasting with the whitewashed towns of the East. The spectacle, materially speaking, was a disappointment: nothing conspicuous appeared but two grey minarets of rude shape: many would have grudged exposing three lives to win so paltry a prize. But of all that have attempted, none ever succeeded in entering that pile of stones: the thorough-bred traveller, dear L., will understand my exultation, although my two companions exchanged glances of wonder.

Spurring our mules, we advanced at a long trot, when Mad Sa'id stopped us to recite the Fatihah in honour of Ao Umar Siyad and Ao Rahmah, two great saints who repose under a clump of trees near the road. The soil on both sides of the path is rich and red: masses of plantains, limes, and pomegranates denote the gardens, which are defended by a bleached cow's skull, stuck upon a short stick and between them are plantations of coffee, bastard saffron, and the graceful Kat. About half a mile eastward of the town appears a burn called Jalah or the Coffee Water: the crowd crossing it did not prevent my companions bathing, and whilst they donned clean Tobes I retired to the wayside, and sketched the town.

These operations over, we resumed our way up a rough *tranchée* ridged with stone and hedged with tall cactus. This ascends to an open plain. On the right lie the holcus fields, which reach to the town wall: the left is a heap of rude cemetery, and in front are the dark defences of Harar, with groups of citizens loitering about the large gateway, and sitting in chat near the ruined tomb of Ao Abdal. We arrived at 3 P.M., after riding about five hours, which were required to accomplish twenty direct miles.

Advancing to the gate, Mad Sa'id accosted a warder, known by his long wand of office, and sent our salaams to the Amir, saying that we came from Aden, and requested the honour of audience. Whilst he sped upon his errand, we sat at the foot of a round bastion, and were scrutinized, derided, and catechized by the curious of both sexes, especially by that conventionally termed the fair. The three Habr Awal presently approached and scowlingly inquired why we had not apprised them of our intention to enter the city. It was now 'war to the knife' – we did not deign a reply.

After waiting half an hour at the gate, we were told by the

returned warder to pass the threshold, and remounting guided our mules along the main street, a narrow up-hill lane, with rocks cropping out from a surface more irregular than a Perote pavement. Long Gulad had given his animal into the hands of our two Bedouin: they did not appear till after our audience, when they informed us that the people at the entrance had advised them to escape with the beasts, an evil fate having been prepared for the proprietors.

Arrived within a hundred yards of the gate of holcus stalks, which opens into the courtyard of this African St. James's, our guide, a blear-eyed, surly-faced, angry-voiced fellow, made signs – none of us understanding his Harari – to dismount. We did so. He then began to trot, and roared out apparently that we must do the same. We looked at one another, the Hammal swore that he would perish foully rather then obey, and – conceive, dear L., the idea of a petticoated pilgrim venerable as to beard and turban breaking into a long 'double!' – I expressed much the same sentiment. Leading our mules leisurely, in spite of the guide's wrath, we entered the gate, strode down the yard, and were placed under a tree in its left corner, close to a low building of rough stone, which the clanking of frequent fetters argued to be a state prison.

This part of the court was crowded with Gallas, some lounging about, others squatting in the shade under the palace walls. The chiefs were known by their zinc armlets, composed of thin spiral circlets, closely joined, and extending in mass from the wrist almost to the elbow: all appeared to enjoy peculiar privileges – they carried their long spears, wore their sandals, and walked leisurely about the royal precincts. A delay of half an hour, during which state affairs were being transacted within, gave me time to inspect a place of which so many and such different accounts are current. The palace itself is, as Clapperton describes the Fellatah Sultan's state hall, a mere shed, a long, single storied, windowless barn of rough stone and reddish clay, with no other insignia but a thin coat of whitewash over the door. This is the royal and wazirial distinction at Harar, where no lesser man may stucco the walls of his house. The courtyard was about eighty yards long by thirty in breadth, irregularly shaped, and surrounded by low buildings: in the centre, opposite the outer entrance, was a circle of masonry against which were propped divers doors.

Presently the blear-eyed guide with the angry voice returned from within, released us from the importunities of certain forward and inquisitive youths, and motioned us to doff our slippers at a stone step, or rather line, about twelve feet distant from the palace wall. We grumbled that we were not entering a mosque, but in vain. Then ensued a long dispute, in tongues mutually unintelligible, about giving up our weapons; by dint of obstinacy we retained our daggers and my revolver. The guide raised a door curtain, suggested a bow, and I stood in the presence of the dreaded chief.

The Amir, or, as he styles himself, the Sultan Ahmad bin Sultan Abibakr, sat in a dark room with whitewashed walls, to which hung – significant decorations – rusty matchlocks and polished fetters. His appearance was that of a little Indian Rajah, an etiolated youth twenty-four or twenty-five years old, plain and thin-bearded, with a yellow complexion, wrinkled brows and protruding eyes. His dress was a flowing robe of crimson cloth, edged with snowy fur, and a narrow white turban tightly twisted round a tall conical cap of red velvet, like the old Turkish headgear of our painters. His throne was a common Indian Kursi, or raised cot, about five feet long, with back and sides supported by a dwarf railing: being an invalid he rested his elbow upon a pillow, under which appeared the hilt of a Cutch sabre. Ranged in double line, perpendicular to the Amir, stood the 'court,' his cousins and nearest relations with right arms bared after the fashion of Abyssinia.

I entered the room with a loud 'Peace be upon ye!' to which H.H. replying graciously, and extending a hand, bony and yellow as a kite's claw, snapped his thumb and middle finger. Two chamberlains stepping forward, held my forearms, and assisted me to bend low over the fingers, which however I did not kiss, being naturally averse to performing that operation upon any but a woman's hand. My two servants then took their turn: in this case, after the back was saluted, the palm was presented for a repetition. These preliminaries concluded, we were led to and seated upon a mat in front of the Amir, who directed towards us a frowning brow and inquisitive eye.

Some inquiries were made about the chief's health: he shook his head captiously, and inquired our errand. I drew from my pocket my own letter: it was carried by a chamberlain, with hands veiled in his Tobe, to the Amir, who after a brief glance laid it upon the couch, and demanded further explanation. I then represented in Arabic that we had come from Aden, bearing the compliments of our Daulah or governor, and that we had entered Harar to see the light of H.H.'s countenance: this information concluded with a little speech, describing the changes of Political Agents in Arabia, and alluding to the friendship formerly existing between the English and the deceased chief Abibakr.

The Amir smiled graciously.

The smile I must own, dear L., was a relief. We had been prepared for the worst, and the aspect of affairs in the palace was by no means reassuring.

Whispering to his Treasurer, a little ugly man with a badly shaven head, coarse features, pug nose, angry eyes, and stubby beard, the Amir made a sign for us to retire. The *baise main* was repeated, and we backed out of the audience-shed in high favour. According to grandiloquent Bruce, 'the Court of London and that of Abyssinia are, in their principles, one': the loiterers in the Harar palace yards who had before regarded us with cut-throat looks, now smiled as though they loved us. Marshalled by the guard, we issued from the precincts, and after walking a hundred yards entered the Amir's second palace, which we were told to consider our home. There we found the Bedouin, who, scarcely believing that we had escaped alive, grinned in the joy of their hearts, and we were at once provided from the chief's kitchen with a dish of Shabta, holcus cakes soaked in sour milk, and thickly powdered with red pepper, the salt of this inland region.

When we had eaten, the treasurer reappeared, bearing the Amir's command, that we should call upon his Wazir, the Gerad Mohammed. Resuming our peregrinations, we entered an abode distinguished by its external streak of chunam, and in a small room on the ground floor, cleanly whitewashed and adorned, like an old English kitchen, with varnished wooden porringers of various sizes, we found a venerable old man whose benevolent countenance belied the reports current about him in Somaliland. Half rising, although his wrinkled brow showed suffering, he seated me by his side upon the carpeted masonry-bench, where lay the implements of his craft, reeds, inkstands and whitewashed boards for paper, politely welcomed me, and gravely stroking his cotton-coloured beard, in good Arabic desired my object.

I replied almost in the words used to the Amir, adding however some details how in the old days one Madar Farih had been charged by the late Sultan Abibakr with a present to the governor of Aden, and that it was the wish of our people to re-establish friendly relations and commercial intercourse with Harar.

'Khayr Inshallah! – it is well if Allah please!' ejaculated the Gerad: I then bent over his hand, and took leave.

Returning, we inquired anxiously of the treasurer about my servants' arms which had not been returned, and were assured that they had been placed in the safest of store-houses, the palace. I then sent a common six-barrelled revolver as a present to the Amir, explaining its use to the bearer, and we prepared to make ourselves as comfortable as possible. The interior of our new house was a clean room, with plain walls, and a floor of tamped earth; opposite the entrance were two broad steps of masonry, raised about two feet, and a yard above the ground, and covered with hard matting. I contrived to make upon the higher ledge a bed with the cushions which my companions used as shabracques, and, after seeing the mules fed and tethered, lay down to rest worn out by fatigue and profoundly impressed with the *poésie* of our position. I was under the roof of a bigoted prince whose least word was death; amongst a people who detest foreigners; the only European that had ever passed over their inhospitable threshold, and the fated instrument of their future downfall.

The Lake Regions of Central Africa,
A Picture of Exploration (1860)

1

The main characteristic of this people is the selfishness which the civilised man strives to conceal, because publishing it would obstruct its gratification. The barbarian, on the other hand, displays his inordinate egotism openly and recklessly; his every action discloses those unworthy traits which in more polished races chiefly appear on public occasions, when each man thinks solely of self-gratification. Gratitude with him is not even a sense of prospective favours; he looks upon a benefit as the weakness of his benefactor and his own strength; consequently, he will not recognise even the hand that feeds him. He will, perhaps, lament for a night the death of a parent or a child, but the morrow will find him thoroughly comforted. The name of hospitality, except for interested motives, is unknown to him: 'What will you give me?' is his first question. To a stranger entering a village the worst hut is assigned, and, if he complains, the answer is that he can find encamping ground outside. Instead of treating him like a guest, which the Arab Bedouin would hold to be a point of pride, of honour, his host compels him to pay and prepay every article, otherwise he might starve in the midst of plenty. Nothing, in fact, renders the stranger's life safe in this land, except the timid shrinking of the natives from the 'hot-mouthed weapon' and the necessity of trade, which induces the chiefs to restrain the atrocities of their subjects. To travellers the African is, of course, less civil than to merchants, from whom he expects to gain something. He will refuse a mouthful of water out of his abundance to a man dying of thirst; utterly unsympathising, he will not stretch out a hand to save another's goods, though worth thousands of dollars. Of his own property, if a ragged cloth or a lame slave be lost, his violent excitement is ridiculous to behold. His egotism renders him parsimonious even in self-gratification; the wretched curs, which he loves as much as his children seldom receive a mouthful of food, and the sight of an Arab's ass feeding on grain elicits a prolonged 'Hi! hi!' of extreme surprise. He is exceedingly improvident, taking no thought for the morrow – not from faith, but rather from carelessness as to what may betide him; yet so greedy of gain is he that he will refuse information about a country or the direction of a path without a present of beads. He also invariably demands prepayment: no one keeps a promise or adheres to an agreement, and, if credit be demanded for an hour, his answer would be, 'There is nothing in my hand.' Yet even greed of gain cannot overcome the levity and laxity of his mind. Despite his best interests, he will indulge the mania for desertion caused by that mischievous love of change and whimsical desire for novelty that characterise the European sailor. Nor can even lucre prevail against the ingrained indolence of the race – an indolence the more hopeless as it is the growth of the climate. In these temperate and abundant lands Nature has cursed mankind with the abundance of her gifts; his wants still await creation, and he is contented with such necessaries as roots and herbs, game, and a few handfuls of grain – consequently improvement has no hold upon him.

In this stage of society truth is no virtue. The 'mixture of a lie' may 'add to pleasure' amongst Europeans; in Africa it enters where neither pleasure nor profit can arise from the deception. If a Mnyamwezi guide informs the traveller that the stage is short, he may make up his mind for a long and weary march, and *vice versâ*. Of course, falsehood is used as a defence by the weak and oppressed; but beyond that, the African desires to be lied to, and one of his proverbs is, ''Tis better to be deceived than to be undeceived.' The European thus qualifies the assertion,

> 'For sure the pleasure is as great
> In being cheated as to cheat.'

Like the generality of barbarous races, the East Africans are wilful, headstrong, and undisciplinable: in point of stubbornness and restiveness they resemble the lower animals. If they cannot obtain the very article of barter upon which they have set their mind, they will carry home things useless to them; any attempt at bargaining is settled by the seller turning his back, and they ask according to their wants and wishes, without regard to the value of goods. Grumbling and dissatisfied, they never do business without a grievance. Revenge is a ruling passion, as the many rancorous fratricidal wars that have prevailed between kindred clans, even for a generation, prove. Retaliation and vengeance are, in fact, their great agents of moral control. Judged by the test of death, the East African is a hardhearted man, who seems to ignore all the charities of father, son, and brother. A tear is rarely shed, except by the women, for departed parent, relative, or friend, and the voice of the mourner is seldom heard in their abodes. It is most painful to witness the complete inhumanity with which a porter seized with small-pox is allowed by his friends, comrades, and brethren to fall behind in the jungle, with several days' life in him. No inducement – even beads – can persuade a soul to attend him. Every village will drive him from its doors; no one will risk taking, at any price, death into his bosom. If strong enough, the sufferer builds a little bough-hut away from the camp, and, provided with his rations – a pound of grain and a gourdful of water – he quietly expects his doom, to feed the hyæna and the raven of the wild. The people are remarkable for the readiness with which they yield to fits of sudden fury; on these occasions they will, like children, vent their rage upon any object, animate or inanimate, that presents itself. Their temper is characterised by a nervous, futile impatience; under delay or disappointment they become madmen. In their own country, where such displays are safe, they are remarkable for a presumptuousness and a violence of manner which elsewhere disappears. As the Arabs say, there they are lions, here they become curs. Their squabbling and clamour pass description: they are never happy except when in dispute. After a rapid plunge into excitement, the brawlers alternatively advance and recede, pointing the finger of threat, howling and screaming, cursing and using terms of insult which an inferior ingenuity – not want of will – causes to fall short of the Asiatic's model vituperation. After abusing each other to their full, both 'parties' usually burst into a loud laugh or a burst of sobs. Their tears lie high; they weep like Goanese. After a cuff, a man will cover his face with his hands and cry as if his heart would break. More furious shrews than the women are nowhere met with. Here it is a great truth that 'the tongues of women cannot be governed.' They work off excitement by scolding, and they weep little compared with the men. Both sexes delight in 'argument,' which here, as elsewhere, means two fools talking foolishly. They will weary out of patience the most loquacious of the Arabs. This development is characteristic of the East African race, and 'maneno marefu!' – long words! – will occur as a useless reproof half a dozen times in the course of a single conversation. When drunk, the East African is easily irritated; with the screams and excited gestures of a maniac he strides about, frantically flourishing his spear and agitating his bow, probably with notched arrow; the spear-point and the arrow-head are often brought perilously near, but rarely allowed to draw blood. The real combat is by pushing, pulling hair, and slapping with a will, and a pair thus engaged require to be torn asunder by half a dozen friends. The settled tribes are, for the most part, feeble and unwarlike barbarians; even the bravest East African, though, like all men, a combative entity, has a valour tempered by discretion and cooled by a high development of cautiousness. His tactics are of the Fabian order: he loves surprises and safe ambuscades; and in common frays and forays the loss of one per cent. justifies a *sauve qui peut*. This people, childlike, is ever in extremes. A man will hang himself from a rafter in his tent, and kick away from under him the large wooden mortar upon which he has stood at the beginning of the operation with as much sang-froid as an Anglo-Saxon in the gloomy month of November; yet he regards annihilation, as all savages do, with loathing and ineffable horror.

'He fears death,' to quote Bacon, 'as children fear to go in the dark; and as that natural fear in children is increased with tales, so is the other.' The African mind must change radically before it can 'think upon death, and find it the least of all evils.' All the thoughts of these negroids are connected with this life. 'Ah!' they exclaim, 'it is bad to die! to leave off eating and drinking! never to wear a fine cloth!' As in the negro race generally, their destructiveness is prominent; a slave never breaks a thing without an instinctive laugh of pleasure; and however careful he may be of his own life, he does not value that of another, even of a relative, at the price of a goat. During fires in the town of Zanzibar, the blacks have been seen adding fuel, and singing and dancing, wild with delight. On such occasions they are shot down by the Arabs like dogs.

It is difficult to explain the state of society in which the civilised 'social evil' is not recognised as an evil. In the economy of the affections and the intercourse between the sexes, reappears that rude stage of society in which ethics were new to the mind of now enlightened man. Marriage with this people – as amongst all barbarians, and even the lower classes of civilised races – is a mere affair of buying and selling. A man must marry because it is necessary to his comfort, consequently the woman becomes a marketable commodity. Her father demands for her as many cows, cloths, and brass-wire bracelets as the suitor can afford; he thus virtually sells her, and she belongs to the buyer, ranking with his other live stock. The husband may sell his wife, or, if she be taken from him by another man, he claims her value, which is ruled by what she would fetch in the slave-market. A strong inducement to marriage amongst the Africans, as with the poor in Europe, is the prospective benefit to be derived from an adult family; a large progeny enriches them. The African – like all barbarians, and, indeed, semi-civilised people – ignores the dowry by which, inverting Nature's order, the wife buys the husband, instead of the husband buying the wife. Marriage, which is an epoch amongst Christians, and an event with Moslems, is with these people an incident of frequent recurrence. Polygamy is unlimited, and the chiefs pride themselves upon the number of their wives, varying from twelve to three hundred. It is no disgrace for an unmarried woman to become the mother of a family; after matrimony there is somewhat less laxity. The mgoni or adulterer, if detected, is punishable by a fine of cattle, or, if poor and weak, he is sold into slavery; husbands seldom, however, resort to such severities, the offence, which is considered to be against vested property, being held to be lighter than petty larceny. Under the influence of jealousy, murders and mutilations have been committed, but they are rare and exceptional. Divorce is readily effected by turning the spouse out of doors, and the children become the father's property. Attachment to home is powerful in the African race, but it regards rather the comforts and pleasures of the house, and the unity of relations and friends, than the fondness of family. Husband, wife, and children have through life divided interests, and live together with scant appearance of affection. Love of offspring can have but little power amongst a people who have no preventive for illegitimacy, and whose progeny may be sold at any time. The children appear undemonstrative and unaffectionate, as those of the Somal. Some attachment to their mothers breaks out, not in outward indications, but by surprise, as it were: 'Mámá! mámá!' – mother! mother! – is a common exclamation in fear or wonder. When childhood is passed, the father and son become natural enemies, after the manner of wild beasts. Yet they are a sociable race, and the sudden loss of relatives sometimes leads from grief to hypochondria and insanity, resulting from the inability of their minds to bear any unusual strain. It is probable that a little learning would make them mad, like Widad, or priest of the Somal, who, after mastering the reading of the Koran, becomes unfit for any exertion of judgment or common sense. To this over-development of sociability must be ascribed the anxiety always shown to shift, evade, or answer blame. The 'ukosa,' or transgression, is never accepted; any number of words will be wasted in proving the worse the better cause. Hence also the favourite phrase, 'Mbáyá we!' – thou art bad! – a pet mode of reproof which sounds simple and uneffective to European ears.

The social position of the women – the unerring test of progress towards civilisation – is not so high in East Africa as amongst the more highly organised tribes of the south. Few parts of the country own the rule of female chiefs. The people, especially the Wanyamwezi, consult their wives, but the opinion of a brother or a friend would usually prevail over that of a woman.

The deficiency of the East African in constructive power has already been remarked. Contented with his haystack or beehive hut, his hemisphere of boughs, or his hide acting tent, he hates

and has a truly savage horror of stone walls. He has the concep-
tion of the 'Madeleine,' but he has never been enabled to be
delivered of it. Many Wanyamwezi, when visiting Zanzibar,
cannot be prevailed upon to enter a house.

The East African is greedy and voracious; he seems, however,
to prefer light and frequent to a few regular and copious meals.
Even the civilised Kisawahili has no terms to express the breakfast, dinner, and supper of other languages. Like most barbarians, the East African can exist and work with a small quantity of
food, but he is unaccustomed, and therefore unable, to bear
thirst. The daily ration of a porter is 1 kubabah (= 1.5 1bs.) of
grain; he can, with the assistance of edible herbs and roots, which
he is skilful in discovering in the least likely places, eke out this
allowance for several days, though generally, upon the
barbarian's impulsive principle of mortgaging the future for the
present, he recklessly consumes his stores. With him the grand
end of life is eating; his love of feeding is inferior only to his
propensity for intoxication. He drinks till he can no longer stand,
lies down to sleep, and awakes to drink again. Drinking-bouts are
solemn things, to which the most important business must yield
precedence. They celebrate with beer every event – the traveller's
return, the birth of a child, and the death of an elephant – a
labourer will not work unless beer is provided for him. A guest is
received with a gourdful of beer, and, amongst some tribes, it is
buried with their princes. The highest orders rejoice in drink, and
pride themselves upon powers of imbibing: the proper diet for a
king is much beer and a little meat. If a Mnyamwezi be asked
after eating whether he is hungry, he will reply yea, meaning that
he is not drunk. Intoxication excuses crime in these lands. The
East African, when in his cups, must issue from his hut to sing,
dance, or quarrel, and the frequent and terrible outrages which
occur on these occasions are passed over on the plea that he has
drunk beer. The favourite hour for drinking is after dawn, – a
time as distasteful to the European as agreeable to the African
and Asiatic. This might be proved by a host of quotations from
the poets, Arab, Persian, and Hindu. The civilised man avoids
early potations because they incapacitate him for necessary
labour, and he attempts to relieve the headache caused by stimu-
lants. The barbarian and the semi-civilised, on the other hand,
prefer them, because they relieve the tedium of his monotonous
day; and they cherish the headache because they can sleep the

longer, and, when they awake, they have something to think of. The habit once acquired is never broken: it attaches itself to the heartstrings of the idle and unoccupied barbarian.

2

Unyanyembe, which rises about 3480 feet above sea-level, and lies 356 miles in rectilinear distance from the eastern coast of Africa, resembles in its physical features the lands about Tura. The plain or basin of Ihárá, or Kwihárá, a word synonymous with the 'Bondei' or low-land of the coast, is bounded on the north and south by low, rolling hills, which converge towards the west, where, with the characteristically irregular lay of primitive formations, they are crossed almost at right angles by the Mfuto chain. The position has been imprudently chosen by the Arabs; the land suffers from alternate drought and floods, which render the climate markedly malarious. The soil is aluminous in the low levels – a fertile plain of brown earth, with a subsoil of sand and sandstone, from eight to twelve feet below the surface; the water is often impregnated with iron, and the higher grounds are uninhabited tracts covered with bulky granite-boulders, bushy trees, and thorny shrubs.

Contrary to what might be expected, this 'Bandari-district' contains villages and hamlets, but nothing that can properly be termed a town. The Mtemi or Sultan Fundikira, the most powerful of the Wanyamwezi chiefs, inhabits a Tembe, or square settlement, called 'Ititenya,' on the western slope of the southern hills. A little colony of Arab merchants has four large houses at a neighbouring place, 'Mawiti.' In the centre of the plain lies 'Kazeh,' another scattered collection of six large hollow oblongs, with central courts, garden-plots, store-rooms, and outhouses for the slaves. Around these nuclei cluster native villages – masses of Wanyamwezi hovels, which bear the names of their founders.

This part of Unyanyembe was first colonised about 1852, when the Arabs who had been settled nearly ten years at Kigandu of P'huge, a district of Usukuma, one long day's march north of Kazeh, were induced by Mpagamo, to aid them against Msimbira, a rival chief, who defeated and drove them from their former seats. The details of this event were supplied by an actor in the scenes; they well illustrate the futility of the people. The Arabs, after five or six days of skirmishing, were upon the point of carrying the boma or palisade of Msimbira, their enemy, when suddenly at night their slaves, tired of eating beef and raw ground-nuts, secretly deserted to a man. The masters awaking in the morning found themselves alone, and made up their minds for annihilation. Fortunately for them, the enemy, suspecting an ambuscade, remained behind their walls, and allowed the merchants to retire without an attempt to cut them off. Their employer, Mpagamo, then professed himself unable to defend them; when, deeming themselves insecure, they abandoned his territory. Snay bin Amir and Musa Mzuri, the Indian, settled at Kazeh, then a desert, built houses, sunk wells, and converted it into a populous place.

It is difficult to average the present number of Arab merchants at Unyanyembe who, like the British in India, visit but do not colonise; they rarely, however, exceed twenty-five in number; and during the travelling season, or when a campaign is necessary, they are sometimes reduced to three or four; they are too strong to yield without fighting, and are not strong enough to fight with success. Whenever the people have mustered courage to try a fall with the strangers, they have been encouraged to try again. Hitherto the merchants have been on friendly terms with Fundikira, the chief. Their position, however, though partly held by force of prestige, is precarious. They are all Arabs from Oman, with one solitary exception, Musa Mzuri, an Indian Kojah, who is perhaps in these days the earliest explorer of Unyamwezi. In July, 1858, an Arab merchant, Silim bin Masud, returning from Kazeh to his home at Msene, with a slaveporter carrying a load of cloth, was, though well armed and feared as a good shot, attacked at a water in a strip of jungle westward of Mfuto, and speared in the back by five men, who were afterwards proved to be subjects of the Sultan Kasanyare, a Mvinza. The Arabs organised a small expedition to revenge the murder, marched out with 200 or 300 slave-musket-eers, devoured all the grain and poultry in the country, and returned to their homes without striking a blow, because each merchant-militant wished his fellows to guarantee his goods or his life for the usual diyat, or blood-money, 800 dollars. This impunity of crime will probably lead to other outrages.

The Arabs live comfortably, and even splendidly, at Unyan-yembe. The houses, though single-storied, are large, substantial, and capable of defence. Their gardens are extensive and well planted; they receive regular supplies of merchandise, comforts, and luxuries from the coast; they are surrounded by troops of concubines and slaves, whom they train to divers crafts and callings; rich men have riding-asses from Zanzibar, and even the poorest keep flocks and herds. At Unyanyembe, as at Msene, and sometimes at Ujiji, there are itinerant fundi, or slave-artisans – blacksmiths, tinkers, masons, carpenters, tailors, potters, and rope-makers, – who come up from the coast with Arab caravans. These men demand exorbitant wages. A broken matchlock can be repaired, and even bullets cast; good cord is purchaseable; and for tinning a set of seventeen pots and plates five shukkah merkani are charged. A pair of Arab stirrups are made up for one shukkah besides the material, and chains for animals at about double the price. Fetters and padlocks, however, are usually imported by caravans. Pack-saddles are brought from Zanzibar: in the caravans a man may sometimes be found to make them. There is, moreover, generally a pauper Arab who for cloth will make up a ridge-tent; and as most civilised Orientals can use a needle, professional tailors are little required. Provisions are cheap and plentiful; the profits are large; and the Arab, when wealthy, is disposed to be hospitable and convivial. Many of the more prosperous merchants support their brethren who have been ruined by the chances and accidents of trade. When a stranger appears amongst them, he receives the 'hishmat l'il gharíb,' or the guest-welcome, in the shape of a goat and a load of white rice; he is provided with lodgings, and is introduced by the host to the rest of the society at a general banquet. The Arab's great deficiency is the want of some man to take the lead. About fifteen years ago Abdullah bin Salim, a merchant from Zanzibar, with his body of 200 armed slaves, kept the whole community in subjection: since his death, in 1852, the society has suffered from all the effects of disunion where union is most required. The Arab, however, is even in Africa a Pantisocrat, and his familiarity with the inferior races around him leads to the proverbial consequences.

The houses of the Arabs are Moslem modifications of the African Tembe, somewhat superior in strength and finish. The deep and shady outside-verandah, supported by stout uprights, shelters a broad bench of raised earthwork, where men sit to enjoy the morning cool and the evening serenity, and where they pray, converse, and transact their various avocations. A portcullis-like door, composed of two massive planks, with chains thick as a ship's cable – a precaution rendered necessary by the presence of wild slaves – leads into the barzah, or vestibule. The only furniture is a pair of clay benches extending along the right and left sides, with pillow-shaped terminations of the same material; over these, when visitors are expected, rush mats and rugs are spread. From this barzah a passage, built at the angle proper to baffle the stranger's curiosity, leads into the interior, a hollow square or oblong, with the several rooms opening upon a courtyard, which, when not built round, is completely closed by a 'liwan' – a fence of small tree-trunks or reeds. The apartments have neither outward doors nor windows: small bull's eyes admit the air, and act as loop-holes in case of need. The principal room on the master's side of the house has a bench of clay, and leads into a dark closet where stores and merchandise are placed. There are separate lodgings for the harem, and the domestic slaves live in barracoons or in their own outhouses. This form of Tembe is perhaps the dullest habitation ever invented by man. The exterior view is carefully removed from sight, and the dull, dirty court-yard, often swamped during the rains, is ever before the tenant's eyes; the darkness caused by want of windows painfully contrasts with the flood of sunshine pouring in through the doors, and at night no number of candles will light up its gloomy walls of grey or reddish mud. The breeze is either excluded by careless frontage, or the high and chilling winds pour in like torrents; the roof is never water-tight, and the walls and rafters harbour hosts of scorpions and spiders, wasps and cockroaches. The Arabs, however, will expend their time and trouble in building rather than trust their goods in African huts, exposed to thieves and to the frequent fires which result from barbarous carelessness: everywhere, when a long halt is in prospect, they send their slaves for wood to the jungle, and superintend the building of a spacious Tembe. They neglect, however, an important precaution, a sleeping-room raised above the mean level of malaria.

Another drawback to the Arab's happiness is the failure of his constitution: a man who escapes illness for two successive months boasts of the immunity; and, as in Egypt, no one enjoys robust health. The older residents have learned to moderate their appetites. They eat but twice a-day – after sunrise, and at noon – the midday meal concluded, they confine themselves to chewing tobacco or the dried coffee of Karagwah. They avoid strong meats, especially beef and game, which are considered heating and bilious, remaining satisfied with light dishes, omelets and pillaus, harisáh, firni, and curded milk, and the less they eat the more likely they are to escape fever. Harisáh, in Kisawahili 'boko-boko,' is the roast beef – the *plat de résistance* – of the Eastern and African Arab. It is a kind of pudding made with finely shredded meat, boiled with flour of wheat, rice, or holcus, to the consistence of a thick paste, and eaten with honey or sugar. Firni, an Indian word, is synonymous with the muhallibah of Egypt, a thin jelly of milk-and-water, honey, rice-flour, and spices, which takes the place of our substantial northern rice-pudding. The general health has been improved by the importation from the coast of wheat, and a fine white rice, instead of the red aborigen of the country, of various fruits, plantains, limes, and papaws; and of vegetables, brinjalls, cucumbers, and tomatos, which relieve the indigenous holcus and maize, manioc and sweet-potato, millet and phaseoli, sesamum and ground-nuts. They declare to having derived great benefit from the introduction of onions, – an anti-febral, which flourishes better in Central than in Maritime Africa. The onion, so thriving in South Africa, rapidly degenerates upon the island of Zanzibar into a kind of houseleek. In Unyamwezi it is of tolerable size and flavour. It enters into a variety of dishes, the most nauseous being probably the sugared onion-omelet. In consequence of general demand, onions are expensive in the interior; an indigo-dyed shukkah will purchase little more than a pound. When the bulbs fail, the leaves chopped into thin circles and fried in clarified butter with salt, are eaten as a relish with meat. They are also inserted into marak or soups, to disguise the bitter and rancid taste of stale ghee. Onions may be sown at all seasons except during the wet monsoon, when they are liable to decay. The Washenzi have not yet borrowed this excellent and healthy vegetable from the Arabs. Garlic has also been tried in Unyanyembe, but with less success; moreover, it is considered too heating for daily use. As might be expected, however, amongst a floating population with many slaves, foreign fruits and vegetables are sometimes allowed to die out. Thus some enterprising merchant introduced into Unyanyembe the date and the mkungu, bidam, or almond-tree of the coast: the former, watered once every third day, promised to bear fruit, when, in the absence of the master, the Wanyamwezi cut up the young shoots into walking-sticks. Sugar is imported: the water-wanting cane will not thrive in arid Unyanyembe, and honey must be used as a succedaneum. Black pepper, universally considered cooling by Orientals, is much eaten with curry-stuffs and other highly-seasoned dishes, whereas the excellent chillies and bird-pepper, which here grow wild, are shunned for their heating properties. Butter and ghee are made by the wealthy; humbler houses buy the article, which is plentiful and good, from the Wanyamwezi. Water is the usual beverage. Some Arabs drink togwa, a sweet preparation of holcus; and others, debauchees, indulge in the sour and intoxicating pombe, or small-beer.

The market at Unyanyembe varies greatly according to the quantity of the rains. As usual in barbarous societies, a dry season, or a few unexpected caravans, will raise the prices, even to trebling; and the difference of value in grain before and after the harvest will be double or half of what it is at par. The price of provisions in Unyamwezi has increased inordinately since the Arabs have settled in the land. Formerly a slave-boy could be purchased for five fundo, or fifty strings of beads: the same article would now fetch three hundred. A fundo of cheap white porcelain-beads would procure a milch cow; and a goat, or ten hens its equivalent, was to be bought for one khete. In plentiful years Unyanyembe is, however, still the cheapest country in East Africa, and, as usual in cheap countries, it induces the merchant to spent more than in the dearest. Paddy of good quality, when not in demand, sells at twenty kayla (120 lbs.) for one shukkah of American domestics; maize, at twenty-five; and sorghum, here the staff of life, when in large stock, at sixty. A fat bullock may be bought for four domestics, a cow costs from six to twelve, a sheep or a goat from one to two. A hen, or its equivalent, four or five eggs, is worth one khete of coral or pink porcelain beads. One fundo of the same will purchase a large bunch of plantains, with which máwá or plantain-wine, and siki or vinegar are made; and the Wanyamwezi will supply about a pint of milk every morning at the rate of one shukkah per mensem. A kind of mud-fish is caught by the slaves in the frequent pools which, during the cold season, dot the course of the Gombe Nullah, lying three miles north of Kazeh; and return-caravans often bring with them stores of the small fry, called Kashwá or Daga'a, from the Tanganyika Lake.

From Unyanyembe twenty marches, which are seldom accomplished under twenty-five days, conduct the traveller to Ujiji, upon the Tanganyika. Of these the fifth station is Msene, the great Bandari of Western Unyamwezi. It is usually reached in eight days; and the twelfth is the Malagarazi River, the western limit of the fourth region.

The traveller, by means of introductory letters to the Doyen of the Arab merchants at Kazeh, can always recruit his stock of country currency, – cloth, beads, and wire, – his requirements of powder and ball, and his supply of spices, comforts, and drugs, without which travel in these lands usually ends fatally. He will pay, it is true, about five times their market-value at Zanzibar: sugar, for instance, sells at its weight in ivory, or nearly one-third more than its weight in beads. But though the prices are exorbitant they preserve the buyer from greater evils, the expense of porterage, the risk of loss, and the trouble and annoyance of personally superintending large stores in a land where 'vir' and 'fur' are synonymous terms.

3

After about an hour's march, as we entered a small savannah, I saw the Fundi before alluded to running forward and changing the direction of the caravan. Without supposing that he had taken upon himself this responsibility, I followed him. Presently he breasted a steep and stony hill, sparsely clad with thorny trees: it was the death of my companion's riding-ass. Arrived with toil, – for our fagged beasts now refused to proceed, – we halted for a few minutes upon the summit. 'What is that streak of light which lies below?' I inquired of Seedy Bombay. 'I am of opinion,' quoth Bombay, 'that that is *the* water.' I gazed in dismay; the remains of my blindness, the veil of trees, and a broad ray of sunshine illuminating but one reach of the Lake, had shrunk its fair proportions. Somewhat prematurely I began to lament my folly in having risked life and lost health for so poor a prize, to curse Arab exaggeration, and to propose an immediate return, with the view of exploring the Nyanza, or Northern Lake. Advancing, however, a few yards, the whole scene suddenly burst upon my view, filling me with admiration, wonder, and delight. It gave local habitation to the poet's fancy:–

'Tremolavano i rai del Sol nascente
    Sovra l'onde del mar purpuree e d'oro,
E in veste di zaffiro il ciel ridente
    Specchiar parea le sue bellezze in loro.
D'Africa i venti fieri e d'Oriente,
    Sovra il letto del mar, prendean ristoro,
E co' sospiri suoi soavi e lieti
Col Zeffiro increspava il lembo a Teti.'

Nothing, in sooth, could be more picturesque than this first view of the Tanganyika Lake, as it lay in the lap of the mountains, basking in the gorgeous tropical sunshine. Below and beyond a short foreground of rugged and precipitous hill-fold, down which the foot-path zigzags painfully, a narrow strip of emerald green, never sere and marvellously fertile, shelves towards a ribbon of glistening yellow sand, here bordered by sedgy rushes, there cleanly and clearly cut by the breaking wavelets. Further in front stretch the waters, an expanse of the lightest and softest blue, in breadth varying from thirty to thirty-five miles, and sprinkled by the crisp east-wind with tiny crescents of snowy foam. The background in front is a high and broken wall of steel-coloured mountain, here flecked and capped with pearly mist, there standing sharply pencilled against the azure air; its yawning chasms, marked by a deeper plum-colour, fall towards dwarf hills of mound-like proportions, which apparently dip their feet in the wave. To the south, and opposite the long low point, behind which the Malagarazi River discharges the red loam suspended in its violent stream, lie the bluff headlands and capes of Uguhha, and, as the eye dilates, it falls upon a cluster of outlying islets, speckling a sea-horizon. Villages, cultivated lands, the frequent canoes of the fishermen on the waters, and on a nearer approach the murmurs of the waves breaking upon the shore give a something of variety, of movement, of life to the landscape, which, like all the fairest prospects in these regions, wants but a little of the neatness and finish of Art, – mosques and kiosks, palaces and villas, gardens and orchards – contrasting with the profuse lavishness and magnificence of nature, and diversifying the unbroken *coup d'œil* of excessive vegetation, to rival, if not to excel, the most admired scenery of the classic regions. The riant shores of this vast crevasse appeared doubly beautiful to me after the silent and spectral mangrove-creeks on the East-African seaboard, and the

melancholy, monotonous experience of desert and jungle
scenery, tawny rock and sun-parched plain or rank herbage and
flats of black mire. Truly it was a revel for soul and sight!
Forgetting toils, dangers, and the doubtfulness of return, I felt
willing to endure double what I had endured; and all the party
seemed to join with me in joy. My purblind companion found
nothing to grumble at except the 'mist and glare before his eyes.'
Said bin Salim looked exulting, – *he* had procured for me this
pleasure, – the monoculous Jemadar grinned his congratulations, and even the surly Baloch made civil salams.

Arrived at Ukaranga I was disappointed to find there a few
miserable grass-huts – used as a temporary shelter by caravans
passing to and from the islets fringing the opposite coast – that
clustered round a single Tembe, then occupied by its proprietor,
Hamid bin Sulayyam, an Arab trader. Presently the motive of the
rascally Fundi, in misleading the caravan, which, by the advice of
Snay bin Amir, I had directed to march upon the Kawele district
in Ujiji, leaked out. The roadstead of Ukaranga is separated from
part of Kawele by the line of the Ruche River, which empties
itself into a deep hollow bay, whose chord, extending from N.W.
to S.E., is five or six miles in length. The strip of shelving plain
between the trough-like hills and the lake is raised but a few feet
above water-level. Converted by the passage of a hundred drains
from the highlands, into a sheet of sloppy and slippery mire,
breast deep in select places, it supports with difficulty a few
hundred inhabitants: drenched with violent rain-storms and
clammy dews, it is rife in fevers, and it is feared by travellers on
account of its hippopotami and crocodiles. In the driest season
the land-road is barely practicable; during and after the wet
monsoon the lake affords the only means of passage, and the port
of Ukaranga contains not a single native canoe. The Fundi, therefore, wisely determined that I should spend beads for rations and
lodgings amongst his companions, and be heavily mulcted for a
boat by them. Moreover, he instantly sent word to Mnya Mtaza,
the principal headman of Ukaranga, who, as usual with the
Lakist chiefs, lives in the hills at some distance from the water, to
come instanter for his Honga or blackmail, as, no fresh fish being
procurable, the Wazungu were about to depart. The latter
manœuvre, however, was frustrated by my securing a conveyance
for the morrow. It was an open solid-built Arab craft, capable of
containing thirty to thirty-five men; it belonged to an absent

merchant, Said bin Usman; it was in point of size the second on
the Tanganyika, and being too large for paddling, its crew rowed
instead of scooping up the water like the natives. The slaves, who
had named four khete of coral beads as the price of a bit of sun-
dried 'baccalà,' and five as the hire of a foul hovel for one night,
demanded four cloths – at least the price of the boat – for
conveying the party to Kawele, a three hours' trip. I gave them
ten cloths and two coil-bracelets, or somewhat more than the
market value of the whole equipage, – a fact which I effectually
used as an *argumentum ad verecundiam.*

At eight A.M., on the 14th February, we began coasting along
the eastern shore of the lake in a north-westerly direction,
towards the Kawele district, in the land of Ujiji. The view was
exceedingly beautiful:

> '... the flat sea shone like yellow gold
> Fused in the sun,'

and the picturesque and varied forms of the mountains, rising
above and dipping into the lake, were clad in purplish blue, set
off by the rosy tints of morning. Yet, more and more, as we
approached our destination, I wondered at the absence of all
those features which prelude a popular settlement. Passing the
low, muddy, and grass-grown mouth of the Ruche River, I could
descry on the banks nothing but a few scattered hovels of miserable construction, surrounded by fields of sorghum and sugar-
cane, and shaded by dense groves of the dwarf, bright-green
plantain, and the tall, sombre elæis or Guinea-palm. By the Arabs
I had been taught to expect a town, a ghaut, a port, and a bazar,
excelling in size that of Zanzibar, and I had old, preconceived
ideas concerning 'die Stadt Ujiji,' whose sire was the 'Mombas
Mission Map.' Presently Mammoth and Behemoth shrank
timidly from exposure, and a few hollowed logs, the monoxyles of
the fishermen, the wood-cutters, and the market-people, either
cut the water singly, or stood in crowds drawn up on the patches
of yellow sand. About 11 A.M. the craft was poled through a hole
in a thick welting of coarse reedy grass and flaggy aquatic plants
to a level landing-place of flat shingle, where the water shoaled off
rapidly. Such was the ghaut or disembarkation quay of the great
Ujiji.

Around the ghaut a few scattered huts, in the humblest beehive shape, represented the port-town. Advancing some hundred yards through a din of shouts and screams, tom-toms and trumpets, which defies description, and mobbed by a swarm of black beings, whose eyes seemed about to start from their heads with surprise, I passed a relic of Arab civilisation, the 'Bazar.' It is a plot of higher ground, cleared of grass, and flanked by a crooked tree; there, between 10 A.M. and 3 P.M. – weather permitting – a mass of standing and squatting negroes buy and sell, barter and exchange, offer and chaffer with a hubbub heard for miles, and there a spear or dagger-thrust brings on, by no means unfrequently, a skirmishing faction-fight. The articles exposed for sale are sometimes goats, sheep, and poultry, generally fish, vegetables, and a few fruits, plantains, and melons; palm-wine is a staple commodity, and occasionally an ivory or a slave is hawked about: those industriously disposed employ themselves during the intervals of bargaining in spinning a coarse yarn with the rudest spindle, or in picking the cotton, which is placed in little baskets on the ground. I was led to a ruinous Tembe, built by an Arab merchant, Hamid bin Salim, who had allowed it to be tenanted by ticks and slaves. Situated, however, half a mile from, and backed by, the little village of Kawele, whose mushroom-huts barely protruded their summits above the dense vegetation, and placed at a similar distance from the water in front, it had the double advantage of proximity to provisions, and of a view which at first was highly enjoyable. The Tanganyika is ever seen to advantage from its shores: upon its surface the sight wearies with the unvarying tintage – all shining greens and hazy blues – whilst continuous parallels of lofty hills, like the sides of a huge trough, close the prospect and suggest the idea of confinement.

FOUR

NORTH AMERICAN ROVER

1860 was a year of destiny for both Burton and his treacherous rival. Speke set out on the second expedition, which would eventually win him a place of honour second only to Livingstone and Stanley among African explorers. Burton travelled in North America, then on his return married and began a new career as a consular official.

For a man with Burton's interests and background, his marriage was the least imaginable one. Isabel Arundel, a member of the family of the Roman Catholic Dukes of Arundel, first met Burton when she was nineteen and he twenty-nine but did not marry him until ten years later. She hero-worshipped him and covered him in blind adulation, but Burton, understandably, did not view a devout Catholic as an ideal wife, quite apart from the fact that the Arundel family opposed the match and regarded Burton as a penniless adventurer and vagabond.

But Isabel persisted through rebuff, inspired by a prophecy made to her in 1850 by a gypsy woman called Hagar Burton that she would first meet her future husband across the sea (it was in Boulogne) and that he would bear the name of the gypsy's tribe. Burton over a decade constantly found excuses not to take the final step towards marriage. He disappeared for the Nile expedition to Africa during the courtship and again, in 1860, absented himself for nine months before finally deciding to take the plunge, this time in the USA, where he toured the West and made a famous study of the polygamous Mormons.

Burton landed in Halifax, travelled through Lower Canada, then journeyed through every single state of the USA. In the South he sympathized with the way of life there and dismissed slavery as a social bagatelle. In the West he revelled in the brushes with Indians, reported on scalpings, lynchings and gunfights, analyzed the short-lived Pony Express and drank hardened mountain men under the table. The highlight of his US tour was his investigation of Mormonism at Salt Lake City. The sect which began with founder Joseph Smith's 'revelations' from the Book of Mormon in 1830 was, thirty years later, a thriving community which had tamed the unyielding deserts of Utah under the aegis of its 'prophet', Brigham Young, playing St Paul to Smith's Jesus Christ. 'This is the place' were Young's famous words when he spotted the Salt Lake Valley in 1847, after taking his persecuted followers beyond the ambit of the USA and its laws. When Burton arrived, the Mormons had won their ten-year battle for survival against drought, locusts and grasshoppers and had tamed the wilderness with massive irrigation schemes.

Burton was a deeply sympathetic observer of Mormonism, and clearly thought of the uneducated Brigham Young as a great man. His prose describing the entry into 'Zion' has an appropriately inspirational glow, while his description of the Mormons' Sunday service suggests an amused cynicism beneath the superficial tolerance. But it was always polygamy for which the sect was famous in the nineteenth century ('their religion is singular, but their wives plural', in Mark Twain's witticism). Burton, who thought climate was the principal determinant of libido, seriously endorsed the desirability of polygamy in pioneer societies, much to the disgust of Isabel and other *bien pensants* in England. His *The City of the Saints* is an invaluable source book for Mormonism in the Brigham Young period. Burton was prepared to give Young's followers the benefit of most doubts; for example, he scouts the notion that the paramilitary arm of the Mormons, the Danites, was simply a disguised death squad. The combination of another 'sacred city', the opportunity to pronounce on the 'woman question', and the many paradoxes thrown up by the 'Saints' enabled Burton to write one of his richest and most imaginative works.

The City of the Saints and Across the Rocky Mountains to California (1861)

1

The End – Hurrah! August 25th.
To-day we are to pass over the Wásách, the last and highest chain of the mountain mass between Fort Bridger and the Gt. S.L. Valley, and – by the aid of St. James of Compostella, who is, I believe, bound over to be the patron of pilgrims in general, – to arrive at our destination, New Hierosolyma, or Jerusalem, alias Zion on the tops of the mountains, the future city of Christ, where the Lord is to reign over the Saints, as a temporal king, in power and great glory.

So we girt our loins and started after a cup of tea and a biscuit at 7 A.M., under the good guidance of Mr. Macarthy, who after a whiskeyless night looked forward not less than ourselves to the run in. Following the course of Bauchmin's Creek, we completed the total number of fordings to thirteen in eight miles. The next two miles were along the bed of a watercourse, a complete fiumara, through a bush full of tribulus, which accompanied us to the end of the journey. Presently the ground became rougher and steeper: we alighted and set our breasts manfully against 'Big Mountain,' which lies about four miles from the station. The road bordered upon the wide arroyo, a tumbled bed of block and boulder, with water in places oozing and trickling from the clay walls, from the sandy soil, and from beneath the heaps of rock, – living fountains these, most grateful to the parched traveller. The synclinal slopes of the chasm were grandly wooded with hemlocks, firs, balsam-pines, and other varieties of abies; some tapering up to the height of ninety feet, with an admirable regularity of form, colour, and foliage. The varied hues of the quaking asp were there; the beech, the dwarf oak, and a thicket of elders and wild roses; whilst over all the warm autumnal tints already mingled with the bright green of summer. The ascent became more and more rugged: this steep pitch, at the end of a thousand miles of hard work and semi-starvation, causes the death of many a wretched animal, and we remarked that the bodies are not inodorous among the mountains as on the prairies. In the most fatiguing part, we saw a handcart halted, whilst the owners, a man, a woman, and a boy, took breath. We exchanged a few consolatory words with them and hurried on. The only animal seen on the line, except the grasshopper, whose creaking wings gave forth an ominous note, was the pretty little chirping squirrel. The trees, however, in places bore the marks of huge talons, which were easily distinguished as the sign of bears. The grizzly does not climb except when young: this was probably the common brown variety. At half-way the gorge opened out, assuming more the appearance of a valley; and in places, for a few rods, were dwarf stretches of almost level ground. Towards the Pass-summit the rise is sharpest: here we again descended from the wagon, which the four mules had work enough to draw, and the total length of its eastern rise was five miles. Big Mountain lies eighteen miles from the city. The top is a narrow crest, suddenly forming an acute based upon an obtuse angle.

From that eyrie, 8000 feet above sea level, the weary pilgrim first sights his shrine, the object of his long wanderings, hardships, and perils, the Happy Valley of the Great Salt Lake. The western horizon, when visible, is bounded by a broken wall of light blue mountain, the Oquirrh, whose northernmost bluff buttresses the southern end of the lake, and whose eastern flank sinks in steps and terraces into a river basin, yellow with the sunlit golden corn, and somewhat pink with its carpeting of heath-like moss. In the foreground a semicircular sweep of hill top, and an inverted arch of rocky wall, shuts out all but a few spans of the Valley. These heights are rough with a shaggy forest, in some places black-green, in others of brownish-red, in others of the lightest ash colour, based upon a ruddy soil; whilst a few silvery veins of snow still streak the bare grey rocky flanks of the loftiest peak.

After a few minutes' delay to stand and gaze, we resumed the footpath way, whilst the mail-wagon, with wheels rough-locked, descended what appeared to be an impracticable slope. The summit of the pass was well nigh cleared of timber; the woodman's song informed us that the evil work was still going on, and that we are nearly approaching a large settlement. Thus stripped of their protecting fringes, the mountains are exposed to the heat of summer, that sends forth countless swarms of devastating crickets, grasshoppers, and blue-worms; and to the wintry cold, that piles up, four to six feet high, – the mountain men speak of thirty and forty, – the snows drifted by the unbroken force of the winds. The pass from November to February can be traversed by nothing heavier than 'sleighs,' and during the snow storms even these are stopped. Falling into the gorge of Big Kanyon Creek, after a total of twelve hard miles from Bauchmin's Fork, we reached at 11.30 the station that bears the name of the water near which it is built. We were received by the wife of the proprietor, who was absent at the time of our arrival; and half stifled by the thick dust and the sun which had raised the glass to 103°, we enjoyed copious draughts – *tant soit peu* qualified – of the cool but rather hard water, that trickled down the hill into a trough by the house side. Presently the station master, springing from his light 'sulky,' entered, and was formally introduced to us by Mr. Macarthy as Mr. Ephe Hanks. I had often heard of this individual, as one of the old triumvirate of Mormon desperadoes, the other two being Orrin Porter Rockwell and Bill Hickman – as the leader of the dreaded Danite band, and in short as a model ruffian. The ear often teaches the eye to form its pictures: I had eliminated a kind of mental sketch of those assassin faces which one sees on the Apennines and Pyrenees, and was struck by what met the eye of sense. The 'vile villain,' as he has been called by anti-Mormon writers, who verily do not try to *ménager* their epithets, was a middle-sized, light-haired, good looking man, with regular features, a pleasant and humorous countenance, and the manly manner of his early sailor life, touched with the rough cordiality of the mountaineer. 'Frank as a bear hunter,' is a proverb in these lands. He had, like the rest of the triumvirate, and like most men (Anglo-Americans) of desperate courage and fiery excitable temper, a clear pale blue eye, verging upon grey, and looking as if it wanted nothing better than to light up, together with a cool and quiet glance that seemed to shun neither friend nor foe.

The terrible Ephe began with a facetious allusion to all our new dangers under the roof of a Danite, to which in similar strain, I made answer that Danite or Damnite was pretty much the same to me. After dining, we proceeded to make trial of the air-cane, to which he took, as I could see by the way he handled it, and by the nod with which he acknowledged the observation, 'almighty convenient sometimes not to make a noise, Mister,' a great fancy. He asked me whether I had a mind to 'have a slap' at his namesake, an offer which was gratefully accepted, under the promise that 'cuffy' should previously be marked down so as to save a long ride and a troublesome trudge over the mountains. His battery of 'killb'ars' was heavy and in good order, so that on this score there would have been no trouble, and the only tool he bade me bring was a Colt's revolver, dragoon size. He told me that he was likely to be in England next year, when he had set the 'ole woman' to her work. I suppose my look was somewhat puzzled, for Mrs. Dana graciously explained that every western wife, even when still, as Mrs. Ephe was, in her teens, commands that venerable title, venerable, though somehow not generally coveted.

From Big Kanyon Creek Station to the city, the driver 'reckoned,' was a distance of seventeen miles. We waited till the bright and glaring day had somewhat burned itself out; at noon heavy clouds came up from the south and south-west, casting a grateful shade and shedding a few drops of rain. After taking friendly leave of the 'Danite' chief, – whose cordiality of manner had prepossessed me strongly in his favour – we entered the mail-wagon and prepared ourselves for the finale over the westernmost ridge of the stern Wasach.

After two miles of comparatively level ground we came to the foot of 'Little Mountain,' and descended from the wagon to relieve the poor devils of mules. The near slope was much shorter, but also it was steeper far than 'Big Mountain.' The counterslope was easier, though by no means pleasant to contemplate with the chance of an accident to the break, which in all inconvenient places would part with the protecting shoe-sole. Beyond the eastern foot, which was ten miles distant from our destination, we were miserably bumped and jolted over the broken ground at the head of Big Kanyon. Down this pass, whose name is a translation of the Yuta name Obitkokichi, a turbulent little mountain-stream tumbles over its boulder-bed, girt with the usual sunflower, vines of wild hops, red and white willows, cotton-wood, quaking-asp, and various bushes near its cool watery margin, and upon the easier slopes of the ravine, with the shin or dwarf oak (*Quercus nana*), mountain mahogany, balsam and other firs, pines, and cedars. The road was a narrow shelf along the broader of the two spaces between the stream and the rock, and frequent fordings were rendered necessary by the capricious wanderings of the torrent. I could not but think how horrid must have been its appearance when the stout-hearted Mormon pioneers first ventured to thread the defile, breaking their way through the dense bush, creeping and clinging like flies to the sides of the hills. Even now accidents often occur; here, as in Echo Kanyon, we saw in more than one place, unmistakable signs of upsets in the shape of broken spokes and yoke bows. At one of the most ticklish turns Macarthy kindly pointed out a little precipice where four of the mail passengers fell and broke their necks, a pure invention on his part, I believe, which fortunately, at that moment, did not reach Mrs. Dana's ears. He also entertained us with many a tale, of which the hero was the redoubtable Hanks; how he had slain a buffalo-bull single-handed with a bowie knife, and how on one occasion, when refused hospitality by his Lamanite brethren, he had sworn to have the whole village to himself, and had redeemed his vow by reappearing *in cuerpo*, with gestures so maniacal that the sulky Indians all fled, declaring him to be 'bad medicine.' The stories had at least local colouring.

In due time, emerging from the gates and portals and deep serrations of the upper course, we descended into a lower level: here Big, now called Emigration, Kanyon gradually bulges out, and its steep slopes of grass and fern, shrubbery and stunted brush, fall imperceptibly into the plain. The valley presently lay full before our sight. At this place the pilgrim emigrants, like the Hajis of Mecca and Jerusalem, give vent to the emotions long pent up within their bosoms by sobs and tears, laughter and congratulations, psalms and hysterics. It is indeed no wonder that the children dance, that strong men cheer and shout, and that nervous women, broken with fatigue and hope deferred, scream and faint; that the ignorant should fondly believe that the 'Spirit of God pervades the very atmosphere,' and that Zion on the tops of the mountains is nearer heaven than other parts of earth. In good sooth, though uninfluenced by religious fervour – beyond the natural satisfaction of seeing a bran new Holy City – even I could not, after nineteen days in a mail-wagon, gaze upon the scene without emotion.

The Sublime and the Beautiful were in present contrast. Switzerland and Italy lay side by side. The magnificent scenery of the past mountains and ravines still floated before the retina, as emerging from the gloomy depths of the Golden Pass – the mouth of Emigration Kanyon is more poetically so called – we came suddenly in view of the Holy Valley of the West.

The hour was about 6 P.M., the atmosphere was touched with a dreamy haze, – as it generally is in the vicinity of the Lake – a little bank of rose-coloured clouds, edged with flames of purple and gold, floated in the upper air, whilst the mellow radiance of an American autumn, that bright interlude between the extremes of heat and cold, diffused its mild soft lustre over the face of earth.

The sun, whose slanting rays shone full in our eyes, was setting in a flood of heavenly light behind the bold jagged outline of 'Antelope Island,' which, though distant twenty miles to the north-west, hardly appeared to be ten. At its feet, and then bounding the far horizon, lay, like a band of burnished silver, the Great Salt Lake, that still innocent Dead Sea. South-westwards, also, and equally deceptive as regards distance, rose the boundary of the valley plain, the Oquirrh Range, sharply silhouetted by a sweep of sunshine over its summits, against the depths of an evening sky, in that direction, so pure, so clear, that vision, one might fancy, could penetrate behind the curtain into regions beyond the confines of man's ken. In the brilliant reflected light, which softened off into a glow of delicate pink, we could distinguish the lines of Brigham's, Coon's and other kanyons, which water has traced through the wooded flanks of the Oquirrh down to the shadows already purpling the misty benches at their base. Three distinct and several shades, light azure, blue, and brown blue, graduated the distances, which extended at least thirty miles.

The undulating valley-plain between us and the Oquirrh Range is 12.15 miles broad, and markedly concave, dipping in the centre like the section of a tunnel, and swelling at both edges into bench-lands, which mark the ancient bed of the Lake. In some parts the valley was green; in others, where the sun shot its oblique beams, it was of a tawny yellowish red, like the sands of the Arabian desert, with scatters of trees, where the Jordan of the West rolls its opalline wave through pasture lands of dried grass dotted with flocks and herds, and fields of ripening yellow corn. Everything bears the impress of handiwork, from the bleak benches behind to what was once a barren valley in front. Truly the Mormon prophecy had been fulfilled: already the howling wilderness – in which twelve years ago a few miserable savages, the half naked Digger Indians, gathered their grass-seed, grasshoppers, and black crickets to keep life and soul together, and awoke with their war cries the echo of the mountains, and the bear, the wolf, and the fox prowled over the site of a now populous city – 'has blossomed like the rose.'

This valley, this lovely panorama of green and azure and gold,
this land, fresh as it were from the hands of God, is apparently
girt on all sides by hills: the highest peaks, raised 7000 to 8000 feet
above the plain of their bases, show by gulches veined with lines
of snow that even in this season winter frowns upon the last smile
of summer.

Advancing, we exchanged the rough cahues, and the frequent
fords of the ravine, for a broad smooth highway, spanning the
easternmost valley-bench: a terrace that drops like a Titanic step
from the midst of the surrounding mountains to the level of the
present valley-plain. From a distance – the mouth of Emigration
Kanyon is about 4.30 miles from the city – Zion, which is not on
a hill, but on the contrary lies almost in the lowest part of the
river-plain, is completely hid from sight, as if no such thing
existed. Mr. Macarthy, on application, pointed out the notabilia
of the scene.

Northwards curls of vapour ascending from a gleaming sheet –
the Lake of the Hot Springs – set in a bezel of emerald green, and
bordered by another lake-bench upon which the glooms of
evening were rapidly gathering, hung like a veil of gauze around
the waist of the mountains. Southwards for twenty-five miles
stretched the length of the valley with the little river winding its
way like a silver thread in a brocade of green and gold. The view
in this direction was closed by 'Mountain Point,' another formation of terraced range, which forms the water gate of Jordan, and
which conceals and separates the fresh water that feeds the Salt
Lake – the Sea of Tiberias from the Dead Sea.

As we descended the Wasach Mountains, we could look back
and enjoy the view of the eastern wall of the Happy Valley. A
little to the north of Emigration Kanyon, and about one mile
nearer the settlement, is the Red Butte, a deep ravine, whose
quarried sides show mottlings of the light ferruginous sandstone
which was chosen for building the Temple wall. A little beyond it
lies the single City of the Dead, decently removed three miles
from the habitations of the living, and further to the north is City-
Creek Kanyon, which supplies the Saints with water for drinking
and for irrigation. South-east of Emigration Kanyon are other
ravines, Parley's, Mill Creek, Great Cottonwood, and Little
Cottonwood, deep lines winding down the timbered flanks of the
mountains, and thrown into relief by the darker and more misty
shading of the farther flank-wall.

The 'Twin Peaks,' the highest points of the Wasach Mountains, are the first to be powdered over with the autumnal snow.
When a black nimbus throws out these piles, with their tilted up
rock strata, jagged edges, black flanks, rugged brows and bald
heads, gilt by a gleam of sunset, the whole stands boldly out with
that phase of sublimity of which the sense of immensity is the
principal element. Even in the clearest weather they are rarely
free from a fleecy cloud, the condensation of cold and humid air
rolling up the heights and vanishing only to be renewed.

The bench-land then attracted our attention. The soil is poor,
sprinkled with thin grass, in places showing a suspicious whiteness, with few flowers, and chiefly producing a salsolaceous plant
like the English samphire. In many places lay long rows of bare
circlets, like deserted tent-floors: they proved to be ant-hills, on
which light ginger-coloured swarms were working hard to throw
up the sand and gravel that everywhere in this valley underlie the
surface. The eastern valley-bench, upon whose western declivity
the city lies, may be traced on a clear day along the base of the
mountains for a distance of twenty miles: its average breadth is
about eight miles.

After advancing about 1.50 mile over the bench ground, the
city by slow degrees broke upon our sight. It showed, one may
readily believe, to special advantage after the succession of Indian
lodges, Canadian ranchos, and log-hut mail-stations of the prairies and the mountains. The site has been admirably chosen for
drainage and irrigation – so well indeed that a 'Deus ex machinâ'
must be brought to account for it. About two miles north, and
overlooking the settlements from a height of 400 feet, a detached
cone called Ensign Peak or Ensign Mount rises at the end of a
chain which, projected westward from the main range of the
heights, overhangs and shelters the north-eastern corner of the
valley. Upon this 'big toe of the Wasach range,' as it is called by a
local writer, the spirit of the martyred prophet, Mr. Joseph Smith,
appeared to his successor Mr. Brigham Young, and pointed out
to him the position of the New Temple, which, after Zion had
'got up into the high mountain,' was to console the Saints for the
loss of Nauvoo the Beautiful. The city – it is about two miles
broad – runs parallel with the right bank of the Jordan, which
forms its western limit. It is twelve to fifteen miles distant from the
western range, ten from the debouchure of the river, and eight to
nine from the nearest point of the lake – a respectful distance,

which is not the least of the position's merits. It occupies the
rolling brow of a slight decline at the western base of the Wasach,
in fact the lower, but not the lowest level of the eastern valley-
bench; it has thus a compound slope from north to south, on the
line of its water supplies, and from east to west, thus enabling it to
drain off into the river.

The city revealed itself, as we approached, from behind its
screen, the inclined terraces of the upper table-land, and at last it
lay stretched before us as upon a map. At a little distance the
aspect was somewhat Oriental, and in some points it reminded
me of modern Athens – without the Acropolis. None of the buildings, except the Prophet's house, were whitewashed. The material – the thick, sun-dried adobe, common to all parts of the
Eastern world – was of a dull leaden blue, deepened by the
atmosphere to a grey, like the shingles of the roofs. The number
of gardens and compounds – each tenement within the walls
originally received 1.50 square acres, and those outside from five to
ten acres, according to their distance – the dark clumps and lines
of bitter cottonwood, locust or acacia, poplars and fruit trees,
apples, peaches, and vines – how lovely they appeared, after the
baldness of the prairies! – and, finally, the fields of long-eared
maize and sweet sorghum strengthened the similarity to an
Asiatic rather than to an American settlement. The differences
presently became as salient. The farm-houses, with their stacks
and stock, strongly suggested the old country. Moreover domes
and minarets – even churches and steeples – were wholly
wanting – an omission that somewhat surprised me. The only
building conspicuous from afar was the block occupied by the
present head of the church. The court-house, with its tinned
Muscovian dome, at the west end of the city; the arsenal, a barn-
like structure, on a bench below the Jebel Nur of the valley –
Ensign Peak; and a saw-mill, built beyond the southern boundary, were the next in importance.

On our way we passed the vestiges of an old moat, from which
was taken the earth for the bulwarks of Zion. A Romulian wall, of
puddle, mud, clay, and pebbles, six miles – others say, 2600 acres
– in length, twelve feet high, six feet broad at the base, and two
and three-quarters at the top, with embrasures five to six feet
above the ground, and semi-bastions at half musket range, was
decided, in 1853–54, to be necessary as a defence against the
Lamanites, whose name in the vulgar is Yuta Indians. Gentiles

declare that the bulwarks were erected because the people wanting work were likely to 'strike' faith, and that the amount of labour expended upon this folly would have irrigated as many thousand acres. Anti-Mormons have, of course, detected in the proceeding treacherous and treasonable intentions. Parenthetically, I must here warn the reader that in Gt. S.L. City there are three distinct opinions concerning, three several reasons for, and three diametrically different accounts of, everything that happens, viz. that of the Mormons, which is invariably one-sided; that of the Gentiles, which is sometimes fair and just; and that of the anti-Mormons, which is always prejudiced and violent. A glance will show that this much talked-of fortification is utterly harmless; it is commanded in half a dozen places; it could not keep out half a dozen sappers for a quarter of an hour; and now, as it has done its work, its foundations are allowed to become salt, and to crumble away.

The road ran through the Big Field, south-east of the city, six miles square, and laid off in five-acre lots. Presently, passing the precincts of habitation, we entered, at a slapping pace, the second ward, called Denmark, from its tenants, who mostly herd together. The disposition of the settlement is like that of the nineteenth century New World cities – from Washington to the future metropolis of the great Terra Australis – a system of right angles, the roads, streets, and lanes, if they can be called so, intersecting one another. The advantages or disadvantages of the rectangular plan have been exhausted in argument; the new style is best suited, I believe, for the New, as the old must, perforce, remain in the Old World. The suburbs are thinly settled; the mass of habitations lie around and south of Temple Block. The streets of the suburbs are mere roads, cut by deep ups and downs, and by gutters on both sides, which, though full of pure water, have no bridge save a plank at the *trottoirs*. In summer the thoroughfares are dusty – in wet weather deep with viscid mud.

The houses are almost all of one pattern – a barn shape, with wings and lean-tos, generally facing, sometimes turned endways to, the street, which gives a suburban look to the settlement; and the diminutive casements show that window-glass is not yet made in the Valley. In the best abodes the adobe rests upon a few courses of sandstone, which prevent undermining by water or ground-damp, and it must always be protected by a coping from the rain and snow. The poorer are small, low, and hut-like;

others are long single-storied buildings, somewhat like stables, with many entrances. The best houses resemble East Indian bungalows, with flat roofs, and low, shady verandahs, well trel-lised, and supported by posts or pillars. All are provided with chimneys, and substantial doors to keep out the piercing cold. The offices are always placed, for hygienic reasons, outside; and some have a story and a half – the latter intended for lumber and other stores. I looked in vain for the outhouse-harems, in which certain romancers concerning things Mormon had informed me that wives are kept, like any other stock. I presently found this but one of a multitude of delusions. Upon the whole the Mormon settlement was a vast improvement upon its contemporaries in the valleys of the Mississippi and the Missouri.

The road through the faubourg was marked by posts and rails, which, as we advanced towards the heart of the city, were replaced by neat palings. The garden plots were small as sweet earth must be brought down from the mountains; and the flowers were principally those of the old country – the red French bean, the rose, the geranium, and the single pink; the ground or winter cherry was common; so were nasturtiums, and we saw tansy, but not that plant for which our souls, well nigh weary of hopes of juleps long deferred, chiefly lusted – mint. The fields were large and numerous, but the Saints have too many and various occup-ations to keep them Moravian-like neat and trim; weeds over-spread the ground; bottles and decanters was not forthcoming; upstairs we found a Gentile ball-room, a tolerably furnished sitting-room, and bed-chambers, apparently made out of a single apartment by partitions too thin to be strictly agreeable. The household had its deficiencies; blacking, for instance, had run out, and servants could not be engaged till the expected arrival of the hand-cart train. However, the proprietor, Mr. Townsend, a Mormon, from the State of Maine – when expelled from Nauvoo, he had parted with land, house, and furniture for $50 – who had married an Englishwoman, was in the highest degree civil and obliging, and he attended personally to our wants, offered his wife's services to Mrs. Dana, and put us all in the best of humours, despite the closeness of the atmosphere, the sadness ever attending one's first entrance into a new place, the swarms of 'emigration flies' – so called because they appear in September with the emigrants, and after living for a month die off with the first snow – and a certain populousness of bedstead, concerning which the less said the better. Such, gentle reader, are the results of my first glance at Zion on the tops of the mountains, in the Holy City of the Far West.

Our journey had occupied nineteen days, from the 7th to the 25th of August, both included; and in that time we had accomplished not less than 1136 statute miles.

2

At 9.45 A.M. we entered the Bowery; it is advisable to go early if seats within hearing are required. The place was a kind of 'hangar,' about a hundred feet long by the same breadth, with a roofing of bushes and boughs supported by rough posts, and open for ventilation on the sides; it can contain about 3000 souls. The congregation is accommodated upon long rows of benches, opposite the dais, rostrum, platform, or tribune, which looked like a long lane of boarding open to the north, where it faced the audience, and entered by steps from the east. Between the people and the platform was a place not unlike a Methodist 'pen' at a camp meeting; this was allotted to the orchestra, a violin, a bass, two women and four men performers, who sang the sweet songs of Zion tolerably well – decidedly well, after a moment's reflection as to latitude and longitude, and after reminiscences of country and town chapels in that land where it is said, had the psalmist heard his own psalms,

'In furious mood he would have tore 'em.'

I was told that 'profane,' *i.e.* operatic and other music is performed at worship, as in the Italian cathedrals, where they are unwilling that Sathanas should monopolise the prettiest airs; on this occasion, however, only hymns were sung.

We – the judge's son and I – took our seats on the benches of the eighth ward, where we could see the congregation flocking in, a proceeding which was not over – some coming from considerable distances – till 10.15 A.M. The people were all *endimanchés*; many a pretty face peeped from the usual sun-bonnet with its long curtain, though the 'mushroom' and the 'pork-pie' had found their way over the plains, and trim figures were clad in neat stuff dresses, sometimes silk: in very few cases there was a little faded finery – gauze, feathers, and gaudy colours – such as one may see on great festivals in an Old Country village. The men were as decently attired: the weather being hot had caused many of them to leave their coats at home, and to open their vests, the costume, however, looked natural to working men and there was no want of cleanliness such as sometimes lurks behind a bulwark of buttons. The elders and dignitaries on the platform affected coats of black broadcloth and were otherwise respectably dressed. All wore their hats till the address began, and then all uncovered. By my side was the face of a blear-eyed English servant girl; *en revanche* in front was a charming American mother and child: she had what I have remarked in Mormon meetings at Saville House and other places in Europe, an unusual development of the organ which phrenologists call veneration. I did not see any Bloomers 'displaying a serviceable pair of brogues,' or 'pictures of Grant Thornburn in petticoats.' There were a few specimens of the 'Yankee woman,' formerly wondrous grim, with a shrewd thrifty grey eye, at once cold and eager, angular in body and mind, tall, bony, and square-shouldered, – now softened and humanised by transplantation and transposition to her proper place. The number of old people astonished me; half a dozen were sitting on the same bench; these broken-down men and decrepit crones had come to lay their bones in the Holy City; their presence speaks equally well for their faith and for the kindheartedness of those who had brought the incumbrance. I remarked some Gentiles in the Bowery; many, however, do not care to risk what they may hear there touching themselves.

At 10 A.M. the meeting opened with a spiritual song. Then Mr. Wallace – a civilised looking man lately returned from foreign travel – being called upon by the presiding elder for the day, opened the meeting with prayer, of which the two shorthand writers in the tribune proceeded to take notes. The matter, as is generally the case with returned missionaries delivering their budget, was good; the manner was somewhat Hibernian; the 'valleys of the mountains' – a stock phrase, appeared and reappeared like the speechifying Patlander's eternal 'emerald green hills and beautiful pretty valleys.' He ended by imploring a blessing upon the (Mormon) President, and all those in authority; Gentiles of course were included. The conclusion was an amen, in which all hands joined: it reminded me of the historical practice of 'humming' in the seventeenth century, which caused the universities to be called '*Hum et Hissimi auditores.*'

Next arose Bishop Abraham O. Smoot, second mayor of Zion, and successor to the late Jedediah M. Grant, who began with 'Brethring,' and proceeded at first in a low and methody tone of voice, 'hardly audible in the gallery,' to praise the saints, and to pitch into the apostates. His delivery was by no means fluent, even when he warmed. He made undue use of the regular Wesleyan organ – the nose; but he appeared to speak excellent sense in execrable English. He recalled past persecutions, without over-asperity, and promised future prosperity without over-prophecy. As he was in the midst of an allusion to the President, entered Mr. Brigham Young, and all turned their faces, even the old lady,–

'Peut-on si bien prêcher qu'elle ne dorme au sermon?'–

who, dear soul! from Hanover Square to far San Francisco, placidly reposes through the discourse.

The prophet was dressed, as usual, in grey homespun and home-woven: he wore, like most of the elders, a tall steeple-crowned straw hat with a broad black ribbon, and he had the rare refinement of black kid gloves. He entered the tribune covered and sat down, apparently greeting those near him. A man in a fit was carried out pumpwards. Bishop Smoot concluded with informing us that we should live for God. Another hymn was sung. Then a great silence, which told us that something was about to happen: *that* old man held his cough; *that* old lady awoke with a start; *that* child ceased to squall. Mr. Brigham Young removed his hat, advanced to the end of the tribune, expectorated stooping over the spittoon, which was concealed from sight by the boarding, restored the balance of fluid by a glass of water from a well-filled decanter on the stand, and leaning slightly forwards upon both hands propped on the green baize of the tribune, addressed his followers.

The discourse began slowly, word crept titubantly after word, and the opening phrases were hardly audible; but as the orator warmed, his voice rose high and sonorous, and a fluency so remarkable succeeded falter and hesitation, that – although the phenomenon is not rare in strong speakers – the latter seemed almost to have been a work of art. The manner was pleasing and animated, and the matter fluent, impromptu, and well turned,

spoken rather than preached: if it had a fault it was rather
rambling and unconnected. Of course colloquialisms of all kinds
were introduced, such as 'he becomes,' 'for you and I,' and so
forth. The gestures were easy and rounded, not without a certain
grace, though evidently untaught; one, however, must be
excepted, namely, that of raising and shaking the forefinger; this
is often done in the Eastern states, but the rest of the world over it
is considered threatening and bullying. The address was long.
God is a mechanic. Mormonism is a great fact. Religion had
made him (the speaker) the happiest of men. He was ready to
dance like a shaker. At this sentence the prophet, who is a good
mimic, and has much of the old New English quaint humour,
raised his right arm, and gave, to the amusement of the congregation, a droll imitation of Anne Lee's followers. The Gentiles had
sent an army to lay waste Zion, and what had they done? Why,
hung one of their own tribe! – and that, too, on the Lord's Day!
The Saints have a glorious destiny before them, and their
morality is remarkable as the beauty of the Promised Land: the
soft breeze blowing over the Bowery, and the glorious sunshine
outside, made the allusion highly appropriate. The Lamanites or
Indians are a religious people. All races know a God and may be
saved. After a somewhat lengthy string of sentences concerning
the great tribulation coming on earth, – it has been coming for
the last 1800 years, – he concluded with good wishes to visitors
and Gentiles generally, with a solemn blessing upon the President of the United States, the territorial governor, and all such as
be in authority over us, and, with an amen which was loudly
reechoed by all around, he restored his hat and resumed his seat.

Having heard much of the practical good sense which characterises the prophet's discourse I was somewhat disappointed:
probably the occasion had not been propitious. As regards the
concluding benedictions, they are profanely compared by the
Gentiles to those of the slave, who whilst being branded on the
hand, was ordered to say thrice, 'God bless the State.' The first
was a blessing. So was the second. But at the third, natural indignation having mastered Sambo's philosophy, forth came a certain
naughty word not softened to 'darn.' During the discourse a
Saint, in whose family some accident had occurred, was called
out, but the accident failed to affect the riveted attention of the
audience.

Then arose Mr. Heber C. Kimball, the second president. He is the model of a Methodist, a tall and powerful man, a 'gentleman in black,' with small dark piercing eyes, and cleanshaven blue face. He affects the Boanerges style, and does not at times disdain the part of Thersites: from a certain dislike to the Nonconformist rant and whine, he prefers an every day manner of speech, which savours rather of familiarity than of reverence. The people look more amused when he speaks than when others harangue them, and they laugh readily, as almost all crowds will, at the thinnest phantom of a joke. Mr. Kimball's movements contrasted strongly with those of his predecessor; they consisted now of a stone-throwing gesture delivered on tiptoe, then of a descending movement, as

'When pulpit, drum ecclesiastic,
Was beat with fist and not with stick.'

He began with generalisms about humility, faithfulness, obeying counsel, and not beggaring one's neighbour. Addressing the hand-cart emigrants, newly arrived from the 'sectarian world,' he warned them to be on the look-out, or that every soul of them would be taken in and shaved (a laugh). Agreeing with the prophet – Mr. Kimball is said to be his echo – in a promiscuous way, concerning the morality of the Saints, he felt it not withstanding his duty to say that amongst them were 'some of the greatest rascals in the world' (a louder laugh, and N.B. the Mormons are never spared by their own preachers). After a long suit of advice, *à propos de rien*, to missionaries he blessed, amen'd and sat down.

I confess that the second president's style startled me. But presently I called to mind Luther's description of Tetzel's sermon, in which he used to shout the words, Bring! bring! bring! with such a horrible bellowing, that one would have said it was a mad bull, rushing on the people and goring them with his horns; and D'Aubigné's neat apology for Luther, who, 'in one of those homely and quaint yet not undignified similitudes which he was fond of using, that he might be understood by the people,' illustrated the idea of God in history by a game of cards! '... Then came our Lord God. He dealt the cards: ... This is the Ace of God ...' Mormons also think it a merit to speak openly of 'those things we know naturally:' they affect what to others appears coarseness and indelicacy. The same is the case with

Oriental nations, even amongst the most modest and moral. After all, taste is in its general development a mere affair of time and place; what is apt to *froisser* us in the nineteenth may have been highly refined in the sixteenth century, and what may be exceedingly unfit for Westminster Abbey and Notre Dame is often perfectly suited to the predilections and intelligence of Wales or the Tessin. It is only fair to both sides to state that Mr. Kimball is accused by Gentiles of calling his young wives, from the pulpit, 'little heifers,' of entering into physiological details belonging to the Dorcas Society, or the clinical lecture-room, rather than the house of worship, and of transgressing the bounds of all decorum when reproving the sex for its *penchants* and *ridicules*. At the same time I never heard, nor heard of, any such indelicacy, during my stay at Gt. S.L. City. The saints abjured all knowledge of the 'fact,' and – in this case, *nefas ab hoste doceri* – so gross a scandal should not be adopted from Gentile mouths.

After Mr. Kimball's address, a list of names for whom letters were lying unclaimed, was called from the platform. Mr. Eldridge, a missionary lately returned from foreign travel, adjourned the meeting till 2 P.M., delivered the prayer of dismissal, during which all stood up, and ended with the benediction and amen. The Sacrament was not administered on this occasion. It is often given and reduced to the very elements of a ceremony; even water is used instead of wine, because the latter is of Gentile manufactory. Two elders walk up and down the rows, one carrying a pitcher, the other a plate of broken bread, and each Saint partakes of both.

Directly the ceremony was over, I passed through the thirty carriages and wagons that awaited at the door the issuing of the congregation, and returned home to write my notes.

FIVE

THE WEST AFRICAN CONSUL

It was depression and aimlessness that finally made Burton vulnerable to Isabel's soothing overtures. The marriage entered into in January 1861 was superficially happy and was very successful at the level of companionship. But there is much evidence that the sexual side of the marriage was a failure, and that Burton, veteran of a hundred trysts and dalliances with Arab women and Indian prostitutes, found the satisfaction of a repressed western Victorian Catholic beyond him. Isabel, for her part, turned a blind eye or pretended not to notice Burton's interest in prostitution, infibulation, cliteridectomy and the like.

After his marriage, Burton joined the consular service in hopes of being sent to Damascus. But in spite of his achievements and the influential connections of his wife, he received the lowly post of consul to the Bights of Benin and Biafra, based at Fernando Po. The Indian Army saw a chance to be rid of him and, instead of putting him on half pay, as was usual, he was removed from the regimental list and given no pension. Consequently, at the age of forty he began a diplomatic career at the bottom rung of the ladder.

The task of consul in such a backwater was not onerous, so Burton devoted himself to travel in West Africa. He climbed peaks in the Cameroons, went up the Gabon river in search of gorillas, explored the Congo estuary, visited Luanda and penetrated Portuguese Angola. His quest for gorillas in 1862 and the ascent of the lower Congo as far as the Yellala rapids in 1863 were particularly important examples of Burton's enterprise.

In the early 1860s gorillas were a sensation in more ways than one. In 1861 the French explorer Paul du Chaillu brought back to Europe the first reports and stuffed specimens of this largest of simians. This was the year after Darwin at the famous Oxford meeting had hinted at how natural selection could account for the descent of man. The existence of the great ape seemed to some circumstantial evidence for the evolutionary link for which Darwin argued. Battle lines were drawn and the devout struck back by portraying the gorilla as a demonic fiend. There is a particularly unpleasant representation of this kind in the 1862 children's book *The Gorilla Hunters* by R.M. Ballantyne. Burton's description of the gorilla is in the form of the douche of cold water poured over this kind of fantasy.

Burton's reconnoitring of the lower reaches of the Congo river pointed the way towards the single greatest feat in African exploration: Stanley's 1876–77 journey down the entire length of the river. In 1863 the Congo was unknown beyond 'Tuckey's Falls', since a long stretch of cataracts made navigation, even by canoe, impossible. To get to Stanley Pool, at the junction of the upper and lower Congo rivers, it was necessary to portage and manhaul the river transport. The contours of the upper Congo were a mystery until 1877. Livingstone had discovered the great feeder to the upper Congo, the Lualaba, but thought it was the source of the Nile, or possibly the Niger. Burton's instincts as to the importance of the Congo were sound, even though he lacked the resources to solve its ultimate mysteries.

In 1864 he was sent on a important mission to Dahomey to attempt to put an end to the slave trade there. He reported on the rites of human sacrifice and the army of female warriors in Dahomey, but his mission was unsuccessful, largely because he was too arrogant and impatient to apply diplomatic niceties to relations with barbarous monarchs. But it produced his best African book by far, a treasure house of arcane information before Dahomey was absorbed by the West, and the only work where his violent prejudice against Africans is largely surmounted. The description of the Amazons is Burton at his scholarly best, and the statement 'seeing the host of women who find a morbid pleasure in attending the maimed and the dying, I must think that it is a tribute paid to sexuality by those who object to the ordinary means' is a clear anticipation of Freud.

During his West African period Burton was alone. He would not allow Isabel to come and live in the 'White Man's Grave', so contented himself with long leaves in her company in the Canaries. Speke meanwhile had further strengthened his claim to be considered the foremost African explorer of his day. Between 1860 and 1862 he led another African expedition, this time in company with James Grant. They marched west from Zanzibar to Tabora, then struck north to Lake Victoria, and came to the court of King Mutesa of Buganda, the most powerful African ruler in Central Africa. After a long period at Mutesa's court on the north-western shores of Lake Victoria, Speke followed the White Nile north to Gondokoro and thence to the sea.

Speke's claim to have discovered the source of the Nile now looked unassailable, but the prestigious figure of Dr Livingstone weighed in on Burton's side. Livingstone claimed that Speke's feeder was but one of several sources of the Nile, the most southerly of which began at the River Lualaba in Katanga. This chimed in perfectly with Burton's theory of a multi-sourced origin for the Nile. A distinguished gathering was arranged by the British Association, to take place at Bath in September 1864. Present would be the three most distinguished African explorers of the day: Livingstone, Burton and Speke. Among other scientific discussions Burton and Speke were invited to debate their differences over the Nile sources.

Speke tried to refuse the invitation, as he feared he would be at a serious disadvantage with the intellectually-gifted Burton in a public debate; there were also many Burton supporters in the audience. The debate never took place. Both men were present in the hall on the opening day, though their discussion was not due until the next day. Speke found the presence of Burton disturbing and left before lunch to go shooting at a cousin's house. The official version of what happened that afternoon was that Speke's concentration was impaired and he accidentally shot himself dead while crossing a stone wall. But the circumstances of Speke's death left strong suspicions that he had committed suicide.

Mr, Mrs, and Master Gorilla
(from *Two Trips to Gorilla Land and the Cataracts of the Congo*
(1876))

The late Count Lavradio informed me that he had heard of it on the banks of the lower Congo River (south latitude 9°), and the 'Soko,' which Dr. Livingstone identifies with the Gorilla, extends to the Lualaba or Upper Congo, in the regions immediately west of the Tanganyika Lake. His friends have suggested that the 'Soko' might have been a chimpanzee, but the old traveller was, methinks, far above making the mistake. The Yorubans at once recognize the picture; they call the anthropoid 'Nákí;' and they declare that, when it seizes a man, it tears the fingers asunder. So M. du Chaillu (chapter vi.) mentions, in the Mpongwe report, that the Njína tears off the toe-nails and the finger-nails of his human captives. We should not believe so scandalous an assertion without detailed proof; it is hardly fair to make the innocent biped as needlessly cruel as man. It is well known to the natives of the Old Calabar River by the name of 'Omon.' In 1860, the brothers Jules and Ambroise Poncet travelled with Dr. Peney to Ab Kúka, the last of their stations near the head of the Luta Nzige (Albert Nyanza) Lake, and Dr. Peney 'brought the hand of the first gorilla which had been heard of' ('Ocean Highways,' p. 482 – February, 1874). The German Expedition (1873) reports Chicambo to be a gorilla country; that the anthropoid is found one day's journey from the Coast, and that the agent of that station has killed five with his own hand. Mr. Thompson of Sherbro ('Palm Land,' chap. xiii.) says of the chimpanzee: 'Some have been seen as tall as a man, from five to seven feet high, and very powerful.' This is evidently the Njína, the only known anthropoid that attains tall human stature; and from the rest of the passage, it is clear that he has confounded the chimpanzee with the Nchígo-mpolo.

The strip of gorilla-country visited by me was an elevated line of clayey and sandy soil, cut by sweet-water streams, and by mangrove-lined swamps, backed inland by thin forest. Here the comparative absence of matted undergrowth makes the landscape sub-European, at least, by the side of the foul tropical jungle; it is exceptionally rich in the wild fruits required by the huge anthropoid. The clearings also supply bananas, pine-apple leaves, and sugar-cane, and there is an abundance of honey, in which, like the Nchígo, the gorilla delights. The villages and the frequent plantations which it visits to plunder limit its reproduction near the sea, and make it exceedingly wary and keen of eye, if not of smell. Even when roosting by night, it is readily frightened by a footstep; and the crash caused by the mighty bound from branch to branch makes the traveller think that a tree has fallen.

The gorilla breeds about December, a cool and dry month: according to my bushmen, the period of gestation is between five and six months. The babe begins to walk some ten days after birth; 'chops milk' for three months and, at the end of that time may reach eighteen inches in height. M. du Chaillu makes his child, 'Joe Gorilla,' 2 feet 6 inches when under the third year: assuming the average height of the adult male at 5 feet to 5 feet 6 inches, this measurement suggests that, according to the law of Flourens, the life would exceed thirty years. I saw two fragmentary skins, thoroughly 'pepper and salt;' and the natives assured me that the gorilla turns silver-white with age.

It is still a disputed point whether the weight is supported by the knuckles of the forehand, like the chimpanzee, or whether the palm is the proper fulcrum. M. du Chaillu says ('First Expedition,' chap. xx.) 'the fingers are only lightly marked on the ground;' yet a few pages afterwards we are told, 'The most usual mode of progression of the animal is on all-fours and resting on the knuckles.' In the 'Second Expedition' (chap. ii.) we read, 'The tracks of the feet never showed the marks of toes, only the heels, and the track of the hands showed simply the impressions of the knuckles.'

The attack of the gorilla is that of the apes and the monkeys generally. The big-bellied satyr advances to the assault as it travels, shuffling on all-fours; 'rocking' not traversing; bristling the crest, chattering, mowing and displaying the fearful teeth and tusks. Like all the Simiads, this Troglodyte sways the body to and fro, and springs from side to side for the purpose of avoiding the weapon. At times Quasimodo raises himself slightly upon the dwarfed 'asthenogenic,' and almost deformed hind limbs, which look those of a child terminating the body of a Dan Lambert: the same action may be seen in its congeners great and small. The wild huntsmen almost cried with laughter when they saw the sketches in the 'Gorilla Book,' the mighty pugilist standing stiff and upright as the late Mr. Benjamin Caunt, 'beating the breast with huge fists till it sounded like an immense bass drum:' and preparing to deal a buffet worthy of Friar Tuck. They asked me if I thought mortal man would ever attempt to face such a thing as that? With respect to drumming with both forehands upon the chest, some asserted that such is the brute's practice when calling Mrs. Gorilla, or during the excitement of a scuffle; but the accounts of the bushmen differ greatly on this point. In a hand-to-hand struggle it puts forth one of the giant feet, sometimes the hinder, as 'Joe Gorilla' was wont to do; and, having once got a hold with its prehensile toes, it bites and worries like any other ape, baboon, or monkey. From this grapple doubtless arose the old native legend about the gorilla drawing travellers up trees and 'quietly choking them.' It can have little vitality, as it is easily killed with a bit of stone propelled out of a trade musket by the vilest gunpowder, and the timid bushmen, when failing to shoot it unawares, do not fear to attack it openly. As a rule, the larger the Simiad, the less sprightly it becomes; and those most approaching man are usually the tamest and the most melancholy – perhaps, their spirits are permanently affected by their narrow escape. The elderly male (for anthropoids, like anthropoi, wax fierce and surly with increasing years) will fight, but only from fear, when suddenly startled, or with rage when slightly wounded. Moreover, there must be rogue-gorillas, like rogue-elephants, lions, hippopotami, rhinoceros, and even stags, *vieux grognards*, who, expelled house and home, and debarred by the promising young scions from the softening influence of feminine society, become, in their enforced widowerhood, the crustiest of old bachelors. At certain seasons they may charge in defence of the wife and family, but the practice is exceptional. Mr. Wilson saw a man who had lost the calf of his leg in an encounter, and one Etia, a huntsman whose left hand had been severely crippled, informed Mr. W. Winwood Reade, that 'the gorilla seized his wrist with his hind foot, and dragged his hand into his mouth, as he would have done a bunch of plantains.' No one, however, could give me an authentic instance of manslaughter by our big brother.

The modifications with which we must read the picturesque pages of the 'Gorilla Book' are chiefly the following. The Gorilla is a poor devil ape, not a 'hellish dream-creature, half man, half beast.' He is not king of the African forest; he fears the Njego or leopard and, as lions will not live in those wet, wooded, and gameless lands, he can hardly have expelled King Leo. He does not choose the 'darkest, gloomiest forests,' but prefers the thin woods, where he finds wild fruits for himself and family. His tremendous roar does not shake the jungle: it is a hollow apish cry, a loudish huhh! huhh! huhh! explosive like the puff of a steam-engine, which, in rage becomes a sharp and snappish bark – any hunter can imitate it. Doubtless, in some exceptional cases, when an aged mixture of Lablache and Dan Lambert delivers his *voce di petto*, the voice may be heard for some distance in the still African shades, but it will hardly compare with the howling monkeys of the Brazil, which make the forest hideous. The eye is not a 'light grey' but the brown common to all the tribe. The Gorilla cannot stand straight upon his rear quarter when attacking or otherwise engaged without holding on to a trunk: he does not 'run on his hind legs;' he is essentially a tree ape, as every stuffed specimen will prove. He never gives a tremendous blow with his immense open paw; doubtless, a native legend found in Battel and Bowdich; nor does he attack with the arms. However old and male he may be, he runs away with peculiar alacrity: though powerfully weaponed with tigerish teeth, with 'bunches of muscular fibre,' and with the limbs of Goliah, the gorilla, on the seaboard at least, is essentially a coward; nor can we be surprised at his want of pluck, considering the troubles and circumstances under which he spends his harassed days. Finally, whilst a hen will defend her chicks, Mrs. Gorilla will fly, leaving son or daughter in the hunter's hands.

The Yellala of the Congo
(from *Two Trips to Gorilla Land and the Cataracts of the Congo*
(1876))

At dawn (September 16), I began the short march leading to the Yellala. By stepping a few paces south of Nkulu, we had a fine view of the Borongwa ya Vivi, the lowest rapids, whose foaming slope contrasted well with the broad, smooth basin beyond. Pala-bala, the village of Nekorado on the other side of the stream, bore south (Mag.), still serving as a landmark; and in this direction the ridges were crowned with palm orchards and settlements. But the great Yellala was hidden by the hill-shoulder.

We at once fell into descent of some 890 feet, which occupied an hour. The ground was red iron-clay, greasy and slippery; dew-dripping grass, twelve to fifteen feet tall, lined the path; the surface was studded with dark ant-hills of the mushroom shape; short sycomores appeared, and presently we came to rough gradients of stone, which severely tried the 'jarrets.' After an hour, we crossed at the trough-foot a brook of pure water, which, uniting with two others, turns to the north-east, and, tumbling over a little ledge, discharges itself into the main drain. An ascent then led over a rounded hill with level summit, and precipitous face all steps and drops of rock, some of them six and seven feet high, opposed to the stream. Another half hour, and a descent of 127 feet placed us under a stunted calabash, 100 feet above the water, and commanding a full view of the Yellala.

On the whole, the impression was favourable. Old Shimbah, the Linguister at Porto da Lenha, and other natives had assured me that the Cataracts were taller than the tallest trees. On the other hand, the plain and unadorned narrative of the 'Expedition' had prepared me for a second-rate stream bubbling over a strong bed. The river here sweeps round from the north-west, and bends with a sharp elbow first to the south-west and then to the south-east, the length of the latter reach being between four and five miles. As far as the eye can see, the bed, which narrows from 900 to 400 and 500 yards, is broken by rocks and reefs. A gate at the upper end pours over its lintel a clear but dwarf fall, perhaps two feet high. The eastern staple rises at first sheer from the water's edge to the estimated altitude of a thousand feet, – this is the 'Crocodile's Head' which we saw on the last march, and already the thin rains are robing its rocky surface with tender green. The strata are disposed at angles, varying from 35° to 45°, and three streaks of bright trees denote Fiumaras about to be filled. Opposite it is the 'Quoin Hill,' bluff to the stream, and falling west with gradual incline. The noise of this higher fall can hardly be heard at Nkulu, except on the stillest nights.

Below the upper gate, the bed, now narrowing to 300 yards, shows the great Yellala; the waters, after breaking into waves for a mile and a half above, rush down an inclined plane of some thirty feet in 300 yards, spuming, colliding and throwing up foam, which looks dingy white against the dull yellow-brown of the less disturbed channel – the movement is that of waves dashing upon a pier. The bed is broken by the Zunga chya Malemba, which some pronounced Sanga chya Malemba, an oval islet in mid-stream, whose greater diameter is disposed along the axis of the bed. The north-western apex, raised about fifty feet above the present level of the waters, shows a little bay of pure sand, the detritus of its rocks, with a flood-mark fifteen feet high, whilst the opposite side bears a few wind-wrung trees. The materials are gneiss and schist, banded with quartz – Tuckey's great masses of slate. This is the 'Terrapin' of the Nzadi. The eastern fork about 150 yards broad, is a mountain-torrent coursing unobstructed down its sandy trough, and, viewed from an eminence, the waters of the mid-channel appear convex, a shallow section of a cylinder, – it is a familiar shape well marked upon the St. Lawrence Rapids. The western half is traversed by a reef, connecting the islets with the right bank. During August, this branch was found almost dry; in mid-September, it was nearly full, and here the water breaks with the greatest violence. The right bank is subtended for some hundred yards by blocks of granite and greenstone, pitted with large basins and pot-holes, delicately rounded, turned as with a lathe by the turbid waters. The people declare that this greenstone contains copper, and Professor Smith found particles in his specimens. The Portuguese agents, to whom the natives carefully submit everything curious, doubt the fact, as well as all reports of gold; yet there is no reason why the latter should not be found.

The current whirls and winds through its tortuous channels, which are like castings of metal, in many distinct flows; some places are almost stagnant, suggesting passages for canoes. Here the fishermen have planted their weirs; some are wading in the pools, others are drying their nets upon the stony ledges. During the floods, however, this *cheval-de-frise* of boulders must all be under water, and probably impassable. Tuckey supposes that the inundation must produce a spectacle which justifies the high-flown description of the people. I should imagine the reverse to be the case; and Dr. Livingstone justly remarked that, when the river was full, the Yellala rapids would become comparatively smooth, as he had found those of the Zambeze; and that therefore a *voyage pittoresque* up the Congo should be made at that season.

Before leaving the Yellala, I wandered along the right bank, and found a cliff, whose overhanging brow formed a fine cavern; it remarkably resembled the Martianez Fountain under the rock near the beautiful Puerto de Orotava. Here the fishermen were disporting themselves, and cooking their game, which they willingly exchanged for beads. All were of the Silurus family, varying from a few inches to two feet. Fish-eagles sat upon the ledges overhanging the stream, and a flight of large cranes wheeled majestically in the upper air: according to the people, they are always to be seen at the Yellalas.

The extent of a few hundred feet afforded a good bird's eye view of the scene. The old river-valley, shown by the scarp of the rocks, must have presented gigantic features, and the height of the trough-walls, at least a thousand feet, gives the Yellala a certain beauty and grandeur. The site is apparently the highest axis of the dividing ridge separating the maritime lowlands from the inner plateau. Looking eastward the land smoothens, the dorsa fall more gently towards the counterslope, and there are none of the 'Morros' which we have traversed.

With the members of the Congo Expedition, I was somewhat startled by the contrast between the apparently shrunken volume of waters and the vast breadth of the lower river; hence Professor Smith's theory of underground caverns and communications, in fact of a subterraneous river, a favourite hobby in those days. But there is not a trace of limestone formation around, nor is there the hollow echo which inevitably would result from such a tunnel. Evidently the difference is to be accounted for by the rapidity of the torrent, the effect of abnormal slope deceiving the eye. At the Mosî-wa-tunya Falls the gigantic Zambeze, from a breadth of a thousand yards suddenly plunges into a trough only forty-five to sixty feet wide: the same is the case with the Brazilian São Francisco, which, a mile wide above the Cachoeira de Paulo Affonso, is choked to a minimum breadth of fifty-one feet. At the Pongo (narrows) de Manseriche also, the Amazonas, 'already a noble river, is contracted at its narrowest part to a width of only twenty-five toises, bounded on each margin by lofty perpendicular cliffs, at the end of which the Andes are fairly passed, and the river emerges on the great plain.' Thus the Yellala belongs to the class of obstructed rapids like those of the Nile, compared with the unobstructed, of which a fine specimen is the St. Lawrence. It reminded me strongly of the Búsa (Boussa) described by Richard Lander, where the breadth of the Niger is reduced to a stone-throw, and the stream is broken by black rugged rocks arising from mid-channel. It is probably a less marked feature than the Congo, for in June, after the 'Malka' or fourteen days of incessant rain, the author speaks of whirlpools, not of a regular break.

I thus make the distance of the Yellala from the mouth

between 116 and 117 miles and the total fall 390 feet, of which about one half (195) occurs in the sixty-four miles between Boma and the Yellala: of this figure again 100 feet belong to the section of five miles between the Vivi and the Great Rapids. The Zambeze, according to Dr. Livingstone ('First Expedition,' p. 284), has a steeper declivity than some other great rivers, reaching even 7 inches per mile. With 3 to 4 inches, the Ganges, the Amazonas, and the Mississippi flow at the rate of three knots an hour in the lowest season and five or six during the flood: what, then, may be expected from the Nzadi?

The Amazons and the Dahoman Army
(from *A Mission to Gelele, King of Dahome* (1864))

The monarch of Yoruba, according to Clapperton, could boast that his wives, of whom some composed his bodyguard, would, linked hand in hand, reach clean across his kingdom. The late King Gezo used to boast that he had organized the Mi-no; but the *History* depicts them before he was born. The Europeans who visited Agaja (1708–30) found the Dahoman court much as it is at the present day. 'If the chief officers wished to speak to the King they first kissed the ground, then whispered their pleasure into the ear of an old woman, who communicated it to the King, and brought his answer.' The same volume also informs us that the warlike monarch, when his force had been reduced by the 'Eyeos', 'armed a great number of women like soldiers, having their proper officers, and furnished like regular troops with drums, colours, and umbrellas, making at a distance a very formidable appearance'. With these, in about A.D. 1728, he attacked and defeated the combined host of the Whydahs and Popos, and since that time the Amazons have ever been a power in the empire.

Doubtless Gezo, one of the most successful amongst the Dahoman monarchs, regarded the feminine force with favouring eye. He depended upon it to check the turbulence and treachery of his subjects, and to ensure his own safety, for

> Qui terret plus ipse timet; sors ista tyrannis
> Convenit.

He may have also wished to cause rivalry, by the example of what is in most cases illogically termed the 'weaker sex'. Perhaps, like the old-school Anglo-Indian Nabob, he may have preferred the maid to the man-servant.

Gezo ordered every Dahoman of note in the kingdom to present his daughters, of whom the most promising were chosen, and he kept the corps clear of the servile and the captive. Gelele, his son, causes every girl to be brought to him before marriage, and, if she pleases, he retains her in the palace: the only subjects exempt from this rule are the old English and French slaves at Whydah. These girls, being royal wives, cannot be touched without danger of death, they never leave their quarters unless preceded by a bell to drive men from the road, and all have slaves who act as spies. The sexes meet on the march and in the field: at parades, as has been shown, they are separated by the typical bamboo. A peculiar fetish, placed by the priests at the Agbodewe gate of the royal abode, induces, by reason of the purity of the place, certain pregnancy in the soldieress that sins. Instances have been known where conscience has made the offender coward enough to sicken, to confess, and to doom her paramour, if not herself, to a cruel death. They have also a 'pundonor'. Like

> That Mary Ambree
> Who marched so free,

many an Amazon captured at Abeokuta has refused to become a wife till the captor, weary of opposition, has killed the *acerba puella* as a useless animal.

Of Gelele's Amazons about two-thirds are said to be maidens, a peculiar body in Africa, where – though 11,000 may have been buried at Cologne – no one expects to find the *integra puella*, much less the old maid. The remaining third has been married. That an element of desperation might not be wanting, women taken in adultery and liable to death, are dashed to the King and duly enlisted. Besides these criminals, the Xanthippes, who make men's eyes yellow, are very properly put into the army, and Africa is well stocked with the noble army of martyrs that begins not with Socrates, and that ends not with Mr. Thomas Sayers.

It is evident that such an organization presents nought of novelty: the systematic organization is more logical and less harmful than the volunteer furies who, as Abolitionists, urge men to ruin and death. The soldieress, at least, joins in the danger: this thing does not. David flying from Absalom left ten of his concubines to guard his palace at Jerusalem. The Greeks probably derived their Amazonian myth from exaggerated reports of the strength and valour of the Caucasian women. With respect to the visit of Thalestris, who desired issue by the conqueror of Asia (which Arrian has exploded), it is no more than what many of Bedawiyah will solicit from the traveller who in fair fight beats off her husband and brother. Amongst the Homerites of South Arabia it was a law for wives to revenge in battle the deaths of their husbands, and mothers their sons. The Suliote women rivalled the men in defending their homes against Osmanli invaders. The Damot or Abyssinian Amazons of Alvarez (1520) would not allow their spouses to fight, as the Jivaro help-mates of Southern America administer caudle to the sex that requires it the least. The native princes of India, especially those of Hyderabad in the Deccan, for centuries maintained a female guard of Urdu-begani, whose courage and devotion were remarkable. Bodies of European fighting women are found in the celebrated 'Female Crusade', organized in 1147 by order of St. Bernard. Temba-Ndumba, among the Jagas of southern inter-tropical Africa, according to old travellers, made her subjects rear and teach their female children war, but she was probably mad. The Tawarik women rank with men like the women of Christianity, and transmit nobility to their children. Denham found the Fellatah wives fighting like males. According to Mr. Thompson (1823), the Mantati host that attacked old 'Lattaku' was led by a ferocious giantess with one eye. M. D'Arnaud (1840) informs us that the King of Behr, on the Upper Nile, was guarded by a battalion of spear women, and that his male ministers never enter the palace, except when required to perform the melancholy duty of strangling their master. At present the Tien-Wang or Heavenly King of the Tae-pings has 1,000 she-soldiers.

Sporadic heroines, like Tomyris and Penthesilea of the Axe, are found in every clime and in all ages, from Semiramis to the artillery-man's wife of Saragossa. Such were Judith and Candace; Kaulah the sister of Derar, and her friend Oserrah; the wife of Aban Ibn Saïb; Prefect Gregory's daughter; Joan of Arc; Margaret of Anjou; Black Agnes; Jeanne Hachette; Begum Sombre; Kara Fatimah; Panna Maryan, and many

A bold virago stout and tall,
As Joan of Arc, or English Moll

– charmers far too numerous to specify. Many a fair form was found stark on the field of Waterloo. During the late Indian mutiny the Ranis were, as a rule, more manly than the Rajahs. And at present the Anglo-American States and Poland show women who, despite every discouragement, still prefer the military profession to all others.

The regimen in which these women are compelled to live doubtless increases their ferocity in fight. It is the essence of training every animal, from a game cock to a pugilist, and a married she-soldier would be useful only as a mother of men. Commander Forbes thus explains the action of forced celibacy: 'The extreme exercise of one passion will generally obliterate the very sense of the others; the Amazons, whilst indulging in the excitement of the most fearful cruelties, forget the other desires of our fallen nature.' But all the passions are sisters. I believe that bloodshed causes these women to remember, not to forget LOVE; at the same time that it gratifies the less barbarous, but, with barbarians, equally animal feeling. Seeing the host of women who find a morbid pleasure in attending the maimed and dying, I must think that it is a tribute paid to sexuality by those who object to the ordinary means. Of course they are savage as wounded gorillas, more cruel far than their brethren in arms.

> For men at most differ as heaven and earth;
> But women, worst and best, as heaven and hell.

The existence of the Amazons is the second great evil of the empire. The first is, or rather was, a thirst for conquest, which, unlike the projections of civilized lands, impoverish and debilitate the country. The object of Dahoman wars and invasions has always been to lay waste and to destroy, not to aggrandize the empire by conquest and annexation. As the *History* puts it, the rulers have ever followed the example of Agaja, the second founder of the kingdom; aiming at conquest and at striking terror, rather than at accretion and consolidation. Hence there has been a decrease of population, with an increase of territory, which is, to nations, the surest road to ruin. In the present days the wars have dwindled to mere slave hunts – a fact which it is well to remember. The women troops, assumed to number 2,500, should represent 7,500 children; the waste of reproduction, and the necessary casualties of 'service', in a region so depopulated, are as detrimental to the body politic as a proportional loss of blood would be to the frame personal. Thus the land is desert, and the raw material of all industry, man, is everywhere wanting. Finally, as regards the Amazons, nothing so outrageously insults manly pride in the adjoining nations than to find that the warriors who attacked them so stoutly are women – and some of them old women.

The dress, the *physique*, and the personal appearance of the Amazons have repeatedly been described in these pages. I have also alluded to the organization of the corps, which requires, however, more detail.

The soldieresses are not divided into regiments, as is supposed by Mr. Duncan. There are, however, in the 'Household Brigade' three distinct divisions or commands, female as well as male.

The Fanti Company takes the centre, and represents the King's bodyguards. These women wear round the hair, which requires scanty confinement, narrow white fillets, with rude crocodiles of blue cloth sewn on to the band.

The right wing, under the Gundeme, or she-Min-gan, and the Khe-tun-gan, or female Gau. It is not distinguished by any peculiarity of costume.

The left wing, in charge of the Yewe or she-Meu and the Akpa-dume, who is the coadjutress of the Po-su.

The King generally pays 'distinguished strangers' the compliment of placing them in command of his bodyguard, which honour, however, does not entitle them even to inspect the corps. The 'Bush-king' has also his captains, both on the men's and on the women's sides. There are lifeguards and commanders for all the deceased sovereigns; moreover, every high official has his head war-man or war-woman, with a recognized title. The *cadre* of commissions, in fact, would become a country numbering twenty-millions instead of some 150,000 souls.

These three corps consist of five arms, under their several officers—

1. The Agbarya or blunderbuss-women, who may be considered the grenadiers. They are the biggest and strongest of the force, and each is accompanied by an attendant carrying ammunition. With the blunderbuss-women rank the Zo-hu-nun, or carbineers, the Gan'u-nlan, or Sure-to-kill Company, and the Achi, or bayoneteers.

2. The elephant huntresses, who are held to be the bravest. Of these women, twenty have been known to bring down, at one volley, with their rude appliances, seven animals out of a herd.

3. The Nyekplo-hen-to, or razor women, who seem to be simply an *épouvantail*.

4. The infantry, or line's-women, forming the staple of the force, from whom, as in France, the *élite* is drawn. They are armed with Tower muskets, and are well supplied with bad ammunition; bamboo fibre, for instance, being the only wadding. They have but little ball practice. They 'manoeuvre with the precision of a flock of sheep', and they are too light to stand a charge of the poorest troops in Europe. Personally, they are cleanly made, without much muscle; they are hard dancers, indefatigable singers, and, though affecting a military swagger, their faces are anything but ferocious – they are rather mild and unassuming in appearance. They fought with fury with Gezo before Abeokuta because there was a jealously between them and their brother soldiers, and because they had been led for many years by that king to small but sure victory. They fled, however, with the rest, when a little per-severance would have retrieved the fortunes of the day.

5. The Go-hen-to, or archeresses, who in Gezo's time were young girls – the parade corps, the pick of the army, and the pink of dancers. They were armed with the peculiar Dahoman bow, a quiver of poisoned light cane shafts – mere birdbolts, with hooked heads, spiny as sticklebacks – and a small knife lashed with a lanyard to the wrist. They were distinguished by scanty attire, by a tattoo extending to the knee, and by an ivory bracelet on the left arm. Their weapon has naturally fallen in public esteem. Under Gezo's son, they are never seen on parade; and when in the field they are used as scouts and porters; like our drummers and doolee-bearers, they also carry the wounded to the rear.

In 1863 I saw all these women troops marching, on service, out of Kana. The officers, distinguished by their white head-cloths, and by an esquiress-at-arms, generally a small slave girl, carrying the musket, led their commands. They were mostly remarkable for a stupendous stratopyga, and for a development of adipose tissue readily believe in fat 'old maids'. I expected to see Penthesileas,

Thalestrises, Dianas – lovely names! I saw old, ugly, and square-built frows, trudging 'grumpily' along, with the face of 'cook' after being much 'knagg'd' by 'the missus'. The privates carried packs on cradles, like those of the male soldiery, containing their bed-mats, clothes, and food for a week or a fortnight, mostly toasted grains and bean-cake, hot with peppers. Cartridge-pouches of two different shapes were girt round their waists, and slung to their sides were water-gourds, fetish-sacks, bullet-wallets, powder-calabashes, fans, little cutlasses, wooden pipe-cases enveloped in leather tobacco-bags, flint, steel, and tinder, and Lilliputian stools, with three or four legs, cut out of single blocks. Their weapons were slung, and behind their backs dangled their hats, scarecrow felts, 'extinguishers' of white cotton useful as *sacs de nuit*, umbrellas of plaited palm leaf, and low-crowned, broad-brimmed, home-made straws, covered with baft more or less blue.

After a careful computation in 1863 I obtained the following results: Before 10 A.M. were counted 1,439, mostly weaponed; they then marched in knots, in all 246; making, when we retired to breakfast, a total of 1,685. The movement was interrupted till our return, when the King set out with a bodyguard of 353. Thus the grand total was 2,038, and at most, allowing for omissions, 2,500. But of these one-third were unarmed, or half-armed, leaving the fighting women at a figure of 1,700. Mr. Bernasko and others, who exaggerate the consequence of the country, asserted that, this being a small campaign, a large corps of Amazons remains at Agbome, but I subsequently ascertained that such was not the case. Mr. Duncan (1845) reckons 6,000 women soldiers (in Vol. I, p. 227), and 8,000 Amazons (Vol. 1, p. 231). Commander Forbes and Mr. Beecroft (1849–50) give 5,000, but the heroines, like the commissariat cattle in Afghanistan, were marched out of one gate and in through another. M. Wallon (1856–58), besides dreaming of twenty to twenty-five howitzers, carronades, and bronze mortars on campaigning beds, assumed the number to be 5,000; but his figures are all seen through a magnifying medium. Mr. Enschott (1862), after inventing a park of artillery, furnished Dahome with 10,000 Amazons, which Commodore Wilmot (1863) reduced to a half. The fact is, these 'most illustrious viragos' are now a mere handful. King Gezo lost the flower of his force under the walls of Abeokuta, and the loss has never been made good.

SIX

TRAVELLER AND WAR CORRESPONDENT IN SOUTH AMERICA

Isabel meanwhile used her influence at the Foreign Office to secure her husband a posting in Brazil. In 1865 Burton departed to take up a position as British consul in Santos, 'the Wapping of the West', as he called it. Isabel joined him a few months later. Burton explored Portugal and the Brazilian state of Bahía *en route* to his post.

Brazil, an independent empire of some forty years, was ruled by the enlightened emperor Pedro II, whom Victor Hugo once called a modern Marcus Aurelius. British pressure had ended the slave trade, but slavery itself was still legal; Brazil was the world's last slave state and would remain so until 1888.

Santos, on the coast, was notoriously unhealthy, so, leaving the consulate in charge of a local official, the Burtons spent most of their time up country in São Paulo. The greatest megalopolis of the late twentieth century was then a sleepy little town of 25,000 inhabitants. Isabel made the first married home in a converted convent. She and Burton lived the life of adventurers. Both were expert riders and fencers. Burton began work on his massive translation of the *Arabian Nights*, which was eventually to see the light of day in 1885. Occasionally there were leaves at Rio, where they enjoyed the diplomatic social round. Burton was lionized by Pedro II, himself an amateur scientist, and shown special favours, much to the fury of his superiors in the diplomatic hierarchy.

In flat defiance of consular regulations, Burton formed a Brazilian mining company, manoeuvred for personal advantage through Pedro, and even floated shares in his mining company on the London Stock Exchange. Sir Edward Thornton, Minister in Rio, issued rebukes that would have wrecked the career of anyone less protected than Burton. Luckily, through the Arundells, he enjoyed the powerful patronage of the Foreign Secretary Lord Stanley.

At last, in the summer of 1867, Burton obtained an extensive local leave to permit him to explore the mines of Minas Gerais province and then float 1,500 miles down the São Francisco river to its mouth in Bahía province. His wife accompanied him on some hard riding as far as Ouro Prêto, where she sprained an ankle and had to return to Rio. Burton then continued north to Pirapora where he joined the São Francisco river and canoed down its length to the great cataract of Paulo Affonso, one of the mightiest waterfalls in the world. 'Powerful, tremendous, inexorable, irresistible,' Burton described the four cascades, 270 feet high. This journey saw Burton at his best – the intrepid traveller describing the Brazilian jungle in all its colour. From the mouth of the Saõ Francisco he proceeded to Salvador and thence to Rio by streamer.

Returning to Saõ Paulo, Burton endured his consulate until August 1868 when he decided he could bear it no longer. He obtained another long leave and, while Isabel returned to England, set out for the River Plate. He travelled widely in Argentina, meeting Bartolome Mitre, Domingo Sarmiento and Justo Urquiza, the leading Argentine political figures of the day, then set off for the seat of the Paraguayan war. Burton's reports on the War of Triple Alliance (Brazil, Uruguay and Argentina against Paraguay) make up a classic of war reporting. In his sympathy for Carlos Lopez, doomed dictator of Paraguay, Burton anticipated much revisionist historiography. In his Argentine writings Burton provides an invaluable sketch of the city of Buenos Aires in 1868-69, on the eve of the massive immigration from Europe that would transform it. He writes testily but wittily of the hardships of travel by river steamer up the River Paraná. And he shows his skills as a war reporter in the description of the great Paraguayan fortress, whose capture by the Allies in 1868 was the turning point of the war.

Back in Buenos Aires Burton made the acquaintance of the noted Arabist Wilfred Blunt and became very friendly with the notorious 'Tichborne Claimant' (Thomas Castro, who laid a claim to the baronetcy of Tichborne by pretending to be the elder brother lost off the coast of South America, but who was found guilty of perjury in a famous Victorian trial in 1872 and was sentenced to fourteen years' hard labour) at whose trial he later testified. After the fall of Asunción, Burton set out for Chile. He encountered hostile Araucanian Indians in the Andes, visited the scene of the recent earthquake in Arica, and ended his tour in Lima, where he received word of his posting to Damascus. He returned via the Straits of Magellan, Buenos Aires and Rio to England, arriving late 1869.

Paulo Affonso, King of Rapids
(from *The Highlands of Brazil* (1869))

Presently we heard a deep hollow sound, soft withal, like the rumbling of a distant storm; but it seemed to come from below the earth, as if we trod upon it: after another mile the ground appeared to tremble at the eternal thunder. Sr. Manuel Leandro led us off to the left of whence came the Voice, and began unloading the mules at the usual halting-place. I looked for the promised 'Traveller's Bungalow,' and saw only the stump of a post, sole remnant of the house run up to receive His Imperial Majesty of the Brazil, who visited the place in October, 1859. The site is a bed of loose sand, which in the height of the floods becomes a torrent. We shall afterwards find where it falls into the main stream. Our rude camp was pitched under the filmy and flickering shade of a tall Carahyba mimosa whose trunk, in places peeled of bark, showed many a name; apparently, however, the great Smithian Gens has been laughed out of cutting and carving its initials and date – here all were Brazilians.

I should advise those who visit Paulo Affonso in the dry season to make at once, with the aid of plan and guide, for the Mãi da Cachoeira, the 'Mother of the Rapids,' where all the waters that come scouring down with their mighty rush are finally gathered together. To see cataracts aright, it is best, I think – though opinions upon this point differ – to begin with the greatest enjoyment, the liveliest emotion, and not to fritter away one's powers, mental and physical, by working up to the grandest feature. Moreover, this one point displays most forcibly the formation which distinguishes Paulo Affonso from all his great brethren and sisterhood.

Stowing my note and sketch-books in a 'Muchíla,' or horse's grain-bag, and hanging it over the guide's shoulder, I struck across the left bank of the river; here a lava-like 'Mal-paiz,' resembling that of the Itaparíca. The stones, polished as if they were mirrors, or marble-slabs, glittered and reflected the burning sun-beams; in places the ridges are walls of turned and worked rock that looks like mouldings of brass, bronze, or iron. Many of the boulders are monster onyxes, or granite banded and ribboned with quartz: they are of an infinite variety in size and shape, in make and hue, rough and smooth, warm-red, rhubarb-yellow, dull-black and polished jet.

Chemin faisant we crossed an Eastern Channel, at this season almost dry, a thread of water striping the bottom. It forms with the main body a large trapèze-shaped Goat Island, which presents its smaller end down stream. Paulo Affonso differs essentially from Niagara, whose regular supply by the inland seas admits little alteration of weight, or size, or strength of stream, except in the rare winters when it is frozen over. About December, as the floods run high, this tiny creek will swell to an impassable boiling rapid, ending in a fine fall about the 'Vampire's Cave.' Upon this 'Goat Island,' where if there are no goats the walking is fit for them only, are short tracts of loose sand alternating with sheets of granite, and of syenite, with here and there a 'courtil' of greener grass. The walk leads to a table of jutting rock on the west side, where we cling to a dry tree-trunk, and peer, fascinated, into the 'hell of waters' boiling below.

The Quebrada, or gorge, is here 260 feet deep, and in the narrowest part it is choked to a minimum breadth of fifty-one feet. It is filled with what seems not water, but the froth of milk, a dashing and dazzling, a whirling and churning surfaceless mass, which gives a wondrous study of fluid in motion. And the marvellous disorder is a well-directed anarchy: the course and sway, the wresting and writhing, all tend to set free the prisoner from the prison walls. Ces eaux! mais ce sont des âmes: it is the spectacle of a host rushing down in 'liquid vastness' to victory, the triumph of motion, of momentum over the immoveable. Here the luminous whiteness of the chaotic foam-crests, hurled in billows and breakers against the blackness of the rock, is burst into flakes and spray, that leap half way up the immuring trough. There the surface reflections dull the dazzling crystal to a thick opaque yellow, and there the shelter of some spur causes a momentary start and recoil to the column, which, at once gathering strength, bounds and springs onwards with a new crush and another roar. The heaped-up centre shows fugitive ovals and progressive circles of a yet more sparkling, glittering, dazzling light, divided by points of comparative repose, like the nodal lines of waves. They struggle and jostle, start asunder, and interlace as they dash with stedfast purpose adown the inclined plane. Now a fierce blast hunts away the thin spray-drift, and puffs it to leeward in rounded clouds, thus enhancing the brilliancy of the gorge-sole. Then the steam boils over and canopies the tremendous scene. Then in the stilly air of dull warm grey, the mists surge up, deepening still more, by their veil of ever ascending vapour, the dizzy fall that yawns under our feet.

The general effect of the picture – and the same may be said of all great cataracts – is the 'realized' idea of power, of power tremendous, inexorable, irresistible. The eye is spellbound by the contrast of this impetuous motion, this wrathful, maddened haste to escape, with the frail stedfastness of the bits of rainbow, hovering above; with the 'Table Rock' so solid to the tread, and with the placid, settled stillness of the plain and the hillocks, whose eternal homes seem to be here. The fancy is electrified by the aspect of this Durga of Nature, this evil working good, this life-in-death, this creation and construction by destruction. Even so, the wasting storm and hurricane purify the air for life: thus the earthquake and the volcano, while surrounding themselves with ruins, rear up earth, and make it a habitation for higher beings.

The narrowness of the chasm is narrowed to the glance by the tall abruptness, yet a well-cast stone goes but a short way across, before it is neatly stopped by the wind. The guide declared, that no one could throw further than three fathoms, and attributed the fact to enchantment. Magic, I may observe, is in the atmosphere of Paulo Affonso: it is the natural expression of the glory and majesty, the splendour and the glamour of the scene, which

Greece would have peopled with shapes of beauty, and which in Germany would be haunted by choirs of flying sylphs and dancing undines. The hollow sound of the weight of whirling water makes it easier to see the lips move than to hear the voice. We looked in vain for the cause; of cataract we saw nothing but a small branch, the Cachoeira do Angiquinho – of the little Angico Acacia – so called from one of the rock islets. It is backed on the right bank by comparatively large trees, and by a patch of vividly green grass and shrubbery, the gift of the spray drifting before the eastern sea-breeze. This pretty gush of water certainly may not account for the muffled thunder which dulls our ears: presently we shall discover whence it comes.

I sat over the 'Quebrada' till convinced it was not possible to become 'one with the waters:' what at first seemed grand and sublime at last had a feeling of awe too intense to be in any way enjoyable, and I left the place that the confusion and emotion might pass away. The rest of the day was spent at 'Carahyba Camp,' where the minor cares of life soon asserted their power. The sand raised by the strong and steady trade wind was troublesome, and the surface seething in the sun produced a constant draught: we are now at the very head of the funnel, the vast ventilator which guides the gale to the upper Rio de São Francisco. Far to seaward we could see the clouds arming for rain. At night the sky showed a fast-drifting scud, and an angry blast dispersed the gathering clouds of blood-thirsty musquitos. Our lullaby was the music of Paulo Affonso; the deep, thundering base produced by the longer and less frequent vibrations from the Falls, and from the Rapids the staccato treble of the shorter wave-sounds. Yet it was no unpleasant crash, the deeper tones were essentially melodious, and at times there rose an expression in the minor key, which might be subjected to musical annotation. I well remember not being able to sleep within ear-shot of Niagara, whose mighty orchestra, during the stillness of night, seemed to run through a repertoire of oratorios and operas.

We will now apply ourselves to the prose of the Great Rapids.

The name, as mostly happens in these regions, is a disputed point. Some make 'Paulo Affonso' a missioner-shepherd, who was hurled down the abyss by the wolves, his 'Red-skin' sheep. Others tell the story of a friar, who was canoeing along the river, when the Indian paddle-men cried, in terror, that they were being sucked into the jaws of the Catadupa; he bade them be of good cheer, and all descended whole. 'Such reverends are now-a-days rare,' observed Sr. Manuel Leandro with an unworthy sneer. Similarly in the Province of São Paulo, the Tiété river has a fierce Rapid, known as 'Avaremandoura' – Cachoeira do Padre, or the Rapid of the Priest. Here, according to Jesuit legend, Padre Anchieta, one of the multitudinous thaumaturgi of the Brazil, was recovered from the water 'some hours afterwards, alive and reading his breviary with a light in his hand.' More sober chronicles declare that the poor man was dragged out half drowned. The gigantic cataract of 'Tequendama,' we may remember, has also its miracle; it was opened by the great Bochica, god of New Granada, a barbarous land, that had hardly any right to have a god. Others pretend that Paulo and Affonso were brothers, and the first settlers, who gave their names to the place. I would, however, observe, that on the right bank of the stream, opposite the Ilha de Tapéra, one of the many that break the river immediately above the upper break, is a village of fishermen and cultivators, whose name, 'Tapéra de Paulo Affonso,' shows that it has occupied the site of a ruined settlement, probably made by the colonist who, happier than Father Hennepin, left his mark upon the Great Rapids near which he squatted. The 'Tapéristas' are still owners of the right bank; the left belongs to one Nicoláo Continguiba, of the Engenho do Pinho, and near 'Carahyba Camp' two properties meet. The Cachoeira is in the Freguezia of the Mata da Agua Branca.

The locale of the Paulo Affonso has been very exactly misrepresented by geographers who write geography for the people. This sudden break in the level of the bed, this divide between the Upper and Lower São Francisco, is not formed by a prolongation of the Serra da Borborema, nor by the Chapada das Mangabeiras, nor by Ibyapaba 'fim da terra,' nor by the Cairirys old or new, nor by the Serra da Borracha, alias Moribéca, so imminent in our maps. The humbler setting of the gem is a rotting plain brown with stone, scrub, and thicket, out of which rise detached blocks, as the Serra do Retiro, about three leagues to the north-west, and to the west the lumpy Serra do Padre. On the southwestern horizon springs, sudden from the flat, a nameless but exceedingly picturesque rangelet of pyramidal hills and peaks, here and there bristling in bare rock, and connected by long blue lines of curtain.

Though our prospect lacks the sublime and glorious natural

beauty of Niagara, tempered by the hand of man, and though we find in Paulo Affonso none of the sapphire and emerald tints that charm the glance in the Horsehoe Falls, still it is original and peculiar. In 'geological' times, the stream must have spread over the valley; even now, extraordinary floods cover a great portion of it. Presently the waters, finding a rock of softer texture and more liable to decay, hollowed out the actual 'Talhadão,' or great fissure, and deepened the glen in the course of ages. We have also here the greatest possible diversity of falling water; it consists, in fact, of a succession of rapids and cauldrons, and a mighty Fall ending in the Mãi da Cachoeira, upon whose terrible tangle of foam we have just looked down. If Niagara be the monarch of cataracts, Paulo Affonso is assuredly a king of rapids; an English traveller who had seen the twain, agreed with me in giving the palm to the latter, as being the more singular and picturesque of the two, which are both so wondrous and so awful. He had not visited the Itaparíca, that foil whose grimness so well sets off its majestic neighbour.

Nature is not in her grandest attire, yet the vestment well suits the shape. Spines predominate. There is the Favelleiro or arboreous Jatropha, with its dark-green oak-like leaves terribly armed; and the Cansanção Maïor (Jatropha urens), a giant nettle, whose white spangles of flowers are scattered in mimicry of snow-flakes upon the sombre verdure. The Cactus is in force; we see the common flat Opuntia, the little Quipá, with its big red fig, the Turk's-head (Cabeça de frade) Melocactus, with the crimson fez, whilst among the rocks project half-domes of a foot in diameter (C. aphananthemum). Some have flowers quaint as orchids, others are clothed in flue, and the rest are hairy and bald, angular and smooth, giant and dwarf, lorded over by the immense Mandracurú (C. brasiliensis), a tree, but strangely different from all our ideas that make up a tree. The Bromelias are abundant, especially the Carauá, banded like a coral snake, and the Macambira with needle thorns and flower-spikes three feet tall; it is loved by monkeys who, they say, make pic-nics to eat the leaves. The feathery elongated Catingueiro, now tender green, then burnished brown, is remarkable near the dense clustering verdure of the rounded Quixabeira, and the Imbuzeiro with the horizontal boughs, a bush twenty feet high. The Carahyba is the monarch of the bush, and its leek-coloured leafage, hung with long bitter pods, and with trumpets of yellow gold, gains beauty seen near the gay red blossom and the velvety foliage of the 'Pinhão bravo,' and the whitey-green catkins of the thorny Acacia, known as the Jurema preta. We also remark the black charred bole of the Paó preto, by the side of the sweet-scented Imburana, hung with flakes of light burnished bronze. The scrub is mostly the hard Araça-guava with its twisted wood, and the Bom-nome, whose 'good name,' I presume, results not from an inedible berry, but because it is found useful for spoons. The cattle straying about the bushes toss their heads, snort, and with raised tails dash through the thicket as we approach; they are sleek, clean-limbed, – much more like the wild animal of the African Gaboon than the European model of bull and cow. Thanks to the drift, they find in the dwarf 'courtils' more succulent fodder than usual; they suffer, however, when not penned for the night in the Cahyçára, from ounces and vampires, and they are sometimes poisoned by the pretty, pink, and innocent-looking blossom, here known as the 'Cebolla brava.' Finish the picture with clouds of spray and vapour, rising from the abyss; and pouring to leeward an incessant shower of silvery atoms; with the burnished stones, here singularly gloomy, there mirroring the dazzles of the sun-beam; and with gay troops of birds, especially the Tanager, the hyacinthine Ararúna, and the red and green parroquet, darting and screaming through the air, whose prevalent hue is a thin warm neutral tint.

My next visit began at the beginning, and thence we followed down the left bank, stepping from slippery stone to stone, and approaching the channel when possible. Here the São Francisco, running swift and smooth out of the north-west, escapes from the labyrinth of islands and islets, rocks and sands, blocks and walls which squeeze it, and receives on the left a smaller branch, separated from the main by a dark ridge. The two, leaping and coursing down a moderate incline of broken bed, burst into ragged, tossing sheets of foam-crested wave, and tumble down the first or upper break, which is about thirty-two feet high. This kind of 'Rideau Fall' is known as the 'Vai-Vem de Cima' – the 'upper go and come.' The waters are compressed in the central channel by the stone courses rising thirty to fifty feet above them, and are driven into a little cove on the left bank. The mouth of a branch during the floods, now it is a baylet of the softest sand hemmed in by high japanned walls, and here the little waves curl and flow, and ebb again, with all the movement of a tide in miniature. I timed and felt the pulse of the flux and reflux, but I could detect no regularity in the circulation. The place tempts to a bath, but strangers must bear in mind that it is treacherous, and that cattle drinking here have been entangled in the waters, from which not even Jupiter himself could save them.

The waters then dashing against the left or south-eastern boulder-pier, are deflected to the south-west in a vast serpentine of tossing foam, and form, a few paces lower down, a similar feature; called by our guide 'Half go and come.' Here insulated rocks and islands, large and small, disposed in long ridges and in rounded towers, black, toothed, and channeled, and wilder far than the Three Sisters or the Bath and Lunar islands of Niagara, split the hurrying tossing course into five distinct channels of white surge, topping the yellow turbid flood. The four to the right topple over at once into the great cauldron. The fifth runs along the left bank in a colossal flume or launders, high raised above the rest; meeting a projection of rock at the south, it is flung round to the west almost at a right angle. Here the parted waters spring over the ledge, and converge in the Chaudière which collects them for the great fall. When the sun and moon are at the favourable angle of 35°, they produce admirable arcs and semi-circles of rainbows in all their prismatic tintage from white to red. These attract the eye by standing in a thin arch of light over the mighty highway of the rushing 'burning' waters; guides to cataracts, however, always make too much of the pretty sight.

The third station is reached by a rough thorny descent, which might easily be improved, and leads to the water's edge, where charred wood shows that travellers have lately nighted in the place. Turning to the north-east we see a furious brown rapid plunging with strange forms, down an incline of forty-nine feet in half a dozen distinct steps: the flood seems as though it would sweep us away. At the bottom, close to where we stand, it bends westward, pauses for a moment upon the billow-fringed lower lip of the Chaudière that rises snow-white from the straw-coloured break, and then the low, deep, thundering roar, shaking the ground and 'sui generis' as the rumbling of the earthquake and the hoarse sumph of the volcano reveal the position of the Great Cataract. The trend is southerly, and the height is calculated to be 192 feet. The waters hurl themselves full upon the right-hand precipice of the trough-ravine, surge high up, fall backwards, fling a permanent mistcloud in the air, and like squadrons of white horses, rush off, roaring and with infinite struggle and confusion, down the Mãi da Cachoeira to the south-east. The latter is the grandest point of view which we prospected from the tablerock overhanging the fracture.

Paulo Affonso is always sketched from our third station, where we 'realize' an unpleasant peculiarity of his conformation; he has here permitted the eye of man to see the main cataract. A little further down, there is a partial view from above, but the normal central mistcloud curling high and always ascending above the lower lip of the cauldron, veils the depth, and we are not satisfied till we have sighted a Fall from its foot. Now much is left to the imagination, and the mystery is so great as to be highly unsatisfactory. In the depth of the dries it is, they say, possible to climb down a portion of the left wall, and to overlook the cataract. I carefully inquired whether it was visible from the right, or Bahian bank; all assured me that a branch stream allowed no approach to the trough-ravine, and all were agreed that from that side nothing is visible. A moveable suspension-bridge, not, I hope, like that of Montmorenci, could be made to span the chasm; wire-ropes fit to bear cradles, could be passed across; or ladders might be let down and act as the winding staircase which leads to the Horseshoe Fall. At present Paulo Affonso is what Niagara was in the days of Père François Piquet: and we can hardly look forward with pleasure to the time when it will have wooden temples and obelisks, vested interests, 25 cents to pay, and monster-hotels.

The next station is that with which I have advised the stranger to begin. Thence he must retrace his steps, the trough up is too rough and broken to be followed. We again crossed the eastern boulder-channel, and walking to the south-east reached, after a few hundred yards, a descent formed by the waters which, in flood-time, sweep over the hollow 'Carahyba Camping ground,' and course down a stony incline to rejoin the parent flood. We found the bed bone-dry, a slippery surface of bare rock, dark and bright after many a freshet, with here and there steps and deep crevasses. There are stagnant pools and corrie-like holes, green with Confervæ, and rich in landshells. These hollows long preserve the rain-water, and though covered with scum-like aquatic growths, they are during the dries, a great resource for cattle. The hands must be used as well as the feet in descending, and the noonday sun will peel the palms.

The zigzag led down to a Ressáca or bulge in the left bank of the river. Here the torrent is less terrible, but still violent, as it dashes against the south-eastern wall of the trough. The light colour of the precipice, not grown, like the rest of the trough, with moss, Bromelia, and thorn bush, shows that, despite the exceeding hardness of the stone, some part has slipped, and more will slip. Sr. Manuel Leandro assured me that it has not changed since the days of his grandfather and his grandmother.

At the trough-foot we reach a baylet formed by the lower 'Go and come' (Vai-Vem de baixo), another back-water of the great rushing tide. People fetching water have fallen into it, but have managed to extricate themselves. No Maid of the Mist, however, will in these ages be able to ascend the line of maëlströms. Now the water recovers from the plunge and dive in the abyss beneath the cascade, it continually rebounds, and as we often noticed in the Cachoeiras of the upper bed, there is no really level surface; the face seems a system of slightly bulging domes.

The little inclined ramp of loose stones at the bottom of the wall is strewed with lumber and with wood brought down by the last floods; its grinding sound and its crash when floods are high, have been compared with the creaking of the ice at the end of a Canadian winter. Light as pumice-stone, the fragments are rounded off and cropped at both ends by the bruising process, and the working takes curious shapes, cheeses and shuttles, nine-pins and skittles. Our guide picturesequely called the heaps 'Cidade de Madeira,' a city of wood, and in them I recognized canoe planks and scantling from the Imperial shed.

The slope ends in a cave opening to the west, and known generically as the 'Casa de Pedra,' specifically as the 'Furna do Morcego,' or Vampire's Grot. Its appearance is singular. The entrance, instead of being low, after the fashion of caverns, is a tall parallelogrammic portal leaning a little to the south. Hence it has its Saintess (uma Santa), who shows herself at times, and the people have heard martial music, and singing which did not, they judged, proceed from mortal wind-pipe. The arch is formed by a thick table of hard, close-grained granite, spread out as though it had been lava, and a cleavage-line extends to the southern corner. Its walls are sandstone, here hard and compact, there soft and mixed with ochreous iron-stained clay, easily cut in the days when the now shrunken and sunken stream filled the trough-ravine with its débâcles. At present the inundations extend only half-way up the floor, where an 'old man' is in the process of degradation. The level sole is strewed with bat's guano, and with ashes where the people have attempted to smoke out the blood-suckers. The greatest height is about 90 feet. The eastern wall overhangs, and the honey-combed upper part shows other branch caves still forming, whilst the western retreats at the easy angle of 8°–9°. I saw no bats in this 'Cave of the Winds,' this 'Devil's Hole;' but the hour of visit was early afternoon, and the plague was probably enjoying its nap. The mouth of the vault has a singular look-out. The fleecy, seething, snow-white torrent, disposed in vorticose-lozenges and ridges, with its spray glittering under the sun like myriads of brilliants, strikes upon a shoulder of polished and intensely black rock, whose parallel and much inclined bands wall the right side of the crevasse. This mass deflects the boiling rapid at nearly a right angle, and sends it roaring between the cliffs of its deep-narrow chasm adown the abrupt redoublings which end its course in the world of waters to the east.

Our last station is upon the 'Paredão,' lower down than the Vampire's Cave, at the place called 'Limpo do Imperador' – the bush having been cleared away for the Imperial visit. There is no shade, and water is far off. A tent and barrels, however, would make all things easy, and a traveller encamped upon this Bellevue would have beneath his eyes by night as well as by day the most beautiful if not the grandest scenery of Paulo Affonso. Here he stands on a level with the stream above the Upper Rapids, and on 800 feet of perpendicular height over the water, which dashes curdling and creaming below. To the westwards the vision strikes full upon the small but graceful Angiquinho branch, which is the American Falls compared with the Horseshoe, and which reminds the traveller of the tall narrow Montmorenci. This offset is the furthest line on the right side of the river, in which, about the Tapéra of Paulo Affonso, a mass of long islands precedes the narrows and the rapids. It encloses an 'Iris Island,' a crag which may easily be confounded with the mainland. It is, however, capped with trees and grass, kept green as emerald by the cease-less drift, and made remarkable by the brown plain forming the distance. Here again the still and silent picture around heightens the effect of the foaming, rushing water. The flood rolls headlong over its own shelf of brown based on jet-black rock, seen in the walls which here jut out and there retire. Dashed to pieces by the drop, it shows about the centre, with the assistance of a projecting rock, at this season clearly visible, a fall within a fall. Puffs of

water-douche, looking as if endless mines were being sprung, rise
to half its height, and the infinite globules, 'spireing up' in shafts,
repeat the prismatic glories of solar and lunar rainbows. At its
foot, from the spectator's right hand, or from north to south, a
section of an arch represents the terminal part of the mysterious
cataract, whose upper two-thirds are hidden by a curtain of rock.
This, the main stream, impinges almost perpendicularly upon
the right-hand wall of the trough-ravine, and the impetus hurls it
in rolls and billows high up the face to be thrown back shattered,
and to add a confusion more confused to the succeeding torrents.
But, subject to the eternal law of gravitation, a sinuous line
perforce undulates down the crevasse, which gradually widens,
and which puts out buttresses from the right and left. Calmed by
the diminished slope, it meets the tall cliffs upon which we stand,
and wheeling from north-west to south-west, it eddies down the
windings of the ravine, which soon conceal it from the sight. The
effect is charming when the moon, rising behind the spectator,
pours upon the flashing line of cascade and rapid full in front, a
flood of soft and silvery light, while semi-opaque shadows, here
purple, here brown, clothe the middle height, and black glooms
hang about the ribs, spines, and buttresses of the chasm-foot.

Not the least interesting part of Paulo Affonso is this terminal
ravine, which reminded me of the gorge of Zambezian Mosiwa-
tunya, as painted by Mr. Baines. It has given rise to a multitude
of wild fables, especially to the legend of the under-ground river,
an Alpheus, a Niger, a Nile, that favourite theme with the 'old
men.' The black sides, footed by boulders which the force of the
flood has hurled in heaps, and in places cut by small white
streams, preserve their uniformity, and wall in the stream as far as
the Porto das Piranhas, forty-two geographical miles below the
cataract. Moreover the elevation profile shows below the actual
cataract, a kieve or deep hollow, and a long succession of similar
abysses, prolonged to the same point, and gradually diminishing
in depth, the effect of a secular filling in. Niagara undermining
the soft shales that support a hard structure of limestone some
ninety feet thick, has eaten back seven miles from the escarpment
known as Queenstown Heights. It is supposed to have expended
4000 years in reaching its present position, and to be receding at
the rate of a foot per annum. Here we find a similar retreat of the
waters. According to the guides, a huge mass of stone above the
Chaudière formed an arch under which birds built their nests.

This disappeared like the old original 'Fall Rock' about ten years ago, and since that time they say the Zoadão, or roar of Paulo Affonso, has not been so loud. Applying, therefore, the rule of the Northern Cataract, we cannot assign to the King of Rapids an age under 2400 years.

My task was done. I won its reward, and the strength passed away from me. Two days of tedious monotonous riding led to the Porto das Piranhas. The steamer had just left it, but a hospitable reception awaited me at the house of Sr. Ventura José Martins, agent to the Bahian Steam Navigation Company. My companion hurried away to catch the American mail at Pernambuco. I descended the lower Rio de São Francisco more leisurely, under the guidance of Sr. Luis Caetano da Silva Campos of Penedo, whose amiable Senhora made me feel at home. Whilst delayed at 'the Rock' I met my excellent friend Dr. A. Moreira de Barros, then President of Alagôas, and visited him at his capital, Maceiò. Thence, with the aid of Mr. Hugh Wilson, I found my way to Aracajú and Bahia, and finally I returned viâ Rio de Janeiro to Santos (São Paulo), alias Wapping in the Far West.

Letters from the Battle-fields of Paraguay (1870)

LETTER V
A Day at Buenos Aires — The Old Engagement Kept

Buenos Aires, Sunday, August 16, 1868

MY DEAR Z———— ,

We prepare to land, and of all self-styled civilized landing-places this at the 'Athens of South America' is perhaps the worst. Vile in fine weather – what must be the abomination when Pampero the storm-blast is out! The wind seems always to blow inwards, and summer shows a worse river than winter; while with rare intervals the air is ever wet, damp, and depressing.

From the 'Canal' or outer roads, distant four or five miles, where the large steamers, including the mails, ride in summer, and whence disembarking is at times almost impossible for a week, you must, as a rule, touch ground at your own expense. There are 'Vaporcitos' or little steamers, the *Jacaré* and the *Baby*, which come, or which come not, as they list. They are never, as they should be, under the control of any great foreign company. The usual landing process is at present composed of three several steps. First you drop with bag and baggage from the ship ladder into a lighter, or into one of the sailing craft which – manned by foreigners, Italians, or worst of all, English – await to devour you. Here, as at Monte Vidéo, the water is far too dangerous for gigs or wherries. After an involuntary douche caused by the least capful of wind, you are transferred, as the boat grounds, to a cart painted blood-red, whose pitiful team of half-drowned and rheumatic horses sticks and dips, rises and struggles painfully along, urged by the screams of the European, who has now ousted the Gaucho. The last transfer is to the northernmost of the two moles, the shallow water utterly disqualifying for use the southern one fronting the large Custom-house. Men and women, loungers and promenaders, gather in groups at the mole-head, adding ridicule to your difficulties as if you were in the tidal boat entering Boulogne. Lads and boys playfully wreathe their bodies in, out, and through the timbers of the main jetty, or bathe and fish in the troubled waters below, or foully bewray the dirty steps. Some thirty or forty excited changadores (porters) and peons (labourers) make a dash at your baggage, and the unsuccessful salute the successful with a volley of foul abuse. These men are the common carriers of the country: it is actionable (with the knife) to call a decent man 'peon' (our pawn from the Persian 'piyádah'), and the Frenchman will, when wishing to say his worst, emphatically declare of the hated rival, 'C'est un pé-on!'

After enduring this savage mobbery, you step probably upon an iron bar, and climb up broken steps to landing-places which are also of the filthiest. The new 'Muelle,' built in 1855 for the local Government by the late Mr. Taylor, C.E., is a wretched affair, some 440 yards long, by 20 wide and 7 to 8 high, composed of soft pine timbers disposed crosswise. There is ever, despite the daily abuse of the daily papers, a hole in the mole, or rather a series of holes, while a system of mighty cracks, crannies, and crevices makes the whole affair a man-trap – but, until lately, anything was 'good enough for the Plate.' The rain-welled surface is slippery as the clay of Fernando Po or the Puy de Dôme, and I have seen a man badly hurt by it, his legs coming from under him as if on ice.

Lastly, your luggage is deposited at the northernmost half of the 'Resguardia,' here represented by two little summer-houses, kiosks, or China tea-rooms, wooden curiosities striped blue and white, queerly attached to the root of the long projection. The kiosk mania has migrated from the banks of the Seine to far Father Plate; at Buenos Aires you see them even in the main square. They sell newspapers and cheap books, Erotic lyrics, and half-naughty photos.; none ever knew a body who had ever entered into one of them. The Custom-house officers are very civil, and slow in proportion; 'nada mas que ropa' will generally do the douanier. They open, however, carefully every box and bag, although they probably consider rummaging not the work of a 'cavalier.' For this 'pitch and toss treatment' you pay your part of boat $50, landing-cart $20, and say four changadores, $90 = $140 (paper) = 1l. 3s., and you at once discover that the sovereign here is the crown in Europe.

The site of Buenos Aires is commercially bad; the 'old men' could hardly have looked forward to the present state of trade. Even for them, either San Fernando to the north or Ensenada to the south-east would have been better. Strangers explain the peculiar choice by the frequency and daring of those days' buccaneers, when shallows, as we shall see up-stream, formed defences. Probably the roads were a long while ago deeper, and have silted up during the course of ages. Yet Dobrizhoffer in 1784 found the port of Buenos Aires shoal water. The internal action of the earth has, however, certainly caused a gradual upheaval of this, the shelf-edge of the Pampas, as well as of the great Prairies themselves. On the Paraná River we shall everywhere see successive marks of former water-levels many yards higher than the highest modern floods. Others have made dust, the incremental material swept up like the silt of the Nile by the storm-wind from the arid sub-Andine wastes to the south-west.

Actual Buenos Aires will soon see a better future when its water-front shall be built up like Californian San Francisco or the levees of New Orleans. Somebody will find her brick, and will, Augustus-like, leave her marble. Evidently, present amelioration is loudly called for. The barques and brigs, brigantines and polaccos, schooners and luggers in port now generally average upwards of 200, and soon they will be 500. The injury to merchandize is enormous; therefore every engineer proposes his nostrum, and naturally enough the authorities, stunned by so much counsel, are deaf to the voice of specific. Similarly the owner of the Great Dragon Tree at Teneriffe — you remember —

over-advised by the host of travellers, allowed it one fine day to fall. The foreigner accuses the native of being a dog in the manger, which perhaps the native is; whilst assuredly the foreigner is mostly anxious about the bone purely for the bone's sake.

The difficulties in the way of constructing a port are certainly enormous. The characteristic feature of the south-eastern or Buenos Airèan shore is deep water in lines and patches – the Outer and Inner Roads, the Pozo, the Catalinas, and others. These are broken and divided by long narrow banks and shallows, incipient islands, whose length is of course disposed down stream. From the mouth of the Corpus Christi, also called the Lujan River – the nearest stream independent of the Paraná delta – a fringing shelf of mud and soft stone, the 'Residencia bank,' so called from an old Hospital, subtends the land. The 'tosca,' in places twenty feet thick and thinning off to three, is a whitish-yellow skin, an upright and raised crust standing out from the mud, like tables of lava. In places it is hard, in others it is so soft that the boring-iron slips through it. Where the bank, cut away by currents, narrows to a mere strip, are the 'Balizas' or inner roads, safe for ships drawing less than eleven feet. Northwards is the Catalinas patch, so called being opposite the old nunnery of St. Catherine in the Calle Templo, *alias* Tacuari, still blessed by a Chapel of Ease. Distant about 2000 yards from the Balizas is the Banco de la Ciudad, a sudden broadening which begins below the northern part of the settlement; this 'City Bank' is very shallow, and beyond it is the 'Canal' or Outer Roads. The whole place is paved with wrecks, and the anchors and ironwork would repay dredging, if the main-d'œuvre were at all reasonable.

Some would clean remove the port to Ensenada, or even to Bahia Blanca; others propose a breakwater eight miles long, one broad, raised on arches above the highest flood, with a 'Tosca' foundation supporting concrete in galvanized iron coffers; upon this they would build piers, steam-cranes, a Custom-house, docks, marine markets, and so forth. Others would form an enclosed harbour – the favourite idea, because it would cause money to be spent. Others advise a semicircular pier from Gasworks Point, convex to the present Mole, with slip and graving dock, and room for two or three streets. This plan is tempting from its proximity to deep water. Others, again, would extend the actual piers; whilst others would build the 'Catalinas

(tidal) Docks,' and warehouses at the point called Bajo de Catalinas.

The most sensible project for improving the channel is that
proposed by my good friend John Coghlan, C.E. His plan shows
a great leg-of-mutton-shaped patch of reclaimed ground,
beginning at the gasworks and ending at the mouth of the
Riachuelo. At an expense of 787,860*l.* − not one-sixth of what is
thrown into many European harbours − he would convert the
City Bank into an island, thus forming a deep channel and
securing anchorage near the shore. He would, moreover, trace a
suitable land-line by throwing out to double the length of the
Moles (880 yards) embankments, with quays and wharfs,
reclaiming ground to the extent of 230 cuadras cuadradas (the
square of 150 varas, each of 34 inches = 22,500 varas). This
emblayement would give room for docks larger than any save
those of Liverpool, for a Grand Central Station where all the rail-
ways would meet, for Custom-house buildings, platforms, and
other necessaries. Moreover, it could spare 120 cuadras for a
promenade, here so much wanted, and to be sold as building
ground at prices which would to a great extent pay off the cost of
the proposed works. But he is persuaded that such changes
should be made in a tentative way. The causes that formed the
delta-islands of the Paraná are still active, and in the natural
order of events banks must be growing up between the mouth of
the Uruguay and the Paraná de las Palmas. Finally, no company
would do justice to such works; they can hardly be entrusted to a
Government which rarely outlasts three years and ends in a
smash − in fact, my friend comes to the wise conclusion that the
scheme is too vast for the young country in its present backward
state.

Meanwhile, in April, 1868, the Government of President
Sarmiento signed a contract with the Impresarios, Messrs.
Madero and Proudfoot, to carry out the plans of Messrs. Miller
and Bell, C.E. The sum is fixed at $7,000,000, which appears
large, but which will not be sufficient. The work is mainly a huge
tidal dock, with a narrow entrance, which will make it a mere silt-
trap, It is, moreover, to be finished in five years, an imprudent
and hasty period. The scour from the north-west and south-east
would be checked by such an obstacle; the diminished flow
would render dredging useless; the fringing bank of the river
would creep towards the eastward, diverting deep water further

from the shore; and in this case, as in many others, unless engineering science can bring the rivers of the future close to existing harbours, Bahia Blanca will become the port of the Buenos Aires that is to be.

As we land we remark a great change from the City of the Past to that of the Present. Instead of the sturdy, rock-like historic fort, 'Santa Trinidad de Buenos Ayres,' which still appears in Sir Woodbine Parish's second edition, there is a new Custom-house of two stories, whitewashed, semicircular, and arched like casemates. Behind it, separated by a kind of stone-revetted moat, is a square, yellow two-storied box − not 'very handsome and commodious' − with a broad verandah, denoting the Government House. Wilcocke (1807) shows in his plan 'the Fort' and the Parade or Paseo. Parish also sketches the increase of growth in his day, and now it is − for South America − enormous, and ever-progressing. The population is generally set down at 200,000. Mr. Coghlan, however, easily reduced it to about half that total, and even to less. He adopted a simple process which may be found useful in lands where the census can hardly be reliable. After counting the cuadras, say 500, he ascertained the area − three and a half square miles − and compared it, by way of maximum, with that of the most crowded part of London − about 30,000 per square mile − from which of course, subtraction must be made. He was, however, astonished at the general expenditure, at the consumption of the inhabitants, and at the number of rooms suiting a city with treble the population which he allows to it.

We step upon the Paseo de Julio, a mixture of Marine Parade and Wapping, badly paved and poorly lighted; this is the city front, now backed by a couple of handsome houses, but mostly by low inns, foundries, cafés, and estaminets, shops, stores, and sailors' haunts, where those amiable beings love to growl, grumble, and knag one another, as only the uneducated classes of England can do; to drink, curse, and fight, occasionally sallying out with foot or fist − foreign Jack prefers the knife − upon the sober, whose sobriety outrages their sensitive feelings. At one time here was an Alameda, which Dictator Rosas proposed prolonging as far as his country palace Palermo; the breakwater and railing, however, were swept away by a gale in 1861, and unfortunately there is now no Rosas to rebuild them.

Sunday is here a crowded day, and the length of your purse determines which of three ways you choose for passing it. Lackcoin discontentedly lounges about the Paseo and the Muelle. Little-money rides the tailor's ride on a hack horse to Palermo or Belgrano. Dives sleeps the Saturday night at his Quinta out of town, or runs down by the Northern Railway to S. Fernando, S. Isidro (summer quarters), or the Tigre. He then idles away the day, visits, perhaps boats, and returns home plenus Bacchi.

We enter by the Calle Cangallo, here pronounced Cajje Cangajjo, 'oppidum seu pagus de Rio de la Plata' – still the title of the Archbishopric. A steep short pitch leads to the longitudinal Calle 25 de Maio, the summit of the true 'barranca,' glacis, or old river bank, which is everywhere traceable between the Tigre and the Riachuelo. It has a similar talus, but of greater slope inland, which is rather puzzling to drainage, and though formerly set down at 70 feet, nowhere does its height exceed 64.2 feet above the water; some reckon 50 feet, but the mean of the barometer is 29.66.

The streets are long, narrow, and ill ventilated; and the tramway of modern progress is as yet unknown to them. The pavement, even after Monte Vídeo, strikes us as truly detestable. It is like a fiumara-bed, bestrewn with accidentally disposed boulders, gapped with dreadful chasms and manholes, bounded on both sides by the trottoirs, narrow ledges of flattish stone, like natural rock 'benches,' flood-levelled on each side of the torrent. In many parts the side walks are raised three and even five feet above the modern street plane, and flush with the doors, which are high up as that of the Kaabah. These trottoirs covered, like the pavement after rain, with a viscid mud, sliding as a ship's deck, dangerous as a freshly waxed parquet for the noble savage, often end at the corners with three or four rude steps, rounded slabs, greasy and slippery by the tread, as though spread with orange peel, and ascended and descended with the aid of an open-mouthed carronade, or a filthy post blacked by the hand of toil. There is a legend of a naval captain who cracked his pate by a header down one of these laderas, these corniches, these precipices, and certainly few places can be more perilous than they are for gentlemen in the state decently termed 'convivial.' Like the trottoirs they want handrails.

More than one street – for instance, Calles Paraguay and Defensa – must be crossed by a drawbridge after rains which drown men, and which carry off carts and horses. Before the days of pavements, when the pantanos or muds were filled up with corn or jerked beef, the earth was converted by showers into slush, and swept down into the general reservoir, the river bed – hence the sunken ways. The crossings are nowhere swept: being slightly raised above the general level they soon dry and cut up the line into deep puddles which lie long, or into segments and parallelograms of mire. The thoroughfares are macadamized with the soil of the suburbs, which cakes under the sun, and crumbles before the wind, dirtying the hands like London smoke. Drainage is left to those Brazilian engineers, Messrs. Sun and Wind. The only washing is by rain rushing down the cross streets. There is absolutely no sewerage; a pit in the patio is dug by way of cesspool, and is filled up with soil, a fair anticipation of the deodorizing earth closet. The 'basura' or sweepings are placed at an early hour in boxes by the doorways to be carried off by the breeze, or to be kicked over by horses driven to water: these offals are used to fill up holes in the road outside the city, and yet the citizens expect 'good airs.' Beyond the town, the unpaved lines thus become quagmires, impasses, and quaking bogs where horses and black cattle are hopelessly fixed.

Street walking becomes at Buenos Aires a study, an art. People prepare for it their toe-nails – excuse the subject – I have a duty to perform – like most duties it is 'unpleasant.' The centre of the nail is scraped thin, so as to weaken the keystone of the arch: the middle edge is cut into a demilune concave, and the corners, generally removed by the vulgar mind, are encouraged to grow square, so as not to penetrate the flesh. Inattention to this general practice may lame you for a month (experto crede!) and all your friends will certainly wag the head, and vote you a 'martyr to the gout.' Another inconvenience is the custom of placing the petticoat on the wall side: the bumptious soutane also claims the honour, so you must perpetually be hopping on and off the lofty trottoir. To escape wind and rain you avoid the side whither the paperslips are whirled: the thoroughfares of the city, roughly speaking, face the cardinal points, whilst the wet and high winds strike them diagonally, and the houses act as screens. Had the lines been fronted more obliquely, one-half of each thoroughfare would not have been in the sun, and the other half in the shade: moreover all the houses facing southwards would not have been mildewed. The prevailing directions are the north-easter especially – like the norther, fine and cool – the wet souther and south-easter and the gusty south-south-wester and south-wester.

Thus one side of the street is dry in wet and is windless in windy weather, and as the height of the houses increases, those at the corners should be rounded off to insure ventilation.

The street scandal is inexcusable in so wealthy a place. The municipality can afford $600,000 (f.) = 120,000*l.* of income, but the city fathers, those posts that point the way to progress without ever progressing, though eternally 'pitched into' give no sign, and fresh blood is still wanted. Buenos Aires sadly requires the Baron de Campy, who is supposed to have paved the Imperial capital further north. The new Custom House, the Moles, the Western Railway, the Gas Works, the Colon Theatre, and the Water Works, with other undertakings carried out by provincial resources, show how much may be done if money be not frittered away. A little macadam, compacted by water and a steam roller, would cheaply remedy the worst evils, and a better material would be the admirable Pedregulho or gravel from Salto of the Uruguay, River of the Missions. Broken brick would be better than nothing in streets which are not much visited by wheeled vehicles, and these could at present be limited. Sufficient care is not taken in naming the thoroughfares: France is the great mistress of that art. As at Rio de Janeiro, the black forefinger points the direction of transit in carriage or cart: this plan, so necessary in narrow streets, might be adopted even in London.

Buenos Aires is evidently a city; it has a civic hurry and excitement; there is a polished manner of citizen in it; the first glance tells us that it is not, like Monte Vídeo, a town. The houses, especially externally, are palazzi, built by Italians, who partly follow the Spanish taste; they appear remarkably fine and solid after the poorer architecture of the Brazil. It is wonderful, at least for these regions, how readily and speedily the tenements are run up, especially the outer shell. The streets give vistas of great length: practically, however, the City is bounded to the stranger north by the Calle del Parque, south by the Calle Belgrano, east by the river and west by Florida, the Regent Street. Thus here again we epitomize long thoroughfares of intense weariness. This is in fact our club-land – our Pall Mall, and within these narrow limits are contained the consulate, the clubs, the cathedral, the museum, the libraries, the chief hotels, the favourite streets, and the offices of the principal periodicals.

LETTER XIII
From Corrientes to Humaitá

Humaitá, August 22, 1868

My dear Z——— ,

We now enter upon the proper scenes of the Paraguayan war. I will tantalise your impatience for a while by recounting our life on board the good ship *Yi*.

The *Yi*, I have told you, is a bran new 'floating hotel,' with her plated silver dazzling, her napkins stiff-starched, and her gilt mouldings upon the untarnished white panels clean as a new sovereign. A common English passenger steamer would have been far plainer, but proportionally much more comfortable. The splendid saloon all along the second deck will presently wax dingy, and there is no possible walking in the open air. The tables draw out and collapse cleverly, but with trouble. The three stewards are expected to do the work of one man; they are exceedingly civil, and they do nothing. Of course, this is the fault of the comisario, or purser, a small Spanish bantam, or rather 'hen-harrier,' who spends all his time in trifling with the feminine heart. The captain, Don Pedro Lorenzo Flores – do not forget the Don, and if you want anything say Señor Don – was an ex-item of that infinitesimal body, the national navy of the Banda Oriental. He brought out *Yi* for its Company from the United States, and he avenges himself upon Northern and Anglo-American coarseness by calling all Yankees 'rascals.' His chief duty is to bale out the soup, to pass cigars, and to send round sherry after dinner. This must be done to everybody at table, or the excluded will take offence and sulk like small boys.

Pleasantly enough passes the se'nnight – perhaps I should call it a fortnight. Every twenty-four hours contains two distinct days and two several nights. First day begins at dawn with coffee and biscuits, by way of breakfast, and a bath, patronized chiefly by the 'yaller' Brazilian passengers. A mighty rush follows the dinner-bell, which sounds with peculiar unpunctuality, between 9 and 10 A.M. (mind). Upon the table are scattered *hors d'œuvres*, olives, ham and sausage, together with gratis wines, sour French 'piquette' called claret, and the rough, ready Catalonian Carlò, here corrupted to Carlon. Port, and similar superior articles, are ridiculously dear; for instance, $8 (32*s.*) per bottle, and of course for a bad bottle. Like the Chilian, the Argentine often calls not for the best, but for the most expensive drink, and makes the call last out the week. We have no soup, but, *en revanche*, we have that eternal puchero, boulli, ragmeat, which, combined with vegetables – potatoes, cabbages, and courges (zavallos) – composes the antiquated olla podrida. It is the national dish, the feijoada of the Brazils, here held to be heavy and indigestible. The rest is hotel fare. The coffee must be made 'coffee royal' if you would drink it; and the tea is the pot-house ('pulperia') style, facetiously termed by foreigners 'cowslip' and 'orange Pekoe:' those who want the real Chinese must bring it for themselves.

Tobacco and a small bout of gambling bring in the first night, which lasts from noon to 3 P.M. During this period all the world of men dressed in faded black is dead and gone. Here the siesta is the universal custom, to the severe injury of picnics. At the mystic hour you see every eye waxing smaller and smaller, till closed by a doze with a suspicion of nasal music. At home, people regularly 'turn in;' and if you have a visit to pay or a favour to ask, do not interrupt the day-night. Strangers soon fall into the habit, and it is evidently required by those climates in which men sit up late and rise early. I have found it an excellent plan in hot countries when hard mental labour was required, and, as every policeman knows, it is a mere matter of habit. In the Brazil the siesta is not the rule, but the Brazilians rarely begin the day at Bengal hours. On this parallel, the further we go westward, and the more back-ward becomes the land, the longer will last the siesta; the cause being simply that the population, having nothing to do, very wisely allows its arteries to contract.

The second day opens with a breakfast of maté. It is drunk *en cachette*; if not, it must be handed all round. Lunch is absolutely unknown; the unsophisticated English stomach therefore clamours for an insult to breakfast and an injury to dinner, in the shape of sherry and biscuits. The second full feed is at 4 P.M., and exactly resembles the first: it lasts an hour and a half. Candles and cigars are then lighted, and preparations made for the *soirée* according to tastes. Some watch the night upon the poop; others converse or mope alone; others play and sing, or listen to music. By far the favourite amusement, however, is hearty, thorough, whole-souled gambling, which makes the fore saloon a standing hell. One passenger is said to have lost during the excursion $8000. The Brazilians are the hottest players, pushing on far into the small hours. Politely admitting the fact that we, thereabouts lodged, may be asleep, or may wish to sleep, they open conversation in a half whisper. This loudens under excitement to an average tone, and the latter speedily gamuts up to a shout and a howl, stintless and remorseless. My only resource was letting a cold draught through the skylight at their feet and ankles, and thus only the roaring, bawling gamblers, who sat lengthening out the night, were cleared away.

LETTER XV
Humaitá

Humaitá, August 24th, 1868

MY DEAR Z——— ,

After a stare of blank amazement, my first question was – where is Humaitá? Where are the 'regular polygons of the Humaitá citadel?' Where is 'the great stronghold which was looked upon as the keystone of Paraguay?' I had seen it compared with Silistria and Kars, where even Turks fought; with Sebastopol in her strength, not in the weakness attributed to her by General Todleben and Mr. Kinglake; with the Quadrilateral which awed Italy; with Luxembourg, dear to France; with Richmond, that so long held the Northerners at bay; and with the armour-plated batteries of Vicksburg and the shielded defences of Gibraltar. Can these poor barbettes, this entrenched camp sans citadel – which the Brazilian papers had reported to have been blown up – be the same that resisted 40,000 men, not to speak of ironclads and gunboats, and that endured a siege of two years and a half? I came to the conclusion that Humaitá was a monstrous 'hum,' and that, with the rest of the public, I had been led into believing the weakest point of the Paraguayan campaign to be the strongest.

As so much that is erroneous has been written about Humaitá, you will not object to a somewhat prolix true description.

The site of the 'Blackstone' batteries is the normal re-entering angle of the eastern bank, but the sweep is more than usually concave, to the benefit of gunnery and the detriment of shipping. Nothing more dangerous than this great bend, where vessels were almost sure to get confused under fire, as happened at Port Hudson to the fleet commanded by Admiral D.G. Farragut. The level bank, twenty to thirty feet above the river, and dipping in places, is bounded by swamps up-stream and down-stream. Earthworks, consisting of trenches, curtains, and redans, disposed at intervals where wanted, and suggesting the lines of Torres Vedras, rest both their extremities upon the river, whose shape here is that of the letter U, and extend in gibbous shape inland to the south. The outline measures nearly eight miles and a half, and it encloses meadow land to the extent of 8,000,000 square yards – a glorious battle-field. This exaggerated enceinte, which required a garrison of at least 10,000 men, was laid out by a certain Hungarian Colonel of Engineers, Wisner de Morgenstern, whom we shall see at Asuncion. He was not so skilful as Mr. Boyle with the billiard-room of Arrah.

Humaitá, in 1854, was a mere Guardia in the Department de los Desmochados (hornless cattle), a river plain, wooded over like the heights of Hampstead and Highgate in the olden time. When Asuncion was threatened in 1855 by the Brazilian fleet, and troubles were expected from the United States, the elder Lopez felled the virgin forest, leaving only a few scattered trees, grubbed up the roots, and laid out the first batteries, to whose completion some two years were devoted. The place does not appear in Mr. Charles Mansfield's map of 1852–53. In 1863, Mr. M. Mulhall describes 'a succession of formidable batteries which frowned on us as we passed under their range; they are placed on a slight eminence, and seem guns of large calibre. First, four batteries *à la barbette*, covered with straw shed, which can be removed at a moment's notice; then a long casemate (the Londres), mounting sixteen guns, with bomb-proof roof; and finally, two more *barbette* batteries, making up a total of seventy-eight batteries. As the canal runs close to the bank, any vessel, unless iron-plated, attempting to force a passage must be sunk by the raking and concentrated fire of this fortification, which is the key to Paraguay and the upper rivers.' (p. 84). At the beginning of the war it had only ninety guns in seven batteries. An exaggerated importance was always attached to it by the Paraguayan Government; it became a great mystery, and strangers were not allowed to visit a settlement which was considered purely military. Mr. William Thompson, of Buenos Aires, narrowly escaped some trouble by strolling about to admire the pretty park-like scenery and the soft beauty of Humaitá, a site then so amene and tranquil.

We will now land and inspect the river-side works, beginning up stream or at the easterly end.

We passed through the merchant fleet, then numbering some 270 hulls, supplying the 3000 booth-tents on shore; this number includes the pontoons of the proveduria or commissariat. There is a line of shop-boats, whose masts support green waterproof awnings; each carries a woman and an anchor, and they sell all small wants and notions – threads, mirrors, and so forth. Two chatas, or barge gun-boats, lie alongside the land, one carries a 10-inch mortar, the other an 8-inch iron gun. It was a hard scramble up the stiff bank, which ignored steps or even a ramp.

At the eastern end we found the corral of commissariat cattle occupying the place where stood the coalsheds and the iron-foundry. Here had been cast the gun 'Cristiano,' lately sent as a trophy to the Brazil, weighing twelve tons, and made of bell-metal taken from the churches; it fired a round shot of 150 lbs. One trunnion was inscribed 'Arsenal Asuncion' (where it was rifled), 1867; on the other appeared the patriotic legend 'La Religion à el Estado' – Church giving to State, somewhat a reversal of the usual rule. Next to the Fundicion de Nierro, a ragged orange-grove showed where the Paraguayan barracks had been; those of the infantry lay further to the south-west. The sheds called barracks which lodged the escort of the Marshal-President were a little north of the church of San Carlos (Borromeo), a namesake of the elder Lopez: on January 1, 1861, it had been consecrated, amidst general rejoicings, by the Bishop. Originally it resembled the Cathedral of Asuncion, as represented by Captain Page (p. 224); the colours are blue and white, whilst the cornices and pilasters evidence some taste. We read in 1863 – 'The church is a splendid edifice with three towers, the middle one being 120 or 150 feet high; the interior is neat, and a colonnade runs round the exterior; there are four large bells, hung from a wooden scaffolding, one bearing the inscription, Sancte Carole, ora pro nobis.' It is now a mere heap of picturesque ruins, with hardwood timber barely supported by cracked walls of brick; the latter is unusually well baked, and the proportions are those of the old Romans – twelve or fourteen inches long, eight broad, and two thick. One belfry, with the roof and façade, has been reduced to heaps; the south-eastern tower still rises above the ruins, but in a sadly shaking condition. The Brazilians banged at the fane persistently as an Anglo-Indian gunner at a flagstaff; and the Paraguayans at times amused themselves with repairing it. The church of S. Carlos lies in Lat. S. 27° 2′, Long. W. (G.), 61° 30′, and here the variation is 7° 50′ E.

Near it is the Presidential 'palace,' a ground-floor shed of brick, with tiled roof, three doors, four windows, and a tall white-washed entrance in token of dignity, leading to a pretty quinta, above whose brick walls peep oranges and a stunted 'curii' (Araucaria Brasiliensis). The 'three enormous tigers,' which each ate a calf for breakfast, are gone; the front is bespattered and pierced with shot, and I see no signs of the bomb-proof 'tanière' in which, they say, the Marshal-President used to lurk. The quarters occupied by Madame Lynch are far to the rear, in the 'women's encampment.' The main sala, whence he drove away with kicks and cuffs the officers who announced to him the destruction of his hopes by the fall of Uruguayana, was shown to us: here the Argentines found unpacked boxes containing furniture from Paris. This was their only civilized 'loot;' the rest was represented by rusty guns, by lean mules, by 100 cases of bottles containing palm oil, and by some fifty tercios or sacks of maté, each holding eight arrobas, and here worth $4.

Westward of the 'palace' lie the quarters of the staff, the arsenal, the Almoxarifado (Custom-house, &c.), and the soap manufacture. These are the 'magnificent barracks' for 12,000 men of which we read in the newspapers, long, low, ground-floor ranchos, with mud walls, and roofed with a mixture of thatch, tile, and corrugated iron. Never even loopholed, they had been much knocked about and torn by shot. The arsenal has now been turned into commissariat and ammunition stores. It is fronted by a guérite or raised sentry-box, and by a huge flagstaff bearing the Brazilian flag.

The batteries are eight in number, and again we will begin with them up-stream. After a scatter of detached guns, some in the open, others slightly parapeted, we find the Bateria Cadenas, or chain-battery of thirteen guns, backed by the Artillery Barracks. The chain, which consisted of seven twisted together, passed diagonally through a kind of brick tunnel. On this side it was made fast to a windlass supported by a house about 100 yards from the bank. Nearer the battery stood a still larger capstan: the latter, however, wanted force to haul taut the chain.

Crossing by one of three dwarf bridges the little nullah Arroyo Humaitá somewhat below the Presidential 'palace,' we come upon the Bateria Londres, that Prince of Humbugs. M. Elisée

Reclus, whose papers in the *Deux Mondes* (October 15, 1866, and August 15, 1868) are somewhat imaginative, makes the London battery deliver fire, even as he carries in his pen the railroad to Villa Rica. It was built for the elder Lopez by a European engineer. The walls were twenty-seven feet thick, of brick (not stone and lime). It was supposed to be rendered bomb-proof by layers of earth heaped upon brick arches, and there were embrasures for sixteen (not twenty-five) guns. Of these ports eight were walled up and converted into workshops, because the artillerymen were in hourly dread of their caving in and crumbling down.

The third battery is the Tacuary of three guns. Then comes the Coimbra mounting eight *bouches à feu*, and directed by the Commandante Hermosa. The three next are the Octava or Madame Lynch, with three guns *en barbette*; the Pesada, five guns, and the Itapirú, seven guns – all partly revetted with brick. Being the westernmost and the least exposed to fire they have suffered but little. Lastly, at the Punta de las Piedars stands the Humaitá redoubt, armed with a single eight-inch gun.

Beyond this point begins the entrenched line running south-south-west along the Laguna Concha, *alias* Ambericaia, and then sweeping round to the east with a gap where the water rendered an attack impossible. The profile is good simply because defended by impenetrable bush. The guns stand in pairs, with a Paiol or magazine to every two, and they had been provided with 200 round of grape, shell, and case. The wet ditch is still black with English gunpowder; some fine, mostly coarse.

The batteries were being rapidly dismantled; the cadenas and its two neighbours had been to a certain extent spared. The guns were all *en barbette*, an obsolete system, showing the usual wilful recklessness of human life. Redoubts and redans, glacis and covered ways, caponnières and traverses, gorge works and épaulements, citadel and entrenchment, were equally unknown, whilst embrasures were rare, although sods for the cheeks might have been cut within a few yards. Where the ramosia or abatis was used, the branches were thrown loosely upon the ground, and no one dreamed of wooden pickets. Though the stockade was employed, the palisade at the bottom of the cunette or ditch was ignored. Thus the works were utterly unfit to resist the developed powers of rifled artillery, the concentrated discharge from shipping, and even the accurate and searching fire of the Spencer carbine. The Londres work, besides being in a state of decay, was an exposed mass of masonry which ought to have shared the fate of the forts from Sumpter to Pulaski, and when granite fails bricks cannot hope to succeed. Had the guns been mounted in Monitor towers, or even protected by sand-bags, the ironclads would have suffered much more than they did in running past them.

Lieutenant Day (1858) gave to the eight batteries on his chart 45 guns; to the casemate (Londres) 15; and to the east battery 50; making a total of 110. In 1868 the river and batteries had 58 cannons, 11 magazines, and 17 brick tanks (depositos de agua). The whole lines of Humaitá mounted 36 brass and 144 iron guns: these 180 were increased to 195 by including the one eight-inch gun and the fourteen 32-pounders found in the Gran Chaco. The serviceable weapons did not however exceed sixty. Many of them had been thrown into deep water, and will be recovered when the level shall fall. Five lay half buried at the foot of the bank, and then remained in position: of these, three were eight-inch, four were short 32 or 36 pounders, and two were long 32-pounder carronades.

The guns barely deserve the name; some of them were so honeycombed that they must have been used as street posts. They varied generally from 4-pounders to 32-pounders, with intermediate calibres of 6, 9, 12, 18, and 24. Not the worst of them were made at Asuncion and Ybicuy, whose furnaces and air chimneys could melt four tons per diem. Some had been converted, but it was a mere patchwork. A few rifled 12-pounders had been cast at Asuncion. There were sundry quaint old tubes bearing the arms of Spain; two hailed from Seville, the *San Gabriel* (A.D. 1671) and the *San Juan de Dios* (1684). The much talked-of 'breech-loading Armstrong' was an English 95 cwt. gun, carrying a 68-lb. ball, and rifled and fitted at Asuncion with a strengthening ring of wrought-iron. The breeching lay like a large mass of pie-crust behind it: the bursting had probably been designed, as the shot remained jammed inside. The captured guns are now being divided into three several parts, each one of the Allies taking about forty, which may be useful for melting up into trophies and memorials. I was told that the Oriental share was twenty-eight guns, of which seven were brass.

I landed with my Blanco friends, who, charmed by my disappointment, despite the natural joy of once more seeing camp life, chaffed me bitterly about this 'chef d'œuvre of an encampment,' this Sebastopol. They were hardly civil to a courteous Brazilian officer of rank – it proved to be General Argolo – who, riding past with his staff, invited us, though perfect strangers, to drink beer at his quarters. They would not even inspect the lines of the Macácos, as they called their Imperial Allies. Again and again they boasted the prowess of their own party, stating how 500 of them had defended Paysandú against a host.

In front of the Marshal-President's 'palace' we found a dozen Whitworth muzzle-loaders, whose shapely lines and highly-finished sights made them look, by the side of other weapons, like racers among cab-horses. Without engaging in the 'battle of the guns,' I may merely state that a few Armstrongs had been tried by the Brazilians, but were not found to succeed; the Krupp, like the Lahitte, was approved of, and the Woolwich gun was unknown to the Allies. The motley armature of the Paraguayans was a curious spectacle. By the side of some Blakely's self-rifling shells and balls, hand-grenades, which were found useful in the triumphant Abyssinian campaign, and the Hall's rotating rockets, without the sticks which merely steer them into the eye of the wind, lay huge Guarani wads, circles of twisted palm, like those which Egyptian peasant-women place between the head and the water-pot; case-shot in leather buckets so quaintly made that it could hardly be efficient at the usual 300 to 400 yards; canister composed of screws and bar-iron chopped up, and grape of old locks and bits of broken muskets, rudely bound in hide with llianas or bush ropes. To be killed by such barbaric appliances would add another sting to that of death. Here were large piles of live shells, some of them lightly loaded with ten to eleven ounces of powder, for the purpose of firing tents and levelling defences. The conquerors had not taken the trouble to wet them, and an old gentleman of the party distinguished himself by scraping the spilt gunpowder with his boot-toes. I ran from him as I never ran before. During the last three days several explosions took place; these extemporised soldiers were careless as Zanzibar blacks.

During the day I saw a review of a Brazilian cavalry corps numbering six full troops; and shortly afterwards all the Argentine army, or rather contingent, marched past. The first at once took my eye; they were mostly Brazilians, Rio Grandenses, not liberated negroes. These Provincials, riders from their babyhood, are reputed as the best cavaliers throughout the Empire, where the 'man on horseback' is universal. Some were lancers; their heavy wooden weapons, not nearly so handy as the bamboo of

Hindostan, were decorated with white stars on red pennons; they carried regulation sabres and coarse horse-pistols, and the European trappings made them look much more soldier-like than the infantry. The lance, so worthless in the hands of raw levies, may be used to great effect by practised troopers: the Poles at Albuera proved it upon Colborne's brigade of British infantry. The dragoons had swords, Spencer (8-round) carbines, and in some cases pistols. As Confederate General Lee, however, truly remarked, 'The sabre is timid before a good revolver,' and the carbine is not to be recommended on horseback. General Beatson foresaw, when commanding the much-abused Bashi Buzéuks in the Crimean campaign, that the revolver is the real arm for cavalry, and it should be accompanied by the yataghan, to be used when ranks lock. In due course of time it will be supplanted by the single or double-barrelled breechloader. I have lately tried the Albini or Belgian rifle, cut short, and provided with a short and heavy saw-handle, and I have had every reason to be pleased with it.

The cattle was in excellent condition; you could play cards or count money, as the Spaniards say, upon their backs. The animals, however, like the men, were light; they would be efficient opposed to Cossacks, but used against heavy cavalry they would dash up, recoil and shatter, as a wave is shivered by a rock.

As a rule the Brazilian cavalry has not seen much service in this war of earthworks. Their principal use has been in raids, reconnaissances, and attacks of outposts. With few exceptions they have behaved remarkably well, and have been ably and gallantly handled by their officers, who acted upon the well-known axiom, that cavalry should never surrender. They are now somewhat in the position of the Crimean cavalry after the Charge of Balaklava. The Argentines, as a rule, were poorly mounted, and being mostly foreigners, were inferior riders. The Paraguayans at the beginning of the war had good cattle, but they were soon annihilated; horses here are rare, and the country supplies for the most part only a diminutive Yaboo. They charged furiously, not with the fine old Spanish war-cry 'Santiago y a Elles!' but with the Zagharit of Egypt and the Kil of Persia, a kind of trille here directly derived from the Red Indians. They exposed themselves with upraised blades, like Mamelukes, careless of what they took, and determined only to give. Their lances are stout weapons of hard heavy wood, eight feet long, with iron heels measuring two and a half spans, and the heads are those of Anglo-Indian boar-spears, not exceeding two inches, and ending in bars that defend it against the sabre.

The Argentine army was variously reported – by its friends as an able and efficient arm; by its enemies as a montonera, or horde of thieves and brigands, who have never had a siege gun in position. They began with 15,000 men, which speedily fell to 9000, of whom some 6000 were Argentines, and as there is no recruiting in election times, they now probably do not exceed 5000. This is a small proportion to be supplied out of nearly 2,000,000 souls – in 1867 it was 1,500,000 – whom the Brazil expected to produce the personnel whilst she contributed the matériel. Yet all are agreed that in case of a war with the Empire, the Confederation could turn out 50,000 men at arms. The Argentine losses in killed, wounded, and missing, are up to this time 2227 – their own calculation.

After hearing much 'bunkum' at Buenos Aires, and reading many diatribes against the 'Marshal of the Army' Caxias, who preserved upon this subject a discreet silence, I was disappointed by the appearance of the force. The Argentine 'Contingent' gave the impression of being fine men, large and strong; the rank and file, however, showed a jumble of nationalities: the tall, raw-boned, yellow-haired German, the Italian Cozinhero, and the Frenchman, who under arms always affects the Zouave, marched side by side with the ignoble negro. Sizing and classing were equally unknown; uniforms were of every description, including even the poncho and chiripá, and the style of progress much resembled that of a flock of sheep. The corps of the fourteen Provinces, or rather their remnants, were separated by drums and bands foully murdering 'Tu che à Dio.' The best were evidently the Santa Fécinos, known by their double tricolor flag; this province has fighting colonies of Frenchmen, Swiss, and Germans, who have been accustomed to hold 'Indians' in check. The officers, some mounted, others on foot, were mostly Argentines, and they rivalled their men in variety of dress: of nether garments, for instance, there were underdrawers, pink trousers, dark overalls, knickerbockers and gaiters, riding boots, and sandals. *Par parenthèse*, the Argentines have only to adopt their national colours, silver and light blue, for an army uniform, which would be neat and handsome as that worn by the cavalry of the defunct East-Indian Company.

The Argentines move easily: they have little commissariat, and foul hides take the place of the neat Brazilian pal-tents. A change of camp is periodically necessary, the ground soon becoming impure in the extreme. The men carried, besides ammunition, arms, and accoutrements, poles to support their mats and skins, raw beef, chairs, tables, and round shot to make hearths. They were followed by women on horse and foot, the hideous lees of civilization, and by carts whose wheel-spokes were bound with hide, and which bore huge heaps of household 'loot.' Being badly paid, and often not paid at all, the men must plunder to live. As might be expected from a force of the kind, there is no ardour for the cause and *esprit de corps* is utterly unknown. As will be seen, they do not even take the trouble to bury their dead. They are kept in order only by the drumhead court-martial, and by the platoon ready at a minute's notice.

As for the 'Oriental' army, I failed to find it. The force commenced under General Flores with 5600 men, and he handled it so recklessly that 600 were sent home, and 4600 were killed or became unfit to serve. The remnant of 300 to 400 is further reduced by some authorities to forty to fifty, of whom most are officers under a certain General D. Enrique Castro, who is characterized as a 'gaucho ordinario.'

The alliance of the Allies is evidently that of dog and cat. The high authorities have agreed not to differ, but the bond of union is political, not sympathetic. An excessive nationality amongst the Brazilians is kept up by their great numerical superiority; whilst the Argentines, like ourselves in the Crimea, are sore about playing a part so palpably 'second fiddle.' Hence the war is nowhere popular on the Plata, and troubles may be expected to accompany its termination. During my first visit to Humaitá, I found that a long entrenched line, with berm, parapet, and other requisites, had been dug to separate Brazilians from Argentines. The reason of the proceeding assigned to me, and probably to the Home Governments, was that the general commanding was fond of keeping his men at work.

Are you tired of Humaitá? Then, *a rivederci!*

SEVEN

CONSUL IN DAMASCUS

Back in London in 1869, Isabel feverishly manoeuvred behind the scenes at the Foreign Office to get Richard the posting he really wanted: the consulate at Damascus. Had Burton made a success of this, it was not beyond possibility that he could eventually have been appointed ambassador in Constantinople. But Burton lasted just two years in Syria. Though superlatively equipped for the task as consul, Burton incurred the deep enmity of the Turkish governor Mohammed Rashid Pasha. Two different contretemps played into Rashid's hands. One of Burton's consular duties was to recover debts on behalf of Jewish creditors. But Burton hated Jews and refused, as he put it, to act as a debt collector. The Jewish community aroused the wrath of their brethren in London against him. Secondly, Isabel Burton foolishly set herself up as the protector of a sect of Syrian Christians against their Muslim persecutors. Rashid was then able to appeal to Constantinople to have the Burtons removed, on the grounds that they were meddling in the internal affairs of the Turkish empire. Burton was recalled in disgrace in 1871. But he left a vivid memoir of daily life at the consulate and a record of a trip to Palmyra, the ruined city forever associated with its fabled queen Zenobia, who defied the Romans.

After a long leave in England and time vainly spent prospecting for sulphur mines in Iceland, Burton was given the consulship of Trieste. Here he remained from 1872 to the end of his career 'chained to his post ... doomed by perverse fate to an isolation that must be almost as irksome as the rock of St Helena to Napoleon.' He made many journeys during his long leaves, to Arabia and India between 1875 and 1876, to Egypt between 1879 and 1880, to the Gold Coast between 1881 and 1882. Many of these expeditions were little more than gold-prospecting or trea-sure-hunting ventures. The problem was that the Foreign Office refused to give him a pension until he had completed thirty years service, which would not be until 1891.

Illness led him increasingly to travel after 1875: to Tangier, Genoa, Naples, Cannes, Geneva, Vevy, Montreux, Berne, Venice, Neuberg, Brindisi, Malta, Tunis, Algiers, Innsbruck, Ragatz, Maloja, never staying in any one place more than three weeks. Lord Salisbury connived at the frequent absences from post and regarded the sinecure as reward for Burton's past services to the crown; he saw to it that Burton was not annoyed with requests for routine consular work, though he still refused to grant him retirement on full pension. Amazingly, while refusing this relatively trivial request, the British establishment was quite prepared to accord him a knighthood. From 1886 he was Sir Richard Burton. But he died in harness, still at Trieste, in October 1890.

Through Syria to Palmyra
(from *Wanderings in Three Continents* (1901))

Beyrut in my day was connected with Damascus by the only carriageable road in the Holy Land, which was supposed to boast of two others, the Jaffa–Jerusalem and the Alexandretto–Aleppo. These two, however, are utterly unfit for wheels, the reason being that they were laid out by native engineers and administered by the Turks, a nation that has succeeded in nothing but destruction. The distance is forty-seven and a half geographical miles, prolonged to sixty by the old road and to seventy-two by the new one.

We could travel to Damascus by night coach or by day dili-gence, preferring the latter, which enables us to see the land. At 4 A.M. we leave the harbour-town, and we shall reach our destination at 6 P.M. The section between the Mediterranean and Damascus, the sea and the Euphrates Desert, is an epitome of Syria, which has been described to be an epitome of the whole world; a volume might be easily written upon what is seen during that day's journey. After a couple of miles through suburbs, cemeteries, and scattered villas, orchards of mulberry and olive, lanes hedged with prickly pear and dense clumps of young stone-pines, the road begins to ascend the westward, or maritime, slope of the Lebanon. It works gradually towards the left bank of the great gorge called Wady Hammánah, in one of whose hamlets Lamartine lived and wrote. After some twelve miles from the Beyrut Plain, we reach the watershed of the Jurd, or Highlands of the Lebanon. Here we are about 5,500 feet above sea-level, and feel immensely relieved, in fine weather at least, from the damp heat of the malarious seaboard, which robs the stranger of appetite and rest. The view, too, is charming: a glimpse of sparkling sea, a well-wooded sandstone region, and a long perspective of blue and purple chain and peak, cut and torn by valley, gorge, and ravine, scarring both flanks of the prism. Looking eastward, we sight for the first time that peculiar basaltic bed which gives rise to the Jordan, the Orontes, and the Litani (a river of Tyre). It appears to be a volcanic depression sunk in the once single range of secondary limestone, and splitting it into two parallel chains, the Libanus and the Anti-Libanus. Viewed from above it is a Spanish viga, a plain of wondrous wealth and fertility, whilst the surface appears smooth as a lake. It is, however, in places dangerously swampy, and though raised some 2,500 to 3,000 feet above sea-level, it is an unwholesome and aguish site, alternately very hot and very cold, curiously damp and distressingly dry. And the same may be said of Damascus, which has to the east the scorching desert, and to the west mountains, mostly snowy: it is no wonder that the old author called it the 'windy.' But the climate of Damascus is complicated by perhaps the worst and hardest water in Syria, by the exceeding uncleanliness of the place, and by the habits of the population. To say that man can exist there at all speaks volumes in his favour.

Rapidly we run down the eastern, or landward, counterslope of the Lebanon, remembering the anti-Jacobin couplet:

And down thy slopes romantic Ashdown glides
The Derby dilly carrying six insides.

Before its lowest folds we find the fifth station, Shtóra; here, as it is now 10 A.M., we breakfast. We at once realise what will be the bill of fare in the interior. Bread? perhaps. Potatoes? possibly. Beef or veal? impossible. Pig? ridiculous. Little, in fact, but lean kid and lamb, mutton, and fowls whose breastbones pierce their skins. Wine? yes – dear and bad. Beer or porter, seltzer or soda? decidedly no. In the winter game is to be had, woodcock and wild duck, hares and gazelles; but the diet is held to be heating and bilious. Vegetables, however, are plentiful, and, during the season, fruit is abundant, with the usual drawback in half-civilised lands: wall fruit is all but unknown, and, with the exception of the excellent grapes and the unwholesome apricots, each kind lasts only a few days.

After breakfast we spin by a straight road – such as old Normandy knew and modern Canada still knows – the breadth of the valley. It is laid out in little fields, copiously irrigated. The little villages which stud the plain are, like those of Egypt, not of Syria, built on mounds, and black with clay plastered over the wickerwork. Every mile or so has some classical ruin; on our right a Báal temple; to our left Chalcis ad Belum; whilst six hours of slow riding northwards, or up the valley, place you at immortal Báalbak, which the Greeks still call Heliopolis.

A rising plane and a bend to the right land us at the first of the Anti-Libanus. Instead of ascending and descending this range, as we did with the Lebanon prism, we thread a ravine called by the Druzes the Valley of Silk, from their favourite article of plunder. An easy up-slope leads to Sahlat Judaydah, the dwarf plateau about 3,600 feet high, where the watershed changes from west to east; farther on to the wild gorge Wady el Karn ('of the Thorn'), so called from its rich ribbings and the wreathing and winding of the bed. We find a stiff climb or a long zigzag at the Akabat el Tin (the Steep of Lime).

The descent of the steep ends with the Daurat el Billau (Zigzag of the Camel Thorn), and hence we fall into the Sahrat el Dimas, so called from a village which may have borrowed a name from the penitent thief. This Sahara has been described with prodigious exaggeration in order to set off by contrast the charms of the so-termed 'sublime Gorge of Abana,' to which it leads. Measuring some ten kilometres, it is undoubtedly a rough bit of ground, dry as dust in the summer, and in winter swept by raving winds and piled with sleet and snow. At its eastern end the

Sahara at once dips into a deep, lateral gorge, which feeds, after rains, the Barada Valley, and here we remark that curious contrast of intense fertility with utter, hopeless barrenness which characterises inner Spain. Life is in that thick line of the darkest and densest evergreen, which, smiling under the fierce and fiery sun-glare, threads the side of the valley, in the wholesome perfume of the wild plants, and in the gush and murmur of waters making endless music. Death is represented by the dull grey formation standing up in tombstones, by the sterile yellow lime-rock, and by the chalk, blinding white; and the proportion of good to bad is as one to twenty. This verdure is, the Arabs say, a cooling to the eye of the beholder; it is like the aspect of the celadon-coloured sea that beats upon the torrid West African shores. With the author of that charming book 'Eothen,' 'you float along (for the delight is as the delight of bathing) through green, wavy fields and down into the cool verdure of groves and gardens, and you quench hot eyes in shade as though in deep, rushing waters.'

The beginning of the end is at the tenth and last station, El Hamah, meaning the Head of the Valley, and we halt here for a cup of coffee. The next place of note is Dummar; here we cross the Barada torrent. This place is, despite its low site and hot and cold air, a favourite for villas; and certain wealthy Damascus usurers have here built large piles, as remarkable for the barbarity of their outer frescoes as for the tawdry decoration of the interior. The witty Damasceines call them 'traps,' because they are periodically let to high officials for other considerations than hire. And now, with its slate-coloured stream, garnished with weirs on our right, the valley becomes broader and more important; the upper cliffs are tunnelled into cut caves. Troglodyte dwellings and sepulchres of the ancients; seven veins at high levels and at low levels branch off from the main artery; and, after passing a natural gateway formed by two shield-like masses of rock, we suspect that Damascus is before us.

The first sight of Damascus was once famous in travel. But then men rode on horseback, and turned, a little beyond Damascus, sharply to the left of the present line. They took what was evidently the old Roman road, and which is still, on account of its being a short cut, affected by muleteers. Now it is nothing but an ugly climb up sheet-rock and rolling stones, with bars and holes dug by the armed hoof of many a generation. They then passed through El Zaarub (the Spout); this is the old way, sunk some ten feet deep in the rock till it resembles an uncovered tunnel, and polished like glass by the traffic and transit of ages. At its mouth you suddenly turn a corner and see Damascus lying in panorama, a few hundred feet below you. 'A flint set in emeralds' is the Damascus citizen's description of what El Islam calls, and miscalls, the 'smile of the Prophet' (Mohammed). Like Stambul, it is beautiful from afar, as it is foul and sore within, morally and physically. The eye at once distinguishes a long head, the northern suburb 'El Salituzzah'; a central nucleus, crescent-shaped and fronting the bed of the Barada; and a long tail, or southern suburb, 'El Maydan.' These three centres of white-washed dwellings and skyline, fretted with dome and minaret, are surrounded and backed by a mass of evergreen orchard, whose outlines are sharply defined by irrigation, whilst beyond the scatter of outlying villages, glare the sunburnt yellow and the parched rich brown of the desert, whose light blue hillocks define the eastern horizon.

The prosaic approach by the French road shows little beyond ruins and graveyards: Damascus outside is a mass of graveyards, the 'Great' and 'Little Camps' of Constantinople, only without their cypresses; whilst within it is all graveyards and ruins, mixed with crowded and steaming bazaars. This world of graves reminds one of Job's forlorn man dwelling 'in desolate cities, and in houses which no man inhabiteth, which are ready to become heaps.' The Barada in olden times had its stone embankment; the walls are now in ruins. On our right is a ruined bridge once leading to a large coffee-house, both also in ruins. As we advance we pass other ruins. But though it was prophesied that Damascus should be a 'ruinous heap,' her position forbids annihilation. The second of Biblical cities, she has been destroyed again and again; her houses have been levelled with the ground, and the Tartar has played hockey with the hearts of her sons. Still she sits upon the eastern folds of the Anti-Libanus and on her gold-rolling river, boldly overlooking the desert at her base. Damascus, not Rome, deserves, if any does, to be entitled the Eternal City.

I passed twenty-three months (October 1st, 1869, to August 20th, 1871), on and off, at this most picturesque and unpleasant of residences. It was then in the transitional state, neither of Asia nor of Europe. To one who had long lived in the outer East, a return to such an ambiguous state of things was utterly disenchanting. Hassan, digging or delving in long beard and long clothes, looks more like an overgrown baby than the romantic being which your fancies paint him. Fatima, with a coloured kerchief (not a nose-bag) over her face, possibly spotted for greater hideousness, with Marseilles gloves and French bottines of yellow satin, trimmed with fringe and bugles, protruding from the white calico which might be her winding-sheet, is an absurdity: she reminded me of sundry 'kings' on the West African shore, whose toilet consists of a bright bandanna and a chimney-pot hat, of the largest dimensions, coloured the liveliest sky-blue.

The first steps to be taken at Damascus were to pay and receive visits, to find a house, to hire servants, to buy horses, and, in fact, to settle ourselves. It proved no easy matter. Certain persons had amused themselves with spreading a report that my pilgrimage to Meccah had aroused Moslem fanaticism, and perhaps might cost me my life. They, as well as I, knew far better, so I was not surprised at the kind and even friendly reception given to me by Emir Abdel Kadir, of Algerine fame, and by the Dean of the great Cathedral el Amahi, the late Shaykh Abdahah el Halati. And I remember with satisfaction that, to the hour of my quitting Damascus, the Moslems never showed for me any but the most cordial feeling.

Other British consuls had been of a stay-at-home disposition, seeing nothing beyond the length of their noses. I was of a roving one, and determined to see all I could, and penetrate to the inner heart of Syria. To be shut up in Damascus was to be in prison; the breath of the desert was liberty. I soon wandered afield. One of my earliest excursions was to Palmyra. Until the spring of 1870 a traveller visiting Syria for the express purpose, perhaps, of seeing Palmyra, 'Tadmor in the Wilderness,' after being kept waiting for months at Damascus, had to return disappointed. Only the rich could afford the large Bedouin escort, for which even six thousand francs and more have been demanded. Add to this the difficulties, hardships, and dangers of the journey, the heat of the arid desert, want of water, chances of attack, the long forced marches by night and hiding by day, ending with a shabby halt of forty-eight hours at a place for which so many sacrifices had been made, and where a fortnight is the minimum required.

Since the beginning of the last century the Porte has had in view a military occupation of the caravan route between

Damascus and the Euphrates. 'The Turk will catch up your best hare on the back of a lame donkey,' say the Arabs, little thinking what high praise they award to the conquering race. The *cordon militaire* was to extend from Damascus, *viâ* Jayrud, Karyatayn, Palmyra, and Sukhnah, to Daye on the great rim. The wells were to be commanded by block houses, the roads to be cleared by movable columns, and thus the plundering Bedouin, who refuse all allegiance to the Sultan, would be kept, perforce, in the dan, or desert, between the easternmost offsets of the Anti-Libanus and the pitch uplands of Nijd. This project was apparently rescued from the fate of good intentions by Osman Bey, a Hungarian officer who had served the Porte since 1848. He moved from Hamah with a body of some 1,600 men – enough to cut his way through half the vermin in Araby the Unblest. Presently, after occupying Palmyra, building barracks, and restoring the old Druze Castle, he proceeded eastward to Suknah, whence he could communicate with the force expected to march westward from Baghdad. The welcome intelligence was hailed with joy: Palmyra, so long excluded from the Oriental tour, lay open to the European traveller; half a step had been taken towards a Euphrates Valley Railway; at Damascus men congratulated themselves upon the new line of frontier, which was naturally expected to strengthen and to extend the limits of Syria; and the merchant rejoiced to learn that his caravan would be no longer liable to wholesale plunder.

A fair vision, doomed so soon to fade! After six months or so of occupation, Osman Bey, whose men were half starving, became tired of Palmyra, and was recalled to Damascus. The garrison was reduced to two hundred men under a captain, whose only friend was the raki bottle, and the last I saw of the garrison was his orderly riding into Hauran, with the huge, empty demijohns dangling at his saddlebow. The Bedouin waxed brave, and, in the spring of 1871, I was obliged to send travellers to Palmyra by a long circuit, *viâ* the north and the north-west.

A certain official business compelled me to visit Karyatayn, which is within jurisdiction of Damascus, and my wife resolved to accompany me. In this little enterprise I was warmly seconded by the Vicomte de Perrochel, a French traveller and author, who had twice visited Damascus in the hope of reaching Tadmor, and by M. Ionine, my Russian colleague. The Governor-General, the Field Marshal commanding the army of Syria, and other high officials, lent us their best aid. We engaged a pair of dragomen, six servants, a cook, and eight muleteers; twelve mules and eight baggage-asses to carry tents and canteen, baggage and provisions; and we rode our own horses, being wrongly persuaded not to take donkeys – on long marches they would have been a pleasant change. We were peculiarly unfortunate in the choice of head dragoman, a certain Anton Wardi, who had Italianised his name to Riza. Originally a donkey-boy at Beyrut, he made, by 'skinning' sundry travellers, some 80,000 francs in ten years. He was utterly spoiled by his French friends, M. de Sauley and M. de Perrochel; he had also dragomaned the then Princess Amadeo, who, in return for his mean conduct, had promised him, and afterwards sent him, greatly to the disgust of every Italian gentleman, the Order of the Rose. This 'native gentleman,' the type of the ignoble *petit bourgeois* of Syria, had been trusted without any contract having been made. He charged us a hundred francs per diem, and the others each fifty francs and forty francs. When the bill was produced for settlement, it proved to be a long list of *des extras*: everything was *un extra*; two bottles of cognac, reported broken, appeared as *des extras*; even the water-camels were *des extras*. The fact was, he had allowed, when galloping about the country, some francs to fall from his pocket, and he resolved that *les extras* should replace them.

We altogether regretted the assistance of Mohammed, Shaykh of the Mezrab tribe, who had systematically fleeced travellers for a score of years. He demanded two napoleons a head for his wretched camels, sending a score when only one was wanted; like all other chiefs, he would not guarantee his protégés, either in purse or person, against enemies, but only against his own friends; he allowed them but two days at Palmyra; he made them march twenty, instead of fifteen, hours between Karyatayn and their destination; he concealed the fact that there are wells the whole way, in order to make them hire camels and buy water-skins; and, besides harassing them with night marches, he organised sham attacks, in order to make them duly appreciate his protection. I rejoice to say that Mohammed's occupation has since gone; his miserable tribe was three times plundered within eighteen months, and, instead of fighting, he fell back upon the desert. May thus end all who oppose their petty interests to the general good – all that would shut roads instead of opening them! With a view of keeping up his title to escort travellers, he sent with us a clansman upon a well-bred mare and armed with the honourable spear. But M. de Perrochel hired the mare; the crestfallen man was put upon a baggage-mare, and the poor spear was carried by a lame donkey.

Armed to the teeth, we set out in a chorus of groans and with general prognostications of evil. Ours was the first party since M. Dubois d'Angus was dangerously wounded, stripped, and turned out to die of hunger, thirst, and cold, because he could not salary the inevitable Bedouin. It would, doubtless, have been the interest of many and the delight of more to see us return in the scantiest of costumes; consequently a false report generally flew abroad that we had been pursued and plundered by the Bedouin.

The first night was passed under canvas near a ruined khan in the fifth valley plain east of the Syrian metropolis. The weather became unusually cold the next morning when we left the foggy lowland and turned to the north-east in order to cross the ridgy line of hills, which, offsetting from the Anti-Libanus, runs from Damascus toward the desert, and afterwards sweeps round to Palmyra. The line of travel was a break in the ridge. Then, gently descending, we fell into a northern depression, a section of that extensive valley in the Anti-Libanus, which, under a variety of names, runs nearly straight north-east (more exactly, 60°), to Palmyra. Nothing can be simpler than the geography of the country. The traveller cannot lose his way in the Palmyra Valley without crossing the high and rugged mountains which hem it in on both sides, and, if he is attacked by raiders, he can easily take refuge, and laugh at the Arab goatees. During the time of our journey the miserable little robber clans Shitai and Ghiyas had completely closed the country five hours' riding to the east of Damascus, whilst the Sorbai and the Anergah bandits were making the Merj a battlefield and were threatening to burn down the peaceful villages. Even as we crossed the pass we were saddened by the report that a troop of Bedouin had the day before murdered a wretched peasant within easy sight of Damascus. This state of things was a national scandal to the Porte, which, of course, was never allowed to know the truth.

We resolved to advance slowly, to examine every object, and to follow the most indirect paths. Hence our march to Palmyra occupied eight days; we returned, however, in four with horses that called loudly for a week's rest. The regular stations are as follows: –

	Hours
1. Damascus to Jayrud	9
2. Jayrud to Karyatayn	10–11
3. Karyatayn to Agu el Waah	8
4. Agu el Waah to Palmyra	9

On the second day we dismissed our escort, one officer and two privates of irregular cavalry, who were worse than useless, and we slept at the house of Daas Agha, hereditary Chief of Jayrud. A noted sabre, and able to bring one hundred and fifty lances into the field, he was systematically neglected by the authorities, because supposed to be friendly with foreigners. Shortly after my departure he barbarously tortured two wretched Arabs, throwing them into a pit full of fire, and practising upon them with his revolver. Thereupon he was at once taken into prime favour, and received a command.

Daas Agha escorted us from Jayrud with ten of his kinsmen mounted upon their best mares. In the upland valley we suffered severely from cold, and the sleety sou'wester which cut our faces on the return was a caution.

At Karyatayn, which we reached on the fifth day, Osman Bey, who was waiting for rations, money, transport, in fact, everything, offered us the most friendly welcome, and I gave official protection to Shaykh Faris, in connection with the English post at Baghdad. The former detached with us eighty bayonets of regulars and twenty-five sabres of Irregulars, commanded by two officers. This body presently put to flight anything in the way of Bedouin; a war party of two thousand men would not have attacked us; and I really believe that a band of thirty Englishmen armed with carbines and revolvers could sweep clean the Desert of the Euphrates from end to end.

At Karyatayn we hired seventeen camels to carry water. This would have been a complete waste of money had we gone, like other travellers, by the Darb el Sultain, or High Way. Some three hours' ride to the right, or south, of the road amongst the hills bounding the Palmyra Valley is a fine cistern (Ibex Fountain), where water is never wanting. There is, however, a still more direct road *viâ* the remains of an aqueduct and a river in the desert. This short cut from Karyatayn to Palmyra may be covered in twenty-four hours of camel walking, fifteen of horse walking, and twelve by dromedary or hard gallop. Travellers would start at

6.30 or 7. A.M., and encamp after being out from twelve to thirteen hours; but this includes breakfast and sundry halts, sometimes to inspect figures, real or imaginary, in the distance, at other times to indulge in a 'spurt' after a gazelle or a wild boar.

We chose, however, the little-known Baghdad, or eastern, road. The next day we rested at a large deserted khan, and on the eighth we made our entrance into Palmyra, where we were hospitably received by Shaykh Faris. Our muleteers, for the convenience of their cattle, pitched their tents close to, and east of, the so-called Grand Colonnade, a malarious and unwholesome site. They should have encamped amongst the trees at a threshing-floor near three palms. Travellers may be strongly advised not to lodge in the native village, whose mud huts, like wasps' nests, are all huddled within the ancient Temple of the Sun, or they may suffer from fever or ophthalmia. The water of Tadmor is sulphurous, like Harrogate, the climate is unhealthy, and the people are ragged and sickly. May there, as in most parts of the northern hemisphere, is the best travelling-season, and in any but a phenomenal year the traveller need not fear to encounter, as we did, ice and snow, siroccos and furious sou'westers.

If asked whether Palmyra is worth all this trouble, I should reply 'No' and 'Yes.' No, if you merely go there, stay two days, and return, especially after sighting noble Báalbak. Certainly not for the Grand Colonnade of weather-beaten limestone, by a stretch of courtesy called marble, which, rain-washed and earth-quake-shaken, looks like a system of galleries. Not for the Temple of the Sun, the building of a Roman emperor, a second-rate affair, an architectural evidence of Rome's declining days. Yes, if you would study the site and the environs, which are interesting and only partially explored, make excavations, and collect coins and relics, which may be bought for a song.

The site of Palmyra is very interesting; she stands between the mountains and the sea; like Damascus, she sits upon the eastern slope of the Anti-Libanus, facing the wilderness, but unhappily she has a dry torrent bed, the Wady el Sayl, instead of a rushing Barada. She is built upon the shore cape, where the sandy sea breaks upon its nearest headlands. This sea is the mysterious Wilderness of the Euphrates, whose ships are camels, whose yachts are high-bred mares, and whose cock-boats are mules and asses. She is on the very threshold of the mountains, which the wild cavalry cannot scour, as they do the level plain. And her position is such that we have not heard the last of the Tadmor, or, as the Arabs call her, Tudmur. Nor will it be difficult to revive her. A large tract can be placed under cultivation, where there shall be protection for life and property; old wells exist in the ruins; foresting the highlands to the north and west will cause rain; and the aqueducts in the old days may easily be repaired.

I am unwilling to indulge in a description of the modern ruin of the great old depôt, which has employed so many pens. But very little has been said concerning the old tomb-towers, which have taken at Palmyra the place of Egyptian pyramids. Here, as elsewhere in ancient Syria, sepulture was extramural, and every settlement was approached by one or more Viâ Appia, much resembling that of ancient Rome. At Palmyra there are, or, rather, were, notably two: one (south-west) upon the high road to Damascus; the other, north-west of the official or monumental city, formed, doubtless, the main approach from Hauran and Hamah. The two are lined on both sides with those interesting monuments, whose squat, solid forms of gloomy and unsquared sandstone contrast remarkably with the bastard classical and Roman architecture, meretricious in all its details, and glittering from afar in white limestone. Inscriptions in the Palmyrian character prove that they date from about A.D. 2 and 102; but they have evidently been restored, and this perhaps fixes the latest restoration. It is highly probable that the heathen method of burial declined under the Roman rule, especially after A.D. 130, when the Great Half-way House again changed its name to Adrianopolis. Still, vestiges of the old custom are found in the Hauran and in the Druze Mountain west of the great valley, extending deep into the second century, when it is believed, Gassanides of Damascus had abandoned their heathen faith for Christianity. I found in the tombs, or cells, fragments of mummies, and these, it is suspected, were the first ever brought to England. Almost all the skulls contained date-stones, more or less, and a peach stone and an apricot stone were found under similar circumstances. At Shathah we picked up in the mummy-towers almond shells with the sharp ends cut off and forming baby cups.

There are three tomb-towers at Palmyra still standing, and perhaps likely to yield good results. The people call them Kasr el Zaynah (Pretty Palace), Kasr el Azin (Palace of the Maiden), and Kasr el Arus (Palace of the Bride). They number four and five stories, but the staircases, which run up the thickness of the walls, are broken, and so are the monolithic slabs which form the lower floors. Explorers, therefore, must take with them ropes and hooks, ladders which will reach to eighty feet, planks to act as bridges, and a short crowbar. We had none of these requirements, nor could the wretched village provide them. I have little doubt that the upper stories would be found to contain bones, coins, and pottery, perhaps entire mummies.

The shortness of our visit allowed me only a day and a half to try the fortune of excavation at Palmyra. It was easy to hire a considerable number of labourers at two and a half piastres a head per diem – say 6d. – when in other places the wages would be at least double. Operations began (April 15th) at the group of tomb-towers bearing west-south-west from the great Temple of the Sun: I chose this group because it appeared the oldest of the series. The fellahs, or peasants, know it as Kusin Ahi Sayl (Palaces of the Father of a Torrent); and they stare when told that these massive buildings are not royal residences but tombs. Here the tombs in the several stages were easily cleared out by my forty-five coolies, who had nothing but diminutive picks and bars, grain-lugs and body-cloths, which they converted into buckets for removing sand and rubbish. But these cells and those of the adjoining ruins had before been ransacked, and they supplied nothing beyond skulls, bones, and shreds of mummy cloth, whose dyes were remarkably brilliant.

The hands were then applied to an adjoining mound: it offered a tempting resemblance to the undulations of ground which cover the complicated chambered catacombs already laid open, and into one of which, some years ago, a camel fell, the roof having given way. After reaching a stratum of snow-white gypsum, which appeared to be artificial, though all hands agreed that it was not, we gave up the task, as time pressed so hard. The third attempt laid open the foundation of a house, and showed us the well, or rain-cistern, shaped, as such reservoirs are still in the Holy Land, like a soda-water bottle. The fourth trial was more successful; during our absence the workmen came upon two oval slabs of soft limestone, each with its kit-cat in high relief. One was a man with straight features, short, curly beard, and hair disposed, as appears to have been the fashion for both sexes, in three circular rolls. The other was a feminine bust, with features of a type so exaggerated as to resemble the negro. A third and similar work of art was brought up, but the head had been removed. It would be hard to explain the excitement caused by these wonderful discoveries; reports flew abroad that gold images of life-size had been dug up, and the least disposed to exaggeration declared that chests full of gold coins and ingots had fallen to our lot.

On the next morning we left Palmyra, and, after a hard gallop which lasted for the best part of four days, we found ourselves, not much the worse for wear, once more at Damascus.

EIGHT

POET, TRANSLATOR AND SEXOLOGIST

The pace of Burton's career as translator began to quicken in South America. Here he began serious work on the translation of *The Thousand and One Nights*, completed an English version of the Sanskrit classic *Vikram or the Art of the Vampire*, and rendered into his native tongue a number of Brazilian classics: *Lacerda's Journey to Cazembe*, *The Captivity of Hans Stade of Hesse among the Wild Tribes of Brazil*, and, most importantly, the 1,400-line epic by Brazil's most important poet, José Basílio da Gama's *The Uruguay*.

But it was only in the limbo of Trieste, and more particularly when he became a semi-invalid at the end of the 1870s, that the flood of translations from his pen really began. Burton's outstanding linguistic gifts led him to translate works in a wide variety of languages: the lyric poetry of Catullus, the epics of Camões, and the Neapolitan folk tales by Basile *Il Pentamerone*, of which a sample is included here. Yet his greatest fame came with the series of translations of erotic classics he began to produce in the early 1880s: the Sanskrit Kama Sutra of Vatsyayana and *The Ananga-Ranga*; the manual of Arabian erotology *The Perfumed Garden of Cheikh Nefzaoui*, plus the Persian sex guides *The Beharistan* and *The Gulistan*, to say nothing of a collectaneous volume of erotica from the Latin poets entitled *Priapeia* or the *Sportive Epigrams* of divers poets on Priapus.

These were risky undertakings in the Victorian era, when even a harmless work like Zola's *La Terre* could be prosecuted for obscenity. With his friends Foster Fitzgerald Arbuthnot and H.S. Ashbee, Burton conceived the idea of a pseudonymous publishing house with a fictitious headquarters. Thus was born the Kama Shastra Society of London and Benares, with printers allegedly in India's Holy City, but in reality in Stoke Newington.

Burton's unembarrassed mind led him to move with ease through the forests of exotic erotica. He had amassed a huge library of oriental works on the art of love and was able to write about sexual practices and variations in a way that even Mrs Grundy found difficult to describe as obscene. Apart from his interests as a scholar and antiquarian, there was a proselytizing element in Burton's writings. Having observed the realistic way sex was treated among oriental peoples and the so-called savages of Africa and North America, Burton was appalled at the depths of sexual ignorance and instinctual repression he observed in the civilized West.

The *Kama Sutra* deals with the role of sexuality and marriage in the life of a young Indian man-about-town of the first century A.D. The fame of the *Kama Sutra* in later years came to rest on the sections in Part Two abut sexual congress. Yet, as the extract below shows, Vatsyayana's attitude to sexuality was the reverse of lubricious or titillatory. If anything it is earnest and po-faced, reflecting the religious and sacramental role sex plays in Hindu culture.

1880, the year of his translation of Camões's *Lusiads* (the Portuguese *Aeneid*) also saw Burton's most sustained attempt ever to establish himself as a poet. His aim was to emulate or surpass the success enjoyed in Victorian England by Edward Fitzgerald's famous *Rubáiyát of Omar Khayyám*. But, uncertain of his talents in this area, he passed the work off as a poem by Hâjî Abdû El-Yerdî, allegedly a Persian from Dhara Ghiral, and ostensibly translated by one Frank Baker (which was Burton's pseudonym). The *Kasîdah* is a *mélange* of western metaphysics and oriental fatalism, which calls to mind the similar syncretism in the 'theosophical' work of Annie Besant and Madame Blavatsky. As the extract shows, Burton's favourite devices are repetition, alliteration and assonance. The poem is shamelessly eclectic and draws on Confucius, Longfellow, Aristotle, Pope, Swinburne, the Tennyson of *In Memoriam* and the Matthew Arnold of *Stanzas from the Grande Chartreuse* as well as, obviously, Fitzgerald himself. The *Kasîdah* seems fated to be regarded by history as an epigone to the *Rubáiyát*, and it is true that its blend of Sufi mysticism and somewhat facile Schopenhauerian pessimism makes an uneasy mixture. At its best, however, it is something more than just a literary curiosity and it has always had its champions.

In 1885 appeared his masterpiece of the translator's art. In ten volumes (and six supplementary tomes of further tales) he produced a complete rendition of the collection of tales known to European culture as *The Thousand and One Nights* and first introduced into the western bloodstream by the French Orientalist Antoine Galland in the early years of the eighteenth century. The nursery stories of Sinbad represented only one strand in the tales. A more dominant motif was the lubricious and the erotic, as in the story of 'The Porter and the Three Ladies of Baghdad' reproduced below. Burton's decision to publish the translation of the *Arabian Nights* complete and unexpurgated was courageous, and he defended his action thus: 'To those critics who complain of these raw vulgarisms and puerile indecencies in the *Nights* I can reply only by quoting the words said to have been said by Dr Johnson (to a woman) who complained of the naughty words in his dictionary – You must have been looking for them, Madam!'

Burton fell foul of his prim detractors only when he published in his 'Terminal Essay' on the *Nights* a long discussion on pederasty and another on the sexual education of women. Otherwise, the Burton edition was hailed by the critics as an outstanding achievement. It was also a commercial success: Burton made a profit of 10,000 guineas on an outlay of 6,000 guineas.

The *Nights* was the perfect subject for Burton. The tales combined the poetry of the *Kasîdah* with the erotology of the *Kama Sutra* and *The Perfumed Garden*. Burton's formidable annotations also allowed him to provide a *tour de force* display of comparative anthropology, culled from four continents. Some critics found the erudition top-heavy, while others damned Burton's linguistic farrago of Chaucerian English, contemporary slang and American neologism. As a sympathetic critic, Jorge Luis Borges, wrote in *Seven Nights*: 'the anthropological and obscene translation by Burton is written in curious English, partly derived from the fourteenth century, an English full of archaism and neologism, an English not devoid of beauty, but which at times is difficult to read.' But the overall consensus is that Burton's translation of the *Nights* is at once monument, model and milestone.

This translation was also important to Burton at a deeper level. Bruno Bettelheim in *The Uses of Enchantment* underlines the likely therapeutic value of these stories to a man like Burton. Many of them can be interpreted at the level of subtext as a yearning for release from fragmented existence into an integrated personality. It is surely significant that in his translation of the *Nights* Burton united the poetic, scholarly, sociological and linguistic aspects of his personality and that for the first time he was prepared to publish a forbidden work under his own name.

The Goose: First Diversion of the Fifth Day
(from *Il Pentamerone; or, the Tale of Tales* (1893))

Lilla and Lolla buy a goose at the market, and the bird shitteth golden coins; a neighbour beggeth them to lend it to her, and finding the contrary, attempteth to slay it, and casts it out of the window. The bird, not being dead, taketh hold of the hindparts of a prince who is doing a thing of need to nature. He crieth aloud for aid, but none of the realm can pull her off from him but Lolla, for which reason he taketh her to wife.

True was the saying of that great man of weal, that 'The craftsman to the locksmith, the musician to the musician, the neighbour to the neighbour, the beggar to the beggar' – there is not an hole in the great building of the world whereupon that accursed spider called envy doth not weave his net, which feedeth on naught else but the ruin of his neighbour: as ye particularly shall hear from the tale, that I am going to relate.

Once upon a time there lived in very reduced circumstances two sisters, and it was as much as they could do to gain a livelihood by spinning flax from morn till night, which they sold; but they dragged on their wretched life, and it was impossible but that some day the ball of necessity would touch that of honour, and send it out; for which matter Heaven, who is so great to recompense good deeds, and so thin and slow in punishing the evil, put into the minds of these two poor children that they should go to the market, and sell some skeins of thread, so that with what they received from it they should buy a goose. The women did so, and carried the goose home, and they loved her so well that they fed her, and let her sleep in their own bed, as if she had been their own sister. But sweep to-day and look to-morrow, the good day came, and the goose began to shit golden crowns, in such manner that one by one they filled a large chest, and the shitting was such that the sisters began to lift their heads, and to look well fed and happy. Such was the show of their prosperity that the gossips began to take notice of it, and one day meeting together, they spake thus amongst themselves, 'Hast thou seen, O gossip Vasta, Lilla with Lolla, who but a few days ago might have dropped down dead with hunger, but who now have become so well-fed and well-dressed that they live in luxury like great ladies? Hast thou seen their windows always ornamented with fowls and barons of beef, which stare thee in the face? What can it be? Either they have laid hands on their honour, or they have found a hoard.' 'I am astonished and am become a mummy with exceeding marvel,' answered Vasta, 'O gossip Pearl mine, when they were ready to sink, I see them in parvenus' splendours, which seem to me a dream.' They said these things and others, stimulated by their surging envy, and they bored a hole in the wall of the house of one of the gossips that corresponded with one of the chambers occupied by the two damsels, so that it might enable them to espy their doings, and to gratify their curiosity; and they played the spy for so long that one evening, when the sun whippeth with its rays the banks of the Indian sea to give rest to the hours of the day, they beheld Lilla and Lolla spreading sheets upon the ground; then they made the goose walk thereon, and as soon as she was on the sheets, the goose began shitting crowns until the very balls of her eyes stood out.

When morning came, and Apollo with his golden wand exorciseth the shadows to withdraw, came Vasta to visit the two damsels, and after twisting and lengthening the conversation, she came to the point, and begged they would kindly lend her the goose for two hours to make a few young ducklings she had bought take affection for the house; and she begged, prayed, and besought so much, that the simpletons, partly because they knew not how to deny, and partly not to cause suspicion on the part of the gossips, lent the bird to her upon the understanding that she should return her at the time appointed. Then Vasta went home

where the other gossips were waiting for her, and they laid clean
sheets upon the floor, and made the goose walk thereon, but
instead of showing a mint and a coining of crowns, out of her
fundament there came a sewer of dirt, which covered the bed-
linen with a dark yellowish matter, the stink of which filled the
whole house like the flavour that cometh forth from the pot of
stew on the holydays. When they beheld that sight, they thought
to feed her well, so that she would make the substance for the
lapis-lasuli philosophorum, to satisfy their desire. And thus they fed
her so well and so much, that she was full up to her throat, and
they then placed her upon a clean sheet; but if the goose had
been rather loose before, she now discovered a new dysentery,
indigestion playing a part. For which reason the gossips were
wroth with exceeding wrath, and twisting the neck of the goose,
threw her out of the window into a narrow street with no outlet,
into which ordure and filth were cast. But as fate and fortune had
decreed, that where least thou thinkest the bean will grow, passed
that way a son of a king, hunting and birding, and on the road he
was taken by a colic, and bidding his groom hold the reins of his
steed and his sword, he entered that narrow street, and emptied
his belly, and completing this service, having no paper in his
pocket to wipe himself with, he beheld the dead goose, whereupon he used it for that purpose.

Now the goose was not dead; so, turning her head, she caught
hold with her bill of the fleshy part of the prince and would not let
it go, and he cried with loud cries, and his suite ran to his assistance, and tried to pull off the bird from him, but it was of no
avail; she held firmly at her booty like a feathery weight or an
hairy hermaphrodite. And the prince, unable to resist the
suffering, and beholding the fruitless efforts made by his suite,
bade them lift him up, and carry him in their arms to the royal
palace, where he sent for all the doctors and sages of his realm to
deliver him. They tried all kinds of ointment, and made use of
pinchers, and used and sprinkled powders, but to no purpose.
And perceiving that the goose was like a tick, and would not let
go for quicksilver, a leech that would not drop for all the vinegar
used, the prince ordered a ban to be proclaimed, that whoso
would deliver him from this annoyance at his bottom, if it should
be a man, he would gift him with half of his realm, if a woman, he
would take her to wife. And folk, having put their noses to the
reward, swarmed to the palace-gate; but the more remedies they

tried, the more the goose tightened her hold, and pinched the wretched prince's back parts, and it seemed as if all the prescriptions of Galen had been gathered together, and all the aphorisms of Hippocrates, and the remedies of Mesoe against the posterior of Aristotiles, to torment that unhappy prince. But by decree of the Decreer, amid so many who came and went to try this trial, came also Lolla, the youngest of the two sisters, and when she beheld the goose she knew her, and cried, 'O Niofatella mine, Niofatella;' and the goose, hearing the voice of her beloved mistress, at once left her prey, and ran to meet her, caressing her and kissing her, well pleased to change the back parts of a prince for the mouth of a country-maid. The prince, seeing this marvel, desired to know how it had occurred, and Lolla related the story from beginning to end, and when she came to the trick played on the gossips, the prince laughed till he fell backwards; and he bade them be taken, and whipped well with switches, and sent into exile; and thereafter amid joyance and feasting he took Lolla to wife, with the goose that could shit so many treasures for her dowry. And he married Lilla to a rich husband, and they lived happily together the most mirthful in the world, in spite of the gossips who tried to shut the road of the two sisters to the riches which Heaven had sent them, and they opened another way so that one should become a queen, knowing in the end that

'An impediment is often an assistance.'

Of the Different Ways of Lying Down, and Various Kinds of Congress
(from *The Kama Sutra of Vatsyayana* (1883))

On the occasion of a 'high congress' the Mrigi (Deer) woman should lie down in such a way as to widen her yoni, while in a 'low congress' the Hastini (Elephant) woman should lie down so as to contract hers. But in an 'equal congress' they should lie down in the natural position. What is said above concerning the Mrigi and the Hastini applies also to the Vadawa (Mare) woman. In a 'low congress' the women should particularly make use of medicine, to cause her desires to be satisfied quickly.

The Deer-woman has the following three ways of lying down.

The widely opened position.
The yawning position.
The position of the wife of Indra.

(1). When she lowers her head and raises her middle parts, it is called the 'widely opened position.' At such a time the man should apply some unguent, so as to make the entrance easy.

(2). When she raises her thighs and keeps them wide apart and engages in congress, it is called the 'yawning position.'

(3). When she places her thighs with her legs doubled on them upon her sides, and thus engages in congress, it is called the position of Indrani, and this is learnt only by practice. The position is also useful in the case of the 'highest congress'.

The 'clasping position' is used in 'low congress,' and in the 'lowest congress,' together with the 'pressing position,' the 'twining position,' and the 'mare's position.'

When the legs of both the male and the female are stretched out over each other, it is called the 'clasping position.' It is of two kinds, the side position and the supine position, according to the way in which they lie down. In the side position the male should invariably lie on his left side, and cause the woman to lie on her right side, and this rule is to be observed in lying down with all kinds of women.

When, after congress has begun in the clasping position, the woman presses her lover with her thighs, it is called the 'pressing position.'

When the woman places one of her thighs across the thigh of her lover, it is called the 'twining position.'

When the woman forcibly holds in her yoni the lingam after it is in, it is called the 'mare's position.' This is learnt by practice only, and is chiefly found among the women of the Andra country.

The above are the different ways of lying down, mentioned by Babhravya; Suvarnanabha, however, gives the following in addition.

When the female raises both her thighs straight up, it is called the 'rising position.'

When she raises both of her legs, and places them on her lover's shoulders, it is called the 'yawning position.'

When the legs are contracted, and thus held by the lover before his bosom, it is called the 'pressed position.'

When only one of her legs is stretched out, it is called the 'half pressed position.'

When the woman places one of her legs on her lover's shoulder, and stretches the other out, and then places the latter on his shoulder, and stretches out the other, and continues to do so alternately, it is called the 'splitting of a bamboo.'

When one of her legs is placed on the head, and the other is stretched out, it is called the 'fixing of a nail.' This is learnt by practice only.

When both the legs of the women are contracted, and placed on her stomach, it is called the 'crab's position.'

When the thighs are raised and placed one upon the other, it is called the 'packed position.'

When the shanks are placed one upon the other, it is called the 'lotus-like position.'

When a man, during congress, turns round, and enjoys the woman without leaving her, while she embraces him round the back all the time, it is called the 'turning position,' and is learnt only by practice.

Thus, says Suvarnanabha, these different ways of lying down, sitting, and standing should be practised in water, because it is easy to do therein. But Vatsyayana is of opinion that congress in water is improper, because it is prohibited by the religious law.

When a man and a woman support themselves on each other's bodies, or on a wall, or pillar, and thus while standing engage in congress, it is called the 'supported congress.'

When a man supports himself against a wall, and the woman, sitting on his hands joined together and held underneath her, throws her arms round his neck, and putting her thighs alongside his waist, moves herself by her feet, which are touching the wall against which the man is leaning, it is called the 'suspended congress.'

When a woman stands on her hands and feet like a quadruped, and her lover mounts her like a bull, it is called the 'congress of a cow.' At this time every thing that is ordinarily done on the bosom should be done on the back.

In the same way can be carried on the congress of a dog, the congress of a goat, the congress of a deer, the forcible mounting of an ass, the congress of a cat, the jump of a tiger, the pressing of an elephant, the rubbing of a boar, and the mounting of a horse. And in all these cases the characteristics of these different animals should be manifested by acting like them.

When a man enjoys two women at the same time, both of whom love him equally, it is called the 'united congress.'

When a man enjoys many women altogether, it is called the 'congress of a herd of cows.'

The following kinds of congress, viz., sporting in water, or the congress of an elephant with many female elephants which is said to take place only in the water, the congress of a collection of goats, the congress of a collection of deer, take place in imitation of these animals.

In Gramaneri many young men enjoy a woman that may be married to one of them, either one after the other, or at the same time. Thus one of them holds her, another enjoys her, a third uses her mouth, a fourth holds her middle part, and in this way they go on enjoying her several parts alternately.

The same things can be done when several men are sitting in company with one courtezan, or when one courtezan is alone with many men. In the same way this can be done by the women of the King's harem when they accidently get hold of a man.

The people in the Southern countries have also a congress in the anus, that is called the 'lower congress.'

Thus ends the various kinds of congress. There are also two verses on the subject as follows.

'An ingenious person should multiply the kinds of congress after the fashion of the different kinds of beasts and of birds. For these different kinds of congress, performed according to the usage of each country, and the liking of each individual, generate love, friendship, and respect in the hearts of women.'

The Kasîdah of Hâjî Abdû El-Yezdî a Lay of the Higher Law Translated and Annotated by His Friend and Pupil F.B. (1880)

> The hour is nigh; the waning Queen walks
> forth to rule the later night;
> Crown'd with the sparkle of a Star, and
> throned on orb of ashen light:
>
> The Wolf-tail sweeps the paling East to
> leave a deeper gloom behind,
> And Dawn uprears her shining head, sighing
> with semblance of a wind:

The highlands catch yon Orient gleam, while
  purpling still the lowlands lie;
And pearly mists, the morning-pride, soar
  incense-like to greet the sky.

The horses neigh, the camels groan, the
  torches gleam, the cressets flare;
The town of canvas falls, and man with din
  and dint invadeth air:

The Golden Gates swing right and left; up
  springs the Sun with flamy brow;
The dew-cloud melts in gush of light; brown
  Earth is bathed in morning-glow.

Slowly they wind athwart the wild, and while
  young Day his anthem swells,
Sad falls upon my yearning ear the tinkling
  of the Camel-bells:

O'er fiery waste and frozen wold, o'er horrid
  hill and gloomy glen,
The home of grisly beast and Ghoul, the
  haunts of wilder, grislier men; –

With the brief gladness of the Palms, that
  tower and sway o'er seething plain,
Fraught with the thoughts of rustling shade,
  and welling spring, and rushing rain;

With the short solace of the ridge, by gentle
  zephyrs played upon,
Whose breezy head and bosky side front
  seas of cooly celadon; –

'Tis theirs to pass with joy and hope, whose
  souls shall ever thrill and fill
Dreams of the Birthplace and the Tomb, –
  visions of Allah's Holy Hill.

But we? Another shift of scene, another
    pang to rack the heart;
Why meet we on the bridge of Time to
    'change one greeting and to part?

We meet to part; yet asks my sprite, Part
    we to meet? Ah! is it so?
Man's fancy-made Omniscience knows who
    made Omniscience nought can know.

Why must we meet, why must we part, why
    must we bear this yoke of MUST,
Without our leave or askt or given, by tyrant
    Fate on victim thrust?

That Eve so gay, so bright, so glad, this
    Morn so dim, and sad, and grey;
Strange that life's Registrar should write
    this day a day, that day a day!

Mine eyes, my brain, my heart, are sad, –
    sad is the very core of me;
All wearies, changes, passes, ends; alas! the
    Birthday's injury!

Friends of my youth, a last adieu! haply
    some day we meet again;
Yet ne'er the selfsame men shall meet; the
    years shall make us other men:

The light of morn has grown to noon, has
    paled with eve, and now farewell!
Go, vanish from my life as dies the tinkling
    of the Camel's bell.

* * *

In these drear wastes of sea-born land, these
    wilds where none may dwell but He,
What visionary Pasts revive, what process
    of the Years we see:

Gazing beyond the thin blue line that rims
    the far horizon-ring,
Our sadden'd sight why haunt these ghosts,
    whence do these spectral shadows spring?

What endless questions vex the thought, of
    Whence and Whither, When and How?
What fond and foolish strife to read the
    Scripture writ on human brow;

As stand we percht on point of Time,
    betwixt the two Eternities,
Whose awful secrets gathering round with
    black profound oppress our eyes.

* * *

We live our lives with rogues and fools,
    dead and alive, alive and dead,
We die 'twixt one who feels the pulse and
    one who frets and clouds the head:

And, – oh, the Pity! – hardly conned the
    lesson comes its fatal term;
Fate bids us bundle up our books, and bear
    them bod'ily to the worm:

Hardly we learn to wield the blade before
    the wrist grows stiff and old;
Hardly we learn to ply the pen ere Thought
    and Fancy faint with cold:

Hardly we find the path of love, to sink the
    Self, forget the 'I',
When sad suspicion grips the heart, when
    Man, *the* Man begins to die;

Hardly we scale the wisdom-heights, and
    sight the Pisgah-scene around,
And breathe the breath of heav'enly air, and
    hear the Spheres' harmonious sound;

When swift the Camel-rider spans the howl-
    ing waste, by Kismet sped,
And of his Magic Wand a wave hurries the
    quick to join the dead.

How sore the burden, strange the strife;
    how full of splendour, wonder, fear;
Life, atom of that Infinite Space that
    stretcheth 'twixt the Here and There.

How Thought is imp'otent to divine the
    secret which the gods defend,
The Why of birth and life and death, that
    Isis-veil no hand may rend.

Eternal Morrows make our Day; our *Is* is
    aye *to be* till when
Night closes in; 't is all a dream, and yet we
    die, – and then and THEN?

And still the Weaver plies his loom, whose
    warp and woof is wretched Man
Weaving th'unpattern'd dark design, so dark
    we doubt it owns a plan.

Dost not, O Maker, blush to hear, amid the
    storm of tears and blood,
Man say Thy mercy made what is, and saw
    the made and said 't was good?

The marvel is that man can smile dreaming
    his ghostly ghastly dream; –
Better the heedless atomy that buzzes in the
    morning beam!

O the dread pathos of our lives! how durst
    thou, Allah, thus to play
With Love, Affection, Friendship, all that
    shows the god in mortal clay?

But ah! what 'vaileth man to mourn; shall
   tears bring forth what smiles ne'er brought;
Shall brooding breed a thought of joy? Ah
   hush the sigh, forget the thought!

Silence thine immemorial quest, contain thy
   nature's vain complaint
None heeds, none cares for thee or thine; –
   like thee how many came and went?

Cease, Man, to mourn, to weep, to wail;
   enjoy thy shining hour of sun;
We dance along Death's icy brink, but is the
   dance less full of fun?

* * *

For Man's Free-will immortal law, Anagkê,
   Kismet, Des'tiny read
That was, that is, that aye shall be, Star,
   Fortune, Fate, Urd, Norn or Need.

'Man's nat'ural State is God's design;'
   such is the silly sage's theme;
'Man's primal Age was Age of Gold,'
   such is the Poet's waking dream:

Delusion, Ign'orance! Long ere Man drew
   upon Earth his earli'est breath
The world was one contin'uous scene of
   anguish, torture, prey and Death;

Where hideous Theria of the wild rended
   their fellows limb by limb;
Where horrid Saurians of the sea in waves
   of blood were wont to swim:

The 'fair young Earth' was only fit to
   spawn her frightful monster-brood;
Now fiery hot, now icy frore, now reeking
   wet with steamy flood.

Yon glorious Sun, the greater light, the
    'Bridegroom' of the royal Lyre,
A flaming, boiling, bursting mine; a grim
    black orb of whirling fire:

That gentle Moon, the lesser light, the
    Lover's lamp, the Swain's delight,
A ruined world, a globe burnt out, a corpse
    upon the road of night.

What reckt he, say of Good or Ill who in
    the hill-hole made his lair,
The blood-fed rav'ening Beast of prey,
    wilder than wildest wolf or bear?

How long in Man's pre-Ad'amite days to
    feed and swill, to sleep and breed,
Were the brute-biped's only life, a perfect
    life sans Code or Creed?

His choicest garb a shaggy fell, his choicest
    tool a flake of stone;
His best of orn'aments tattoo'd skin and
    holes to hang his bits of bone;

Who fought for female as for food when
    Mays awoke to warm desire;
And such the Lust that grew to Love when
    Fancy lent a purer fire.

Where *then* 'Th'Eternal nature-law by God
    engraved on human heart?'
Behold his simiad sconce and own the Thing
    could play no higher part.

Yet, as long ages rolled, he learnt from
    Beaver, Ape and Ant to build
Shelter for sire and dam and brood, from
    blast and blaze that hurt and killed;

And last came Fire; when scrap of stone
    cast on the flame that lit his den,
Gave out the shining ore, and made the
    Lord of beasts a Lord of men.

The 'moral sense,' your Zâhid-phrase, is
    but the gift of latest years;
Conscience was born when man had shed
    his fur, his tail, his pointed ears.

What conscience has the murd'erous Moor,
    who slays his guest with felon blow,
Save sorrow he can slay no more, what
    prick of pen'itence can he know?

You cry the 'Cruelty of Things' is myst'ery
    to your purblind eye,
Which fixed upon a point in space the gen-
    eral project passes by:

For see! the Mammoth went his ways,
    became a mem'ory and a name;
While the half-reasoner with the hand
    survives his rank and place to claim.

Earthquake and plague, storm, fight and fray,
    portents and curses man must deem
Since he regards his self alone, nor cares to
    trace the scope, the scheme;

The Quake that comes in eyelid's beat to
    ruin, level, 'gulf and kill,
Builds up a world for better use, to general
    Good bends special Ill:

* * *

'You all are right, you all are wrong,' we
    hear the careless Soofi say,
'For each believes his glimmering lamp to
    be the gorgeous light of day.'

'*Thy* faith why false, *my* faith why true?
    't is all the work of Thine and Mine,
'The fond and foolish love of self that
    makes the Mine excel the Thine.'

Cease then to mumble rotten bones; and
    strive to clothe with flesh and blood
The skel'eton; and to shape a Form that all
    shall hail as fair and good.

'For gen'erous youth,' an Arab saith,
    'Jahim's the only genial state;
'Give us the fire but not the shame with
    the sad, sorry blest to mate.'

And if your Heav'en and Hell be true, and
    Fate that forced me to be born
Force me to Heav'en or Hell – I go, and
    hold Fate's insolence in scorn.

I want not this, I want not that, already sick
    of Me and Thee;
And if we're both transform'd and changed,
    what then becomes of Thee and Me?

Enough to think such things may be: to say
    they are not or they are
Were folly; leave them all to Fate, nor wage
    on shadows useless war.

Do what thy manhood bids thee do, from
    none but self expect applause;
He noblest lives and noblest dies who makes
    and keeps his self-made laws.

All other Life is living Death, a world where
    none but Phantoms dwell,
A breath, a wind, a sound, a voice, a tinkling
    of the camel-bell.

* * *

From self-approval seek applause; What ken
    not men thou kennest, thou!
Spurn ev'ry idol others raise: Before thine
    own Ideal bow:

Be thine own Deus: Make self free, liberal
    as the circling air:
Thy Thought to thee an Empire be; break
    every prison'ing lock and bar;

Do thou the Ought to self aye owed; here
    all the duties meet and blend,
In widest sense, withouten care of what
    began, for what shall end.

Thus, as thou view the Phantom-forms
    which in the misty Past were thine,
To be again the thing thou wast with honest
    pride though may'st decline;

And, glancing down the range of years, fear
    not thy future self to see;
Resign'd to life, to death resign'd, as though
    the choice were nought to thee.

On Thought itself feed not thy thought;
    nor turn from Sun and Light to gaze,
At darkling cloisters paved with tombs,
    where rot the bones of bygone days:

'Eat not thy heart,' the Sages said: 'nor
    mourn the Past, the buried Past;'
Do what thou dost, be strong, be brave;
    and, like the Star, nor rest nor haste.

Pluck the old woman from thy breast: Be
    stout in woe, be stark in weal;
Do good for Good is good to do: Spurn
    bribe of Heav'en and threat of Hell.

To seek the True, to glad the heart, such is
    of life the HIGHER LAW,
Whose differ'ence is the Man's degree, the
    Man of gold, the Man of straw.

See not that something in Mankind that
    rouses hate or scorn or strife,
Better the worm of Izrâil than Death that
    walks in the form of life.

Survey thy kind as One whose wants in the
    great Human Whole unite;
The Homo rising high from earth to seek
    the Heav'ens of Life-in-Light;

And hold Humanity one man, whose univer-
    sal agony
Still strains and strives to gain the goal,
    where agonies shall cease to be.

Believe in all things; none believe; judge
    not nor warp by 'Facts' the thought;
See clear, hear clear, tho' life may seem
    Mâyâ and Mirage, Dream and Naught.

Abjure the Why and seek the How: the
    God and gods enthroned on high,
Are silent all, are silent still; nor hear thy
    voice, nor deign reply.

The Now, that indivis'ible point which studs
    the length of inf'inite line
Whose ends are nowhere, is thine all, the
    puny all thou callest thine.

Perchance the law some Giver hath: Let
    be! let be! what canst thou know?
A myriad races came and went; this Sphinx
    hath seen them come and go.

Haply the Law that rules the world allows
   to man the widest range;
And haply Fate's a Theist-word, subject to
   human chance and change.

This 'I' may find a future Life, a nobler
   copy of our own,
Where every riddle shall be ree'd, where
   every knowledge shall be known;

Where't will be man's to see the whole of
   what on Earth he sees in part;
Where change shall ne'er surcharge the
   thought; nor hope defer'd shall hurt the heart.

But! – faded flow'er and fallen leaf no more
   shall deck the parent tree;
And man once dropt by Tree of Life what
   hope of other life has he?

The shatter'd bowl shall know repair; the
   riven lute shall sound once more;
But who shall mend the clay of man, the
   stolen breath to man restore?

The shiver'd clock again shall strike; the
   broken reed shall pipe again:
But we, we die, and Death is one, the doom
   of brutes, the doom of men.

Then, if Nirwânâ round our life with
   nothingness, 't is haply best;
Thy toils and troubles, want and woe at
   length have won their guerdon – Rest.

Cease, Abdû, Cease! Thy song is sung, nor
   think the gain the singer's prize;
Till men hold Ignor'ance deadly sin, till man
   deserves his title 'Wise:'

In Days to come, Days slow to dawn, when
    Wisdom deigns to dwell with men,
These echoes of a voice long stilled haply
    shall wake responsive strain:

Wend now thy way with brow serene, fear
    not thy humble tale to tell: –
The whispers of the Desert-wind; the Tink-
    ling of the camel's-bell.

The Porter and the Three Ladies of Baghdad
(from *A Plain and Literal Translation of the Arabian Nights'
Entertainments, Now Entitled The Book of The Thousand Nights and a
Night* (1885))

Once upon a time there was a Porter in Baghdad, who was a
bachelor and who would remain unmarried. It came to pass on a
certain day, as he stood about the street leaning idly upon his
crate, behold, there stood before him an honourable woman in a
mantilla of Mosul silk, broidered with gold and bordered with
brocade; her walking-shoes were also purfled with gold and her
hair floated in long plaits. She raised her face-veil and, showing
two black eyes fringed with jetty lashes, whose glances were soft
and languishing and whose perfect beauty was ever blandishing,
she accosted the Porter and said in the suavest tones and choicest
language, 'Take up thy crate and follow me.' The Porter was so
dazzled he could hardly believe that he heard her aright, but he
shouldered his basket in hot haste saying in himself, 'O day of
good luck! O day of Allah's grace!' and walked after her till she
stopped at the door of a house. There she rapped, and presently
came out to her an old man, a Nazarene, to whom she gave a
gold piece, receiving from him in return what she required of
strained wine clear as olive oil; and set it safely in the hamper,
saying, 'Lift and follow.' Quoth the Porter, 'This, by Allah, is
indeed an auspicious day, a day propitious for the granting of all
a man wisheth.' He again hoisted up the crate and followed her;
till she stopped at a fruiterer's shop and bought from him Shámi
apples and Osmáni quinces and Ománi peaches, and cucumbers
of Nile growth, and Egyptian limes and Sultáni oranges and
citrons; besides Aleppine jasmine, scented myrtle berries,

Damascene nenuphars, flower of privet and camomile, blood-red anemones, violets, and pomegranate-bloom, eglantine and narcissus, and set the whole in the Porter's crate, saying, 'Up with it.' So he lifted and followed her till she stopped at a butcher's booth and said, 'Cut me off ten pounds of mutton.' She paid him his price and he wrapped it in a banana-leaf, whereupon she laid it in the crate and said 'Hoist, O Porter.' He hoisted accordingly, and followed her as she walked on till she stopped at a grocer's, where she bought dry fruits and pistachio-kernels, Tihámah raisins, shelled almonds and all wanted for dessert, and said to the Porter, 'Lift and follow men.' So he up with his hamper and after her till she stayed at the confectioner's, and she bought an earthen platter, and piled it with all kinds of sweetmeats in his shop, open-worked tarts and fritters scented with musk and 'soap-cakes,' and lemon-loaves and melon-preserves, and 'Zaynab's combs,' and 'ladies' fingers,' and 'Kazi's tit-bits' and goodies of every description; and placed the platter in the Porter's crate. Thereupon quoth he (being a merry man), 'Thou should-est have told me, and I would have brought with me a pony or a she-camel to carry all this market-stuff.' She smiled and gave him a little cuff on the nape saying, 'Step out and exceed not in words, for (Allah willing!) thy wage will not be wanting.' Then she stopped at a perfumer's and took from him ten sorts of waters, rose scented with musk, orange-flower, water-lily, willow-flower, violet and five others; and she also bought two loaves of sugar, a bottle for perfume-spraying, a lump of male incense, aloe-wood, ambergris and musk, with candles of Alexandria wax; and she put the whole into the basket, saying, 'Up with thy crate and after me.' He did so and followed until she stood before the green-grocer's, of whom she bought pickled safflower and olives, in brine and in oil; with tarragon and cream-cheese and hard Syrian cheese; and she stowed them away in the crate saying to the Porter, 'Take up thy basket and follow me.' He did so and went after her till she came to a fair mansion fronted by a spacious court, a tall, fine place to which columns gave strength and grace: and the gate thereof had two leaves of ebony inlaid with plates of red gold. The lady stopped at the door and, turning her face-veil sideways, knocked softly with her knuckles whilst the Porter stood behind her, thinking of naught save her beauty and loveli-ness. Presently the door swung back and both leaves were opened, whereupon he looked to see who had opened it; and behold, it was a lady of tall figure, some five feet high; a model of beauty and loveliness, brilliance and symmetry and perfect grace. Her forehead was flower-white; her cheeks like the anemone ruddy bright; her eyes were those of the wild heifer or the gazelle, with eyebrows like the crescent-moon which ends Sha'abán and begins Ramazán; her mouth was the ring of Sulayman, her lips coral-red, and her teeth like a line of strung pearls or of camomile petals. Her throat recalled the antelope's, and her breasts, like two pomegranates of even size, stood at bay as it were, her body rose and fell in waves below her dress like the rolls of a piece of brocade, and her navel would hold an ounce of benzoin ointment. In fine she was like her of whom the poet said:–

On Sun and Moon of palace cast thy sight / Enjoy her flower-like face, her fragrant light:
Thine eyes shall never see in hair so black / Beauty encase a brow so purely white:
The ruddy rosy cheek proclaims her claim / Though fail her name whose beauties we indite:
As sways her gait I smile at hips so big / And weep to see the waist they bear so slight.

When the Porter looked upon her his wits were waylaid, and his senses were stormed so that his crate went nigh to fall from his head, and he said to himself, 'Never have I in my life seen a day more blessed than this day!' Then quoth the lady-portress to the lady-cateress, 'Come in from the gate and relieve this poor man of his load.' So the provisioner went in followed by the portress and the Porter and went on till they reached a spacious ground-floor hall, built with admirable skill and beautified with all manner of colours and carvings; with upper balconies and groined arches and galleries and cupboards and recesses whose curtains hung before them. In the midst stood a great basin full of water surrounding a fine fountain, and at the upper end on the raised daís was a couch of juniper-wood set with gems and pearls, with a canopy like mosquito-curtains of red satin-silk looped up with pearls as big as filberts and bigger. Thereupon sat a lady bright of blee, with brow beaming brilliancy, the dream of philosophy, whose eyes were fraught with Babel's gramarye and her eyebrows were arched as for archery; her breath breathed ambergris and perfumery and her lips were sugar to taste and carnelian to see.

Her stature was straight as the letter and her face shamed the noon-sun's radiancy; and she was even as a galaxy, or a dome with golden marquetry or a bride displayed in choicest finery or a noble maid of Araby. Right well of her sang the bard when he said:–

Her smiles twin rows of pearls display / Chamomile-buds or
   rimey spray
Her tresses stray as night let down / And shames her light the
   dawn o' day.

The third lady rising from the couch stepped forward with graceful swaying gait till she reached the middle of the saloon, when she said to her sisters, 'Why stand ye here? take it down from this poor man's head!' Then the cateress went and stood before him, and the portress behind him while the third helped them, and they lifted the load from the Porter's head; and emptying it of all that was therein, set everything in its place. Lastly they gave him two gold pieces, saying, 'Wend thy ways, O Porter.' But he went not, for he stood looking at the ladies and admiring what uncommon beauty was theirs, and their pleasant manners and kindly dispositions (never had he seen goodlier); and he gazed wistfully at that good store of wines and sweet-scented flowers and fruits and other matters. Also he marvelled with exceeding marvel, especially to see no man in the place and delayed his going; whereupon quoth the eldest lady, 'What aileth thee that goest not; haply thy wage be too little?' And, turning to her sister the cateress, she said, 'Give him another dinar!' But the Porter answered, 'By Allah, my lady, it is not for the wage; my hire is never more than two dirhams; but in very sooth my heart and my soul are taken up with you and your condition. I wonder to see you single with ne'er a man about you and not a soul to bear you company; and well you wot that the minaret toppleth o'er unless it stand upon four, and you want this same fourth; and women's pleasure without man is short of measure, even as the poet said:–

Seest not we want for joy four things all told / The harp and lute,
   the flute and flageolet;
And be they companied with scents four-fold / Rose, myrtle,
   anemone and violet;

Nor please all eight an four thou wouldst withold / Good wine
 and youth and gold and pretty pet.

You be three and want a fourth who shall be a person of good
sense and prudence; smart witted, and one apt to keep careful
counsel.' His words pleased and amused them much; and they
laughed at him and said, 'And who is to assure us of that? We are
maidens and we fear to entrust our secret where it may not be
kept, for we have read in a certain chronicle the lines of one Ibn
al-Sumam:–

Hold fast thy secret and to none unfold / Lost is a secret when
 that secret's told:
An fail thy breast thy secret to conceal / How canst thou hope
 another's breast shall hold?

And Abu Nowás said well on the same subject:–

Who trusteth secret to another's hand / Upon his brow deserveth
 burn of brand!'

When the Porter heard their words he rejoined, 'By your lives! I
am a man of sense and a discreet, who hath read books and
perused chronicles; I reveal the fair and conceal the foul and I act
as the poet adviseth:–

None but the good a secret keep / And good men keep it unre-
 vealed:
It is to me a well-shut house / With keyless locks and door
 ensealed.'

When the maidens heard his verse and its poetical application
addressed to them they said, 'Thou knowest that we have laid out
all our monies on this place. Now say, hast thou aught to offer us
in return for entertainment? For surely we will not suffer thee to
sit in our company and be our cup-companion, and gaze upon
our faces so fair and so rare without paying a round sum. Wottest
thou not the saying:–

> Sans hope of gain
> Love's not worth a grain?'

Whereto the lady-portress added, 'If thou bring anything thou art a something; if no thing, be off with thee, thou art a nothing;' but the procuratrix interposed, saying, 'Nay, O my sisters, leave teasing him, for by Allah he hath not failed us this day, and had he been other he never had kept patience with me, so whatever be his shot and scot I will take it upon myself.' The Porter, over-joyed, kissed the ground before her and thanked her saying, 'By Allah, these monies are the first fruits this day hath given me.' Hearing this they said, 'Sit thee down and welcome to thee,' and the eldest lady added, 'By Allah, we may not suffer thee to join us save on one condition, and this it is, that no questions be asked as to what concerneth thee not, and frowardness shall be soundly flogged.' Answered the Porter, 'I agree to this, O my lady, on my head and my eyes be it! Lookye, I am dumb, I have no tongue.' Then arose the provisioneress and tightening her girdle set the table by the fountain and put the flowers and sweet herbs in their jars, and strained the wine and ranged the flasks in row and made ready every requisite. Then sat she down, she and her sisters, placing amidst them the Porter who kept deeming himself in a dream; and she took up the wine flagon, and poured out the first cup and drank it off, and likewise a second and a third. After this she filled a fourth cup which she handed to one of her sisters; and, lastly, she crowned a goblet and passed it to the Porter, saying:–

Drink the dear draught, drink free and fain / What healeth every
    grief and pain.

He took the cup in his hand and, louting low, returned his best thanks and improvised:–

Drain not the bowl save with a trusty friend / A man of worth
    whose good old blood all know:
For wine, like wind, sucks sweetness from the sweet / And stinks
    when over stench it haply blow:

Adding:–

Drain not the bowl, save from dear hand like thine / The cup
    recalls thy gifts; thou, gifts of wine.

After repeating this couplet he kissed their hands and drank and was drunk and sat swaying from side to side and pursued:—

All drinks wherein is blood the Law unclean / Doth hold save
    one, the bloodshed of the vine:
Fill! fill! take all my wealth bequeathed or won / Thou fawn! a
    willing ransom for those eyne.

Then the cateress crowned a cup and gave it to the portress, who
took it from her hand and thanked her and drank. Thereupon
she poured again and passed to the eldest lady who sat on the
couch, and filled yet another and handed it to the Porter. He
kissed the ground before them; and, after drinking and thanking
them, he again began to recite:—

Here! Here! by Allah, here! / Cups of the sweet, the dear!
Fill me a brimming bowl / The Fount o' Life I speer.

Then the Porter stood up before the mistress of the house and
said, 'O lady, I am thy slave, thy Mameluke, thy white thrall, thy
very bondsman;' and he began reciting:—

A slave of slaves there standeth at thy door / Lauding thy
    generous boons and gifts galore:
Beauty! may he come in awhile to 'joy / Thy charms? for Love
    and I part nevermore!

She said to him, 'Drink; and health and happiness attend thy
drink.' So he took the cup and kissed her hand and recited these
lines in sing-song:—

I gave her brave old wine that like her cheeks / Blushed red or
    flame from furnace flaring up:
She bussed the brim and said with many a smile / How durst
    thou deal folk's cheek for folk to sup?
'Drink!' (said I) 'these are tears of mine whose tinct / Is heart-
    blood sighs have boilèd in the cup.'

She answered him in the following couplet:—

'An tears of blood for me, friend, thou hast shed / Suffer me sup
    them, by thy head and eyes!'

Then the lady took the cup, and drank it off to her sister's health, and they ceased not drinking (the Porter being in the midst of them), and dancing and laughing and reciting verses and singing ballads and ritornellos. All this time the Porter was carrying on with them, kissing, toying, biting, handling, groping, fingering; whilst one thrust a dainty morsel in his mouth, and another slapped him; and this cuffed his cheeks, and that threw sweet flowers at him; and he was in the very paradise of pleasure, as though he were sitting in the seventh sphere among the Houris of Heaven. They ceased not doing after this fashion until the wine played tricks in their heads and worsted their wits; and, when the drink got the better of them, the portress stood up and doffed her clothes till she was mother-naked. However, she let down her hair about her body by way of shift, and throwing herself into the basin disported herself and dived like a duck and swam up and down, and took water in her mouth, and spurted it all over the Porter, and washed her limbs, and between her breasts, and inside her thighs and all around her navel. Then she came up out of the cistern and throwing herself on the Porter's lap said, 'O my lord, O my love, what callest thou this article?' pointing to her slit, her solution of continuity. 'I call that thy cleft,' quoth the Porter, and she rejoined, 'Wah! wah! art thou not ashamed to use such a word?' and she caught him by the collar and soundly cuffed him. Said he again, 'Thy womb, thy vulva;' and she struck him and bashed him. Then cried the Porter, 'Thy clitoris,' is there no shame in thee?' Quoth he, 'Thy coynte;' and she cried, 'O thou! art wholly destitute of modesty?' and thumped him and bashed him. Then cried the Porteer, 'Thy clitoris,' whereat the eldest lady came down upon him with a yet sorer beating, and said, 'No;' and he said, ' 'Tis so,' and the Porter went on calling the same commodity by sundry other names, but whatever he said they beat him more and more till his neck ached and swelled with the blows he had gotten; and on this wise they made him a butt and a laughing-stock. At last he turned upon them asking, 'And what do you women call this article?' Whereto the damsel made answer, 'The basil of the bridges.' Cried the Porter, 'Thank Allah for my safety: aid me and be thou propitious, O basil of the bridges!' They passed round the cup and tossed off the bowl again, when the second lady stood up; and, stripping off all her clothes, cast herself into the cistern and did as the first had done; then she came out of the water and throwing her naked form on the Porter's lap pointed to her machine and said, 'O light of mine eyes, do tell me what is the name of this concern?' He replied as before, 'Thy slit,' and she rejoined 'Hath such term no shame for thee?' and cuffed him and buffeted him till the saloon rang with the blows. Then quoth she, 'O fie! O fie! how canst thou say this without blushing?' He suggested, 'The basil of the bridges;' but she would not have it and she said, 'No! no!' and struck him and slapped him on the back of the neck. Then he began calling out all the names he knew, 'Thy slit, thy womb, thy coynte, thy clitoris;' and the girls kept on saying, 'No! no!' So he said, 'I stick to the basil of the bridges;' and all the three laughed till they fell on their backs and laid slaps on his neck and said, 'No! no! that's not its proper name.' Thereupon he cried, 'O my sisters, what *is* its name?' and they replied, 'What sayest thou to the husked sesame-seed?' Then the cateress donned her clothes and they fell again to carousing, but the Porter kept moaning, 'Oh! and Oh!' for his neck and shoulders, and the cup passed merrily round and round again for a full hour. After that time the eldest and handsomest lady stood up and stripped off her garments, whereupon the Porter took his neck in his hand, and rubbed and shampoo'd it, saying, 'My neck and shoulders are on the way of Allah!' Then she threw herself into the basin, and swam and dived, sported and washed; and the Porter looked at her naked figure as though she had been a slice of the moon and at her face with the sheen of Luna when at full, or like the dawn when it brighteneth, and he noted her noble stature and shape, and those glorious forms that quivered as she went; for she was naked as the Lord made her. Then he cried 'Alack! Alack!' and began to address her, versifying in these couplets:–

'If I liken thy shape to the bough when green / My likeness errs
    and I sore mistake it;
For the bough is fairest when clad the most / And thou art fairest
    when mother-naked.'

When the lady heard his verses she came up out of the basin and, seating herself upon his lap and knees, pointed to her genitory and said, 'O my lordling, what be the name of this?' Quoth he, 'The basil of the bridges;' but she said, 'Bah, bah!' Quoth he, 'The husked sesame;' quoth she, 'Pooh, pooh!' Then said he,

'Thy womb?' and she cried, 'Fie, Fie! art thou not ashamed of
thyself?' and cuffed him on the nape of the neck. And whatever
name he gave declaring 'Tis so,' she beat him and cried 'No! no!'
till at last he said, 'O my sisters, and what *is* its name?' She
replied, 'It is entitled the Khan of Abu Mansur;' whereupon the
Porter replied, 'Ha! ha! O Allah be praised for safe deliverance!
O Khan of Abu Mansur!' Then she came forth and dressed and
the cup went round a full hour. At last the Porter rose up, and
stripping off all his clothes, jumped into the tank and swam about
and washed under his bearded chin and armpits, even as they
had done. Then he came out and threw himself into the first
lady's lap and rested his arms upon the lap of the portress, and
reposed his legs in the lap of the cateress and pointed to his
prickle and said, 'O my mistresses, what is the name of this
article?' All laughed at his words till they fell on their backs, and
one said, 'Thy pintle!' But he replied, 'No!' and gave each one of
them a bite by way of forfeit. Then said they, 'Thy pizzle!' but he
cried 'No,' and gave each of them a hug; – And Shahrazad
perceived the dawn of day and ceased saying her permitted say.

NOW WHEN IT WAS THE TENTH NIGHT

Quoth her sister Dunyazad, 'Finish for us thy story;' and she
answered, 'With joy and goodly gree.' It hath reached me, O
auspicious King, that the damsels stinted not saying to the Porter
'Thy prickle, thy pintle, thy pizzle,' and he ceased not kissing and
biting and hugging until his heart was satisfied, and they laughed
on till they could no more. At last one said, 'O our brother, what,
then, is it called?' Quoth he, 'Know ye not?' Quoth they, 'No!'
'Its veritable name,' said he, 'is mule Burst-all, which browseth
on the basil of the bridges, and muncheth the husked sesame,
and nighteth in the Khan of Abu Mansur.' Then laughed they till
they fell on their backs, and returned to their carousal, and
ceased not to be after this fashion till night began to fall. Thereupon said they to the Porter, 'Bismillah, O our master, up and on
with those sorry old shoes of thine and turn thy face and show us
the breadth of thy shoulders!' Said he, 'By Allah, to part with my
soul would be easier for me than departing from you: come let us
join night to day, and to-morrow morning we will each wend our
own way.' 'My life on you,' said the procuratrix, 'suffer him to
tarry with us, that we may laugh at him: we may live out our lives

and never meet with his like, for surely he is a right merry rogue and a witty.' So they said, 'Thou must not remain with us this night save on condition that thou submit to our commands, and that whatso thou seest, thou ask no questions thereanent, nor enquire of its cause.' 'All right,' rejoined he, and they said, 'Go read the writing over the door.' So he rose and went to the entrance and there found written in letters of gold wash; WHOSO SPEAKETH OF WHAT CONCERNETH HIM NOT, SHALL HEAR WHAT PLEASETH HIM NOT!' The Porter said, 'Be ye witnesses against me that I will not speak on whatso concerneth me not.' Then the cateress arose, and set food before them and they ate; after which they changed their drinking place for another, and she lighted the lamps and candles and burned ambergris and aloes-wood, and set on fresh fruit and the wine service, when they fell to carousing and talking of their lovers. And they ceased not to eat and drink and chat, nibbling dry fruits and laughing and playing tricks for the space of a full hour when lo! a knock was heard at the gate. The knocking in no wise disturbed the seance, but one of them rose and went to see what it was and presently returned, saying, 'Truly our pleasure for this night is to be perfect.' 'How is that?' asked they; and she answered, 'At the gate be three Persian Kalandars with their beards and heads and eyebrows shaven; and all three blind of the left eye – which is surely a strange chance. They are foreigners from Roum-land with the mark of travel plain upon them; they have just entered Baghdad, this being their first visit to our city; and the cause of their knocking at our door is simply because they cannot find a lodging. Indeed one of them said to me: – Haply the owner of this mansion will let us have the key of his stable or some old out-house wherein we may pass this night; for evening had surprised them and, being strangers in the land, they knew none who would give them shelter. And, O my sisters, each of them is a figure o' fun after his own fashion; and if we let them in we shall have matter to make sport of.' She gave not over persuading them till they said to her, 'Let them in, and make thou the usual condition with them that they speak not of what concerneth them not, lest they hear what pleaseth them not.' So she rejoiced and going to the door presently returned with the three monoculars whose beards and mustachios were clean shaven. They salam'd and stood afar off by way of respect; but the three ladies rose up to them and welcomed them and wished them joy of their safe arrival and made them sit down. The Kalandars looked at the room and saw that it was a pleasant place, clean swept and garnished with flowers; and the lamps were burning and the smoke of perfumes was spireing in air; and beside the dessert and fruits and wine, there were three fair girls who might be maidens; so they exclaimed with one voice, 'By Allah, 'tis good!' Then they turned to the Porter and saw that he was a merry-faced wight, albeit he was by no means sober and was sore after his slappings. So they thought that he was one of themselves and said, 'A mendicant like us! whether Arab or foreigner.' But when the Porter heard these words, he rose up, and fixing his eyes fiercely upon them, said, 'Sit ye here without exceeding in talk! Have you not read what is writ over the door? surely it befitteth not fellows who come to us like paupers to wag your tongues at us.' 'We crave thy pardon, O Fakír,' rejoined they, 'and our heads are between thy hands.' The ladies laughed consumedly at the squabble; and, making peace between the Kalandars and the Porter, seated the new guests before meat and they ate. Then they sat together, and the portress served them with drink; and, as the cup went round merrily, quoth the Porter to the askers, 'And you, O brothers mine, have ye no story or rare adventure to amuse us withal?' Now the warmth of wine having mounted to their heads they called for musical instruments; and the portress brought them a tambourine of Mosul, and a lute of Irák, and a Persian harp; and each mendicant took one and tuned it; this the tambourine and those the lute and the harp, and struck up a merry tune while the ladies sang so lustily that there was a great noise. And whilst they were carrying on, behold, some one knocked at the gate, and the portress went to see what was the matter there. Now the cause of that knocking, O King (quoth Shahrazad) was this, the Caliph, Hárún al-Rashíd, had gone forth from the palace, as was his wont now and then, to solace himself in the city that night, and to see and hear what new thing was stirring; he was in merchant's gear, and he was attended by Ja'afar, his Wazir, and by Masrúr his Sworder of Vengeance. As they walked about the city, their way led them towards the house of the three ladies; where they heard the loud noise of musical instruments and singing and merriment; so quoth the Caliph to Ja'afar, 'I long to enter this house and hear those songs and see who sing them.' Quoth Ja'afar, 'O Prince of the Faithful; these folk are surely drunken with wine, and I fear some mischief betide us if we get amongst them.'

'There is no help but that I go in there,' replied the Caliph, 'and I desire thee to contrive some pretext for our appearing among them.' Ja'afar replied, 'I hear and I obey;' and knocked at the door, whereupon the portress came out and opened. Then Ja'afar came forward and kissing the ground before her said, 'O my lady, we be merchants from Tiberias-town: we arrived at Baghdad ten days ago; and, alighting at the merchants' caravanserai, we sold all our merchandise. Now a certain trader invited us to an entertainment this night; so we went to his house and he set food before us and we ate: then we sat at wine and wassail with him for an hour or so when he gave us leave to depart; and we went out from him in the shadow of the night and, being strangers, we could not find our way back to our Khan. So haply of your kindness and courtesy you will suffer us to tarry with you this night, and Heaven will reward you!' The portress looked upon them and seeing them dressed like merchants and men of grave looks and solid, she returned to her sisters and repeated to them Ja'afar's story; and they took compassion upon the strangers and said to her, 'Let them enter.' She opened the door to them, when they said to her, 'Have we thy leave to come in?' 'Come in,' quoth she; and the Caliph entered followed by Ja'afar and Masrur; and when the girls saw them they stood up to them in respect and made them sit down and looked to their wants, saying, 'Welcome, and well come and good cheer to the guests, but with one condition!' 'What is that?' asked they, and one of the ladies answered, 'Speak not of what concerneth you not, lest ye hear what pleaseth you not.' 'Even so,' said they; and sat down to their wine and drank deep. Presently the Caliph looked on the three Kalandars and, seeing them each and every blind of the left eye, wondered at the sight; then he gazed upon the girls and he was startled and he marvelled with exceeding marvel at their beauty and loveliness. They continued to carouse and to converse and said to the Caliph, 'Drink!' but he replied, 'I am vowed to Pilgrimage;' and drew back from the wine. Thereupon the portress rose and spreading before him a table-cloth worked with gold, set thereon a porcelain bowl into which she poured willow flower water with a lump of snow, and a spoonful of sugar-candy. The Caliph thanked her and said in himself, 'By Allah, I will recompense her to-morrow for the kind deed she hath done.' The others again addressed themselves to conversing and carousing; and, when the wine gat the better of them, the eldest lady who

ruled the house rose and making obeisance to them took the cateress by the hand, and said, 'Rise, O my sister and let us do what
is our devoir.' Both answered 'Even so!' Then the portress stood
up and proceeded to remove the table-service and the remnants
of the banquet; and renewed the pastiles and cleared the middle
of the saloon. Then she made the Kalandars sit upon a sofa at the
side of the estrade, and seated the Caliph and Ja'afar and Masrur
on the other side of the saloon; after which she called the Porter,
and said, 'How scant is thy courtesy! now thou art no stranger;
nay, thou art one of the household.' So he stood up and, tightening his waist-cloth, asked, 'What would ye I do?' and she
answered, 'Stand in thy place.' Then the procuratrix rose and set
in the midst of the saloon a low chair and, opening a closet, cried
to the Porter, 'Come help me.' So he went to help her and saw
two black bitches with chains round their necks; and she said to
him, 'Take hold of them;' and he took them and led them into
the middle of the saloon. Then the lady of the house arose and
tucked up her sleeves above her wrists and, seizing a scourge, said
to the Porter, 'Bring forward one of the bitches.' He brought her
forward, dragging her by the chain, while the bitch wept, and
shook her head at the lady who, however, came down upon her
with blows on the sconce; and the bitch howled and the lady
ceased not beating her till her forearm failed her. Then, casting
the scourge from her hand, she pressed the bitch to her bosom
and, wiping away her tears with her hands, kissed her head. Then
said she to the Porter, 'Take her away and bring the second;' and,
when he brought her, she did with her as she had done with the
first. Now the heart of the Caliph was touched at these cruel
doings; his chest straitened and he lost all patience in his desire to
know why the two bitches were so beaten. He threw a wink at
Ja'afar wishing him to ask, but the Minister turning towards him
said by signs, 'Be silent!' Then quoth the portress to the mistress
of the house, 'O my lady, arise and go to thy place that I in turn
may do my devoir.' She answered, 'Even so'; and, taking her seat
upon the couch of juniper-wood, pargetted with gold and silver,
said to the portress and cateress, 'Now do ye what ye have to do.'
Thereupon the portress sat upon a low seat by the couch side;
but the procuratrix, entering a closet, brought out of it a bag of
satin with green fringes and two tassels of gold. She stood up
before the lady of the house and shaking the bag drew out from it
a lute which she tuned by tightening its pegs; and when it was in

perfect order, she began to sing these quatrains:–

Ye are the wish, the aim of me / And when, O love, thy sight I see
The heavenly mansion openeth; / But Hell I see when lost thy
sight.
From thee comes madness; nor the less / Comes highest joy,
comes ecstasy:
Nor in my love for thee I fear / Or shame and blame, or hate and
spite.
When Love was throned within my heart / I rent the veil of
modesty;
And stints not Love to rend that veil / Garring disgrace on grace
to alight;
The robe of sickness then I donned / But rent to rags was secrecy:
Wherefore my love and longing heart / Proclaim your high
supremest might:
The tear-drop railing adown my cheek / Telleth my tale of
ignomy:
And all the hid was seen by all / And all my riddle ree'd aright.
Heal then my malady, for thou / Art malady and remedy!
But she whose cure is in thy hand / Shall ne'er be free of bane
and blight;
Burn me those eyne that radiance rain / Slay me the swords of
phantasy;
How many hath the sword of Love / Laid low, their high degree
despite?
Yet will I never cease to pine / Nor to oblivion will I flee.
Love is my health, my faith, my joy / Public and private, wrong
or right.
O happy eyes that sight thy charms / That gaze upon thee at
their gree!
Yea, of my purest wish and will /The slave of Love I'll aye be
hight.

When the damsel heard this elegy in quatrains she cried out
'Alas! Alas!' and rent her raiment, and fell to the ground fainting;
and the Caliph saw scars of the palm-rod on her back and welts of
the whip; and marvelled with exceeding wonder. Then the portress arose and sprinkled water on her and brought her a fresh and
very fine dress and put it on her. But when the company beheld
these doings their minds were troubled, for they had no inkling of

the case nor knew the story thereof; so the Caliph said to Ja'afar, 'Didst thou not see the scars upon the damsel's body? I cannot keep silence or be at rest till I learn the truth of her condition and the story of this other maiden and the secret of the two black bitches.' But Ja'afar answered, 'O our lord, they made it a condition with us that we speak not of what concerneth us not, lest we come to hear what pleaseth us not.' Then said the portress, 'By Allah, O my sister, come to me and complete this service for me.' Replied the procuratrix, 'With joy and goodly gree;' so she took the lute; and leaned it against her breasts and swept the strings with her finger-tips, and began singing:—

Give back mine eyes their sleep long ravishèd / And say me whither be my reason fled:

I learnt that lending to thy love a place / Sleep to mine eyelids mortal foe was made.

They said, 'We held thee righteous, who waylaid / Thy soul?' 'Go ask his glorious eyes,' I said.

I pardon all my blood he pleased to spill / Owning his troubles drove him blood to shed.

On my mind's mirror sun-like sheen he cast / Whose keen reflection fire in vitals bred

Waters of Life let Allah waste at will / Suffice my wage those lips of dewy red:

An thou address my love thou'lt find a cause / For plaint and tears or ruth or lustihed.

In water pure his form shall greet your eyne / When fails the bowl nor need ye drink of wine.

Then she quoted from the same ode:—

I drank, but the draught of his glance, not wine; / And his swaying gait swayed to sleep these eyne;

'Twas not grape-juice gript me but grasp of Past / 'Twas not bowl o'erbowled me but gifts divine:

His coiling curl-lets my soul ennetted / And his cruel will all my wits outwitted.

After a pause she resumed:—

If we 'plain of absence what shall we say? / Or if pain afflict us where wend our way?

An I hire a truchman to tell my tale / The lovers' plaint is not told
    for pay:
If I put on patience, a lover's life / After loss of love will not last a
    day:
Naught is left me now but regret, repine / And tears flooding
    cheeks for ever and aye:
O thou who the babes of these eyes hast fled / Thou art homed in
    heart that shall never stray;
Would heaven I wot hast thou kept our pact / Long as stream
    shall flow, to have firmest fay?
Or hast forgotten the weeping slave / Whom groans afflict and
    whom griefs waylay?
Ah, when severance ends and we side by side / Couch, I'll blame
    thy rigours and chide thy pride!

Now when the portress heard her second ode she shrieked aloud
and said, 'By Allah! 'tis right good!'; and laying hands on her
garments tore them, as she did the first time, and fell to the
ground fainting. Thereupon the procuratrix rose and brought her
a second change of clothes after she had sprinkled water on her.
She recovered and sat upright and said to her sister the cateress,
'Onwards, and help me in my duty, for there remains but this
one song.' So the provisioneress again brought out the lute and
began to sing these verses:–

How long shall last, how long this rigour rife of woe / May not
    suffice thee all these tears thou seest flow?
Our parting thus with purpose fell thou dost prolong / Is't not
    enough to glad the heart of envious foe?
Were but this lying world once true to lover-heart / He had not
    watched the weary night in tears of woe:
Oh pity me whom overwhelmed thy cruel will / My lord, my
    king, 'tis time some ruth to me thou show:
To whom reveal my wrongs, O thou who murdered me? / Sad,
    who of broken troth the pangs must undergo!
Increase wild love for thee and phrenzy hour by hour / And days
    of exile minute by so long, so slow;
O Moslems, claim *vendetta* for this slave of Love / Whose sleep
    Love ever wastes, whose patience Love lays low:
Doth law of Love allow thee, O my wish! to lie / Lapt in
    another's arms and unto me cry 'Go!'?

Yet in thy presence, say, what joys shall I enjoy / When he I love
  but works my love to overthrow?

When the portress heard the third song she cried aloud; and,
laying hands on her garments, rent them down to the very skirt
and fell to the ground fainting a third time, again showing the
scars of the scourge. Then said the three Kalandars, 'Would
Heaven we had never entered this house, but had rather nighted
on the mounds and heaps outside the city! for verily our visit hath
been troubled by sights which cut to the heart.' The Caliph
turned to them and asked, 'Why so?' and they made answer,
'Our minds are sore troubled by this matter.' Quoth the Caliph,
'Are ye not of the household?' and quoth they, 'No; nor indeed
did we ever set eyes on the place till within this hour.' Hereat the
Caliph marvelled and rejoined, 'This man who sitteth by you,
would he not know the secret of the matter?' and so saying he
winked and made signs at the Porter. So they questioned the man
but he replied, 'By the All-might of Allah, in love all are alike! I
am the growth of Baghdad, yet never in my born days did I
darken these doors till to-day and my companying with them was
a curious matter.' 'By Allah,' they rejoined, 'we took thee for one
of them and now we see thou art one like ourselves.' Then said
the Caliph, 'We be seven men, and they only three women
without even a fourth to help them; so let us question them of
their case; and, if they answer us not, fain we will be answered by
force.' All of them agreed to this except Ja'afar who said, 'This is
not my recking; let them be; for we are their guests and, as ye
know, they made a compact and condition with us which we
accepted and promised to keep: wherefore it is better that we be
silent concerning this matter; and, as but little of the night
remaineth, let each and every of us gang his own gait.' Then he
winked at the Caliph and whispered to him, 'There is but one
hour of darkness left and I can bring them before thee tomorrow,
when thou canst freely question them all concerning their story.'
But the Caliph raised his head haughtily and cried out at him in
wrath, saying, 'I have no patience left for my longing to hear of
them: let the Kalandars question them forthright.' Quoth Ja'afar,
'This is not my rede.' Then words ran high and talk answered
talk, and they disputed as to who should first put the question,
but at last all fixed upon the Porter. And as the jangle increased
the house-mistress could not but notice it and asked them, 'O ye

folk! on what matter are ye talking so loudly?' Then the Porter stood up respectfully before her and said, 'O my lady, this company earnestly desire that thou acquaint them with the story of the two bitches and what maketh thee punish them so cruelly; and then thou fallest to weeping over them and kissing them; and lastly they want to hear the tale of thy sister and why she hath been bastinado'd with palm-sticks like a man. These are the questions they charge me to put, and peace be with thee.' Thereupon quoth she who was the lady of the house to the guests, 'Is this true that he saith on your part?' and all replied, 'Yes!' save Ja'afar who kept silence. When she heard these words she cried, 'By Allah, ye have wronged us, O our guests, with grievous wronging; for when you came before us we made compact and condition with you, that whoso should speak of what concerneth him not should hear what pleaseth him not. Sufficeth ye not that we took you into our house and fed you with our best food? But the fault is not so much yours as hers who let you in.' Then she tucked up her sleeves from her wrists and struck the floor thrice with her hand crying, 'Come ye quickly;' and lo! a closet door opened and out of it came seven negro slaves with drawn swords in hand to whom she said, 'Pinion me those praters' elbows and bind them each to each.' They did her bidding and asked her, 'O veiled and virtuous! is it thy high command that we strike off their heads?', but she answered, 'Leave them awhile that I question them of their condition, before their necks feel the sword.' 'By Allah, O my lady!' cried the Porter, 'slay me not for other's sin; all these men offended and deserve the penalty of crime save myself. Now by Allah, our night had been charming had we escaped the mortification of those monocular Kalandars whose entrance into a populous city would convert it into a howling wilderness.' Then he repeated these verses:–

How fair is ruth the strong man deigns not smother! / And
    fairest, fair when shown to weakest brother:
By Love's own holy tie between us twain, / Let one not suffer for
    the sin of other.

When the Porter ended his verse the lady laughed – And Shahrazad perceived the dawn of day and ceased to say her permitted say.

BIBLIOGRAPHY

PRIMARY SOURCES

Published collections of contemporary memoirs, eye-witness
reports, journals, correspondence, etc.

Arbuthnott, Foster Fitzgerald, *Persian Portraits* (1887)
Baker, Samuel, *The Rifle and the Hound in Ceylon* (1854), *The Albert
  Nyanza*, 2 vols (1866)
Beatson, W.F., *Lord Stratford de Redcliffe, the War Department and
  the Bashi Bazouks* (1856)
Beke, C.T., *Discoveries of Sinai in Arabia and of Midian* (1878)
Besant, Sir Walter, *The Life and Achievements of Edward Henry
  Palmer* (1883), ed., *Literary Remains of Charles Tyrwhitt-Drake*
  (1877)
Bey, Ali, *Voyages d'Ali Bey et Abassi en Afrique et en Asie pendant les
  années 1803, 1804, 1805, 1806 et 1807*, 2 vols (Paris, 1814)
Blunt, Wilfred Scawen, *My Diaries*, 2 vols (N.Y., 1921)
Broca, Paul, *Memoires d'anthropologie* (1871), *Hybridity in genus homo*
  (1864)
Bruce, James, *Travels to Discover the Source of the Nile in the Years
  1768, 1769, 1770, 1771, 1772, and 1773* (Edinburgh, 1890)
Burdo, Adolphe, *Les Belges dans l'Afrique Centrale* (Paris, 1885)
Burkhardt, Jacob, *Travels in Syria and the Holy Land* (1822), *Travels
  in Arabia* (1829), *Travels in Arabia Petrae.*
Burton, Isabel, *The Inner Life of Syria, Palestine and the Holy Land*, 2
  vols (1876), *Arabia, Egypt, India* (1879), *Life of Captain Sir Richard
  F. Burton*, 2 vols (1893)
Cameron, Verney Lovett, *Across Africa*, 2 vols (1877)
Carlyle, Thomas, *On Heroes and Hero Worship* (1841)
Cromer, Lord, *Modern Egypt* (1908)
Coulbois, François, *Dix Années au Tanganika* (Limoges, 1901)
Doughty, Charles, *Travels in Arabia Deserta*, 2 vols (1888)

Fitzgerald, Edward, *The Rubáiyát of Omar Khayyám* (1859)

Galton, Francis, *Memories of My Life* (1908)

Goncourt, Edmond & Jules, *Journal et Memoires de la vie littéraire* (Monaco, 1956)

Grant, James Augustus, *A Walk Across Africa* (Edinburgh, 1864)

Grosskurth, Phyllis, ed., *The Memoirs of John Addington Symonds* (1984)

Hare, Augustus J.C., *The Story of My Life* (1896)

Harris, Frank, *Contemporary Portraits* (N.Y., 1920), *My Life and Loves* (1964)

Harrison, W.H., *Psychic Facts* (1880)

Hitchman, Francis, *Richard Burton*, 2 vols (1897)

Hobart-Hampden, August Charles, *Sketches from My Life* (1887)

Jackson, Frederick, *Early Days in East Africa* (1930)

Johnston, Harry H., *The Nile Quest* (1903), *The Story of My Life* (1923)

Kelvin, Norman, ed., *The Collected Letters of William Morris*, 2 vols (Princeton, 1984–87)

Kinglake, Alexander William, *Eothen* (1844)

Kingsley, Mary, *Travels in West Africa* (1897)

Krapf, J.L., *Travels and Researches and Missionary Labours during an eighteen years' residence in Eastern Africa* (1860)

Lake, H.A., *Narrative of the Defence of Kars* (1857), *Kars and Our Captivity in Russia* (1857)

Lamartine, Alphonse Marie Louis de, *Souvenirs, impressions, pensées et paysages pendant un voyage en Orient 1832–33* (Paris, 1835)

Lang, Cecil Y., ed., *The Swinburne Letters*, 6 vols (Yale, 1959)

Lindsay, Alexander William Crawford, 8th Earl of Crawford and Balcarres, *Letters on Egypt, Edom and the Holy Land* (1838)

Lombroso, Cesare, *L'Uomo Delinquente* (1875)

McCarthy, Justin, *Reminiscences* (1900), *Portraits of the Sixties* (1903)

Maltzan, Heinrich von, *Meine Wallfalist nach Mekka* (Leipzig, 1865), *Reisen in Arabien* (Brunswick, 1873)

Marx, Karl & Engels, Friedrich, *Collected Works*, Laurence and Wishart edition (1979)

Melville, Herman, *Whitejacket* (1850)

Mill, John Stuart, *Autobiography* (1873)

Morris, William, *Journal of Travel in Iceland* (1871)

Myall, Laura Friswell, *In the Sixties and Seventies, Impressions of Literary People and Others* (Boston, 1906)

Napier, William, *Life and Opinions of Charles Napier*, 4 vols (1857)

Newman, John Henry, *Apologia pro vita sua* (1864)

Palgrave, William Gifford, *Narrative of a Year's Journey through Central and Eastern Arabia 1862–63*, 2 vols (1866)

Petherick, John, *Travels in Central Africa*, 2 vols (1869)

Playfair, Lambert, *A History of Arabia Felix* (1859)

Rainy, William, *The Censor Censored, or the Calumnies of Captain Burton on the Africans of Sierra Leone refuted and his conduct relative to the purchase money of the brig 'Harriet' tested and Examined* (1865)

Reade, Winwood, *Savage Africa* (1863)

Redesdale, Lord Algernon, *Memoirs*, 2 vols (1915)

Richards, Alfred Bates, *A Short Sketch of the Career of Captain Richard F. Burton . . . by an old Oxonian* (1880)

Roe, Henry, *West African Scenes* (1874)

Russell, Bertrand and Patricia, eds., *The Amberley Papers*, 2 vols (1937)

Russell, C.E.B., *General Rigby, Zanzibar and the Slave Trade* (1935)

Sandwith, H., *Narrative of the Siege of Kars* (1856)

Schueller, Herbert M & Peters, Robert L., *The Letters of John Addington Symonds*, 3 vols (Indiana, 1969)

Schynse, A., *À Travers l'Afrique avec Stanley et Emin-Pacha* (Paris, 1890)

Seetzen, U.G., *A Brief Account of the countries adjoining the lake of Tiberias, the Jordan and the Dead Sea* (Bath, 1810)

Skene, J.H., *With Lord Stratford in the Crimea* (1883)

Skertchly, J.A., *Dahomey as it is: being a narrative of eight months' residence in that country* (1874)

Slatin, Carl, *Fire and Sword in the Soudan* (1896)

Speke, John Hanning, *What Led to the Discovery of the Source of the Nile* (Edinburgh, 1864), *Journal of the Discovery of the Source of the Nile* (1864)

Stanley, Henry Morton, *Autobiography* (1909), *How I Found Livingstone in Central Africa* (1872), *Through the Dark Continent*, 2 vols (1878), *In Darkest Africa*, 2 vols (1890)

Stisted, Georgiana, *The True Life of Captain Sir Richard F. Burton* (N.Y., 1897)

Stoker, Bram, *Personal Reminiscences of Henry Irving*, 2 vols (1906)

Stuhlmann, Franz, *Mit Emin Pascha ins Herz von Afrika* (Berlin, 1894)

Symonds, J.A., *A Problem in Greek Ethics* (1883), *A Problem in Modern Ethics* (1896)

Thomson, Joseph, *Through Masailand* (1885)

Timmins, Douglas, ed., *A Traveller of the Sixties: The Journals of F.J. Stevenson* (1929)

Vambery, Arminius, *Travels and Adventures in Central Asia* (1864)

Waller, Horace, ed., *Livingstone's Last Journals*, 2 vols (1874)

Wilkins, W.H., *The Romance of Isabel, Lady Burton*, 2 vols (1897)

Wolf, James, B., *Missionary to Tanganyika 1877–78* (1971)

Wolseley, Sir Garnet, *The Story of a Soldier's Life*, 2 vols (1903)

Wright, Thomas, *The Life of Sir Richard Burton*, 2 vols (1906), *The Life of John Payne* (1919)

Wright, William, *The Empire of the Hittites* (N.Y., 1884)

SECONDARY SOURCES

Abdullah, Achmed & Pakenham, Compton T., *Dreamers of Empire* (N.Y., 1929)

Abrahams, R.G., *The Peoples of Greater Unyamwezi, Tanzania (Nyamwezi, Sukuma, Sumbwa, Kimbu, Konongo* (1967), *The Political Organisation of Unyamwezi* (1967)

Alder, Lory, *The Dervish of Windsor Castle: the life of Arminius Vambery* (1979)

Allan, Mea, *Palgrave of Arabia: The Life of William Gifford Palgrave 1826–88* (1972)

Allgrove, G., *Love in the East* (1962)

Andrews, Norwood, *The Case against Camoens* (N.Y., 1988)

Arens, Thomas, *The Man Eating Myth* (1979)

Arvin, Newton, *Herman Melville* (N.Y., 1950)

Assad, Thomas J., *Three Victorian Travellers* (1964)

Bacon, Leonard, *The Lusiads of Luiz de Camoens* (N.Y., 1950)

Baumann, Oscar, *Der Sansibar Archipel*, 3 vols (Leipzig, 1896–97)

Baumann, H. & Westermann, D., *Les Peuplades et les Civilisations de l'Afrique* (Paris, 1948)

Beachey, R.W., *The Slave Trade of Eastern Africa* (1976)

Beidelmann, Thomas O., *The Matrilineal Peoples of Eastern Tanzania* (1967)

Bennett, Norman R., *Studies in East African History* (Boston, 1963), *A History of the Arab State of Zanzibar* (1978), *The Arab State of Zanzibar* (Boston, 1984), *Arab versus European* (1986)

Bethell, Leslie, *Britain and the Abolition of the Brazilian Slave Trade* (Cambridge, 1970)

Bettelheim, Bruno, *The Uses of Enchantment* (1976)

Biobaku, S.O., *The Egba and their Neighbours 1842–72* (Oxford, 1957)

Blohm, Wilhelm, *Die Nyamwezi, Land und Wirtschaft* (Hamburg, 1931), *Die Nyamwezi, Gesellschaft und Weltbild* (Hamburg, 1933)

Borges, Jorge Luis, *Translators of the Thousand and One Nights* (1970), *Seven Nights* (1987)

Bosch, Fr., *Les Banyamwezi* (Munster, 1930)

Box, Pelham Horton, *The Origins of the Paraguayan War* (Illinois, 1929)

Bridges, Roy C., edition of Johann Ludwig Krapf, *Travels, Researches and Missionary Labours during an eighteen years' residence in Eastern Africa* (1968)

Brodie, Fawn M., *The Devil Drives* (1967)

Brome, Vincent, *Havelock Ellis: philosopher of sex* (1979)

Brown, H.F., *Life Of John Addington Symonds* (1923), *Letters of John Addington Symonds* (1925)

Burton, Jean, *Sir Richard Burton's Wife* (N.Y., 1941)

Caracciolo, Peter, ed., *The Arabian Nights in English Literature* (1988)

Clauss, Heinrich, *Die Wagogo* (Leipzig, 1911)

Conacher, J.B., *Britain and the Crimea 1855–56* (1987)

Compton, Piers, *Cardigan of Balaclava* (1972)

Cook, Frank, *Casualty Roll for the Crimea* (1976)

Cruse, A., *The Victorians and their Books* (1935)

Cunliffe, Marcus, *American Presidents and the Presidency* (1972)

Curtiss, John S., *Russia's Crimean War* (1979)

Dearden, Seton, *Burton of Arabia* (N.Y., 1937)

Dike, K.O., *Trade and Politics in the Niger Delta 1830–1885* (Oxford, 1956)

Dodge, Walter, *The Real Sir Richard Burton* (1907)

Downey, Fairfax, *Burton, Arabian Nights Adventurer* (N.Y., 1931)

Drake-Brockman, *British Somaliland* (1912)

Ellman, Richard, *Oscar Wilde* (1987)

Elwin, Verrier, *The Baiga* (1939)

Erikson, Erik, *Young Man Luther* (N.Y., 1958)

Fairchild, H.N., *A Study in Romantic Naturalism* (N.Y., 1961)

Farwell, Byron, *Burton* (1963)

Ford, Jeremiah, *The Lusiads* (Harvard, 1940)

Fowkes, Charles, ed., *The Illustrated Kama Sutra, Ananaga Ranga, Perfumed Garden: The Burton translations* (1987)

Gail, Marzieh, *Persia and the Victorians* (1951)

Gay, Peter, *Freud: A Life for Our Time* (1988)

Geikie, A., *Life of Sir Roderick Murchison* (1875)

Gerhardt, M., *The Art of Story Telling: a literary study of the Thousand and One Nights* (Leyden, 1963)

Gorer, Geoffrey, *The Lepchas of Sikkim* (1938)

Gournay, Jean-François, *L'Appel du Proche-Orient* (Paris, 1983)

Graves, Robert, *Lawrence and the Arabs* (1927)

Greene, Graham, *Journey without Maps* (1936)

Grosskurth, Phyllis, *John Addington Symonds* (1964), *Havelock Ellis* (1980)

Hall, Richard, *Lovers on the Nile* (1979)

Harbord, R.E., *A Reader's Guide to Rudyard Kipling* (1962)

Harris, John, *The Gallant Six Hundred* (1973)

Hastings, Michael, *Sir Richard Burton* (1978)

Haxsall, Christopher, *Rupert Brooke* (1964)

Herskovits, Melville, *Dahomey: An Ancient West African Kingdom*, 2 vols (N.Y., 1938)

Hibbert, Christopher, *The Destruction of Lord Raglan* (1961), *George IV, Regent and King* (1973)

Hilbrecht, H.V., *Exploration in Bible Lands during the Nineteenth Century* (Philadelphia, 1903)

Hitti, Philip K., *A Short History of the Arabs* (1937)

Hogarth, D.G., *The Penetration of Arabia* (Cambridge, 1904)

Honan, Park, *Matthew Arnold* (1981)

Jeal, Tim, *Livingstone* (1973)

Kandt, Richard, *Caput Nili* (Berlin, 1914)

Ker, Ian, *John Henry Newman* (Oxford, 1988)

Khuhro, Hamida, ed., *Sind Through the Ages* (Oxford, 1981)

Klein, Melanie, *Love, Guilt and Reparation* (1975)

Lambrick, H.T., *Sir Charles Napier and Sind* (Oxford, 1952)

Lawrence, T.E., *Seven Pillars of Wisdom* (1935)

Le Herisse, *L'Ancien Royaume du Dahomey* (Paris, 1911)

Lene, A., *Dar-es-Salaam* (Berlin, 1903)

Lewis, I.M., *A Pastoral Democracy* (Oxford, 1961), *Islam in Tropical Africa* (1966)

Longford, Elizabeth, *A Pilgrimage of Passion: The Life of Wilfred Scawen Blunt* (1979)

McLynn, Frank, *Stanley, The Making of An African Explorer* (1989)

McGovern, W. Montgomery, *To Lhasa in Disguise* (1924)

Maitland, Alexander, *Speke* (1971)

Malinowski, Bronislaw, *The Sexual Lives of Savages in North-Western Melanesia* (1932)

Manning, Patrick, *Slavery, Colonialism and Economic Growth in Dahomey 1640–1960* (Cambridge, 1982)

Marcus, Steven, *The Other Victorians: A Study of Sexuality and Pornography in Mid-Nineteenth Century England* (N.Y., 1964)

Marek, Curt V., *The Secret of the Hittites* (N.Y., 1956)

Martin, Robert B., *With Friends Possessed* (1985)

Mayes, Stanley, *The Great Belzoni* (1959)

Meyer, Bernard C., *Joseph Conrad: A Psychoanalytic Biography* (Princeton, 1967)

Moorehead, Alan, edition of Burton's *Lake Regions* (1960), *The White Nile* (1960), *The Blue Nile* (1962)

Newbury, C.W., *The Western Slave Coast and its Rulers* (Oxford, 1961), edition of Burton's *A Mission to Gelele* (1966)

Oliver, Roland, *Sir Harry Johnston and the Scramble for Africa* (1957)

Penzer, Norman, *An Annotated Bibliography of Sir Richard Francis Burton* (1923), *Selected Papers on Anthropology, Travel and Exploration by Sir Richard Burton* (1924)

Phelps, Gilbert, *Tragedy of Paraguay* (1975)

Philby, H. St. John, *Heart of Arabia*, 2 vols (1922), *The Empty Quarter* (1933), *The Land of Midian* (1957)

Plowden, Alison, *Caroline and Charlotte* (1989)

Pope-Hennessy, James, *Monkton Milnes: The Years of Promise, 1809–1851* (1940), *Monkton Milnes: The Flight of Youth, 1851–1885* (1951)

Pound, Ezra, *The Spirit of Romance* (N.Y., 1968)

Praz, Mario, *The Romantic Agony* (1962)

Pritchard, James B., *Ancient Near Eastern Texts Relating to the Old Testament* (Princeton, 1955), *Archaeology of the Old Testament* (Princeton, 1958)

Ralli, Auguste, *Christians at Mecca* (1909)

Ransford, Oliver, *Livingstone, The Dark Interior* (1979)

Rich, Norman, *Why the Crimean War* (Hanover, N.H., 1985)

Rigby, Peter, *Cattle and Kinship among the Gogo* (Ithaca, N.Y., 1969)

Ronen, Dor, *Dahomey between Tradition and Modernity* (Lovell, 1975)

Rotberg, *Africa and its Explorers* (Harvard, 1970)

Rowbotham, Sheila, *Socialism and the New Life: the personal and sexual politics of Edward Carpenter and Havelock Ellis* (1977)

Russell, Bertrand, *In Praise of Idleness and Other Essays* (1935)

Sackville-West, Vita, *Passage to Teheran* (1926)

Schmitz, Robert, *Les Bahololo* (Brussels 1912)

Schroeder, Paul W., *Austria, Great Britain and the Crimean War* (1972)

Schubert, Von, *Heinrich Barth* (1897)

Scwhapper, Bernard, *La politique et le commerce français dans le Golfe de Guinée de 1838 à 1871* (Paris, 1961)

Shorter, Aylward, *A Political History of the Kimbu* (Oxford, 1972)

Sim, Catherine, *Desert Traveller: The Life of J.L. Burkhardt* (1969)

Simpson, Donald, *Dark Companions* (1975)

Spoto, Donald, *The Life of Alfred Hitchcock: The Dark Side of Genius* (1983)

Stark, Freya, *The Coasts of Incense* (1953)

Strachey, James, ed., *Standard Edition of the Complete Psychological Works of Sigmund Freud* (1953–74)

Symons, A.J., *Dramatis Personaes* (1925), *Essays and Biographies* (1969)

Symonds John & Grant, Kenneth, eds., *Confessions of Aleister Crowley: An Autobiography* (1979)

Taylor, Anne, *Laurence Oliphant* (1982)

Thesiger, Wilfred, *Arabian Sands* (1959), *The Life of My Choice* (1988)

Thomas, Bertram, *Arabia Felix* (1932)

Trench, Richard, *Arabian Travellers* (1986)

Treneer, Anne, *Charles M. Doughty* (1935)

Trimingham, Spencer, *Islam in Ethiopia* (Oxford, 1952)

Walker, Kenneth, *Love, War and Fancy: The Social and Sexual Customs of the East by Sir Richard Burton* (1964)

Waterfield, Gordon, edition of Burton's *First Footsteps in Africa* (1966)

Wemyss-Reid, T., *Life, Letters and Friendships of Richard Monkton Milnes, 1st Lord Houghton*, 2 vols (1891)

Woodham-Smith, Cecil, *The Reason Why* (1963)

Woodruff, Douglas, *The Tichborne Claimant, a Victorian Mystery* (1957)

Yapp, M.E., *Strategies of British India* (Oxford, 1980)